To a
Dark
Place

To a Dark Place

Experiences from Survivors of The Troubles

Ken Wharton

First published 2022

The History Press
97 St George's Place, Cheltenham,
Gloucestershire, GL50 3QB
www.thehistorypress.co.uk

British Library Cataloguing in Publication Data.
A catalogue record for this book is available from the British Library.

ISBN 978 0 7509 9819 2

Typesetting and origination by The History Press
Printed and bound in Great Britain by TJ Books Limited, Padstow, Cornwall.

Trees for LYfe

I can see you, you're dead inside, but still you won't look at me. Ignoring me won't change the facts that I took your dad away from you. There's more of me at the front door; I smashed the glass and took a life; I settled in your wall. You know I'm here. Don't look, don't look all you want, but I'm inside your head.

Laura Burns, whose father was murdered by Republican terrorists

The thing which hit me the most was the empty shell which had once been my mummy, sitting in a corner.

Mary McCurrie, whose father was murdered by Republican terrorists

I am often asked: do I forgive? I can't forgive, no, not for them taking those young lives away. My emotions have never changed: I am still very, very sad, and what my poor mother and father went through; I can never forget their agony.

Anthony O'Reilly is the brother of Geraldine O'Reilly, murdered in a UVF bombing in Belturbet

My family didn't know where I lived so I heard it from the news. My father and my young brother went to identify him; on a mortuary slab awash from Terence's blood. My father never got over it. At 62 years he suffered a brain haemorrhage and died soon afterwards. No one was ever charged with his murder.

Denis Maguire, brother of former UDR soldier killed by the UFF

There were bodies all around me. Some crying out for help. It was the quiet ones who scared me. Just lying still. The men of evil came to our town that day. They stole the lives of many.

Laura Hamilton, who was badly injured alongside her sister Nicola in the RIRA Omagh bombing

Paramilitaries don't realise that they're not only murdering one person, they're tearing a whole family apart. It has been a very difficult thing for us to live with, but talking about Gavin helps me. It is difficult even now to realise that he has been dead longer than he was alive.

Phyllis Brett, mother of Gavin who was murdered by UFF terrorists in Belfast

Mum falteringly told us 'I've got something to tell, you … 'Your Daddy's dead, kids' … and then collapsed into tears. I was scooped into the arms of Sheila Jackson, whilst my Mother hugged the boys. I didn't want to cry, but felt I should. I felt numb and very strange as I had not witnessed this kind of emotion in adults before. I remember also feeling angry that nobody had warned me that my Daddy might lose his life in Northern Ireland.

Anita Haughey, whose soldier father was killed by the IRA when she was just 7

He wasn't coming home, my boy, our boy wasn't coming home, as he lay covered in a tartan blanket in the Army barracks.

Claire Monteith, whose brother Alan was killed in the Omagh blast

There is no difference at all in a broken heart; they are still broken, whoever you are.

Mary Hull, whose husband was murdered by the UVF in Belfast

I was praying that David would be alive, no matter how serious his injuries were; how selfish of me. At exactly 9 p.m., my sister Heather phoned; her exact words were: 'Ruth, it's all over, David is dead.'

Ruth Forrest, whose brother David was killed by the IRA in the
Teebane crossroads massacre

The hurt is still there, but we have had to learn to live with it. I have a little cry about Patrick every now and then.

Geraldine Ferguson, whose son Patrick was shot dead by the Real IRA
at Massereene Barracks in 2009

Contents

Imagine

I would like the reader to picture how life might have felt, living in an alien world, a world of suspicion and fear. Can you imagine what life would be like, in that alien world, where a seemingly innocent knock at the door might herald something more that the postman or the milk-man coming to collect his money? Imagine that insistent rapping on the door might herald violent death; are you able to look inside of your worst nightmares? Can you picture a man with a black hood showing only his eyes? Can you imagine the shock of seeing a weapon in his or her hand? Could you even begin to process the brain-freezing realisation that they were there to rob you of life's most precious gift? Imagine your shocked stare, with your brain and legs simultaneously locking, that cold stab of fear as your own life-clock suddenly clicked on to midnight?

The man standing there, at your front door had come with but one purpose: to end your life. Your premature demise was now almost inevi-table and imminent. It could be as a consequence of several factors: the church at which you worshipped, your job, or the uniform you wore; even the company that you kept. Imagine a place or a time, where vio-lent death could be meted out with such a frightening casualness. A time when life could be taken with the same unthinking ease as one might swat a wasp or a fly. If the reader can picture this nightmare scenario then it will be easy to understand that, for many thousands of people living in a part of the United Kingdom, this was a frequent occurrence. For many ordinary civilians, this was everyday life in Northern Ireland during the final three decades of the twentieth century.

In those dreadful times, violent death was a very real possibility; it was random, it came calling in many shapes and forms, in different places and at different times; but the one constant was that it was going to call. Imagine a world in which men and women would wake from their sleep, with but one thought: that of violent death uppermost in their minds. A world in which they, in good conscience, carried explosive devices to place under vehicles, or plant inside shops and pubs. These actions were carried out, in the full knowledge that the end result would be the termination of lives, young and old, or the shredding of limbs or torso, young as well as old.

Try to imagine shoppers walking blissfully and casually along city streets and markets; occasionally passing the ubiquitous waste bins. At places as diverse as the centre of Enniskillen, Victoria train station or in the centre of sleepy Warrington,* fellow human beings chose these same receptacles in which to place deadly explosive devices; designed to kill and maim.

Try to imagine being an 81-year-old man, enjoying a pint of beer with your family, neighbours and friends; imagine your eyes rising from that cooling drink, possibly to share a joke with your companions, but instead, meeting the cold, steely gaze of a man with a deadly automatic weapon in his hand. That sudden, chilling realisation that the weapon was aimed at your body, as your heart begins to pound, your pulse races, as adrenaline attempts to force your inert body to react, to survive, to move.

Imagine a world in which police officers, legitimately going about their business, investigating break-ins or vandalism, even delivering a court summons, being cut down by snipers, or torn to pieces by hidden explosive devices. Imagine a soldier on routine patrol, meeting death in the same violent and unforgiving manner.

---

* On 20 March 1993, two no-warning PIRA bombs that detonated in one of Warrington's main shopping areas – Bridge Street – killed Jonathan Ball (3) and Tim Parry (12); Bronwen Vickers (32) was dreadfully injured, losing both legs; she died twelve months later.

I have purposely used the word 'imagine' no fewer than eleven times in the past few paragraphs, because I want you, the reader, to put yourself in the body of a Catholic resident of Belfast or mid-Ulster; I want you to put yourself in the body of a Protestant in the Co. Fermanagh area or in Londonderry's Fountains Estate. If you can do so, then you might understand life during the Northern Ireland Troubles between 1969 and 1998.

What follows are but a mere handful of the countless sectarian murders that were committed during The Troubles; murders that took place in pubs, in shops, at work and even while people were relaxing in the comfort of their homes. You will read stories of people who died while having a quiet drink, on a trip to pick up tasty seafood, out for an outing to watch a football match, or while turning up at their place of employment. Some of the murders took place as people prayed in their chosen places of worship. Each one of the aforementioned scenarios were actually the real-life scenes of sectarian and political murder; all were seemingly innocuous places that would become forever associated with violent death. These were not scenes from the cinema; this was real life.

In this book, I have added a brief description of the reported events for each testimony, to give the reader the background to the individual contributor's account. The words that follow my factual description are their own words; their own individual but shared pain. Their words have not been cropped or censored, nor have they been chosen to fit my own narrative. Their pain is immense, but their resilience and courage is without comparison.

It is axiomatic that military historians must be passionate about their chosen subject, but they must always maintain a weather eye on neutrality. For argument's sake, it would be almost impossible to debate or analyse Auschwitz, Dachau, Belsen or indeed any aspect of the Holocaust, without displaying at least some emotion. There must, however, be an element of academic neutrality, objectivity, possibly even a touch of what might be considered to be callous indifference. When writing about a highly emotive topic such as The Troubles, with the inextricably linked obscenity of sectarian murder, it has proven almost impossible not to suffuse one's comments with condemnation, horror and an inevitable emotional involvement. Moreover, I find it exceedingly problematic to find any sort of 'middle ground' when discussing those turbulent years.

It is, quite correctly, a crime today – both legally and morally – in the western world to publicly claim that the murder of more than 6 million people by the Nazis is an untruth. Quite correctly these people are subject to legal and moral outrage as Holocaust deniers. I recognise and concede that there can be no comparison between the catastrophic loss of life in the Nazi death camps and the numbers killed during the Northern Ireland Troubles. However, this author believes that both moral and legal outrage should also be directed at those who are Troubles' deniers, and to those who deny their role in them, whether it be from a lack of conscience or from political expedience.

Finally, picture a smoke-filled room in a dingy house in a hard-line Republican or Loyalist area; there are men and women seated around a table, planning to shatter someone's idyllic life, for their own selfish objectives. Picture the conversation, as they outline their plans to kill a policeman or soldier, or even an ordinary civilian on the very fringes of Nationalism. As they plot murder, the countdown to the end of their intended victim's life begins to tick, tick, tick away.

In closing, I must echo Melanie Anan's disgust, that in both Northern Ireland and the Irish Republic, convicted and suspected terrorists hold positions of power and responsibility. With the slave-like adoration of their voters, this responsibility is not accompanied by their account-ability, as they rewrite their versions of history without let or hindrance. The British Government and the devolved rulers of Northern Ireland indulge and encourage men and women who have committed terrorist acts, as one might indulge a spoiled child for the sake of harmony within the household. In this case, that household is the United Kingdom.

This is not a book for the easily offended; it is a book about the attempted destruction of family lives. It is a book showing how the paramilitaries attempted to destroy the future, and how the resilience of human nature defeated their attempts.

Foreword by Kenny Donaldson, Director of Services, SEFF

The Voices of the Innocent Must Soar

In the context of Northern Ireland, we are conditioned to believe that we must divide on religion, that we must divide on our position of the constitutional future of this place. Rather than focus on division, there is a greater power to building on those values which unify us.

Within this publication are contained the authentic voices of The Troubles, those who carry trauma and a searing pain of loss and injustice. But also, within their primary testimony can be found shoots of hope, a quiet yet steely determination never to allow terrorism and violence to triumph.

'The Past' is shorthand language which Government, the Churches and others have used in relaying what occurred over the period commonly referred to as The Troubles otherwise understood by vast swathes of the population as the 'years of the terror campaign'. But for victims and survivors of Terrorism, 'The Past' is very much 'Their Present'. Others may talk in the past tense, but for victims and survivors the sense of loss, the pain, the sense of injustice is a daily fixture of their lives.

An accord/public acknowledgement must be agreed and communicated by the UK and Republic of Ireland Governments and all terrorist organisations that the use of criminal violence in the furtherance of or defence of a 'political' objective was never justified.

SEFF War Widows Campaign, fighting for justice. (SEFF)

I view the actions of Republican or Loyalist terrorists and individual members of the security forces who broke the code and engaged in wanton acts of criminality in exactly the same light. None of that was legitimate and Justice, Truth and Accountability must prevail.

Were this public acknowledgement to happen then we would have a foundation stone from which to build. Whilst organisations or individuals remain in denial of this fundamental point, there remains a serious threat of history repeating itself and of a further generation reverting to the sins perpetrated by their forebears.

It is essential that in order to build genuine reconciliation that organisations and individuals must be prepared to submit to the 3 Rs: expressing Remorse for wrong words and deeds, showing genuine Repentance and then engaging in acts of Restitution. If our society were to follow this template, then we would all have a very different future ahead of us.

Those of us who live in and around this place have a vested interest in ensuring that the integrity of 'The Past' is preserved. We must resist pressure being exerted by 'The Establishment' to laud once terrorists who now assume the mantle of 'Peacemakers'. Rather, we should reserve our humble praise and thanks for those who held the line against Terrorism and Anarchy; we must understand the heroes and martyrs of this Society to be those who rejected violence, those who refused to inflict harm upon their fellow neighbour, including those who have courageously contributed to this publication, in-so-doing entrusting the most intimate aspect of themselves with the author, Ken Wharton.

For too long shelves in our bookshops have been filled with autobiographies and other publications which feature the bleating of terrorists, their political annexes or others who portray themselves as being impartial academics or human rights campaigners. The core driver and net result of their contributions has been of seeking to romanticise terrorism and criminal violence, to rewrite history and to airbrush away responsibility from the chief protagonists of The Troubles – terrorist organisations and their personnel.

For a quarter of a century the political system has subverted the criminal justice system: early prisoner releases through the Belfast Agreement and there followed a maximum two-year sentence for pre-1998 Troubles related crimes (those committed in Northern Ireland anyway), protracted decommissioning which enabled terrorism to have armaments destroyed which held the evidential secrets to their heinous crimes.

Then there were the OTR Assurance letters which were a covert way of bypassing the expressed will of Parliament who would not back the Labour Government's official efforts to finalise the issue in 2006. We have also had Royal Prerogatives of Mercy with ten years of records in the run up to the Belfast Agreement having magically disappeared – supposedly no back up copy of recipients exists.

The Blair Administration presided over the wanton appeasement of terrorism, believing that the ends justify the means at all costs, there was laid the foundation for the moral abyss to which our Society has fallen. Successive UK Governments since then have also sought to divide and conquer people by teasing them into accepting particular positions, conditioning them to believe that nothing better is possible. But is this the case, is what we have now really good enough? The death rate from terror related actions and other unrest has certainly dissipated since the

Above and opposite: SEFF memorial tapestries to remember the dead. (SEFF)

1998 Belfast/Good Friday Agreement but as the penultimate chapter within this publication illustrates, there were new victims/survivors created post that supposed milestone political settlement.

Aside from the threat of physical violence, the terror campaign is being fought through psychological terrorism and historical rewrite with the objective of cleansing the actions of perpetrators. Whether it's terror memorials or communal public displays of memorialisation to individuals such as Seamus McElwaine, PIRA; Billy Wright, LVF; or those responsible for the Miami Showband attack, all are wrong and must cease. The daily glorification of violence and revisionism of our history is what hurts innocent victims and survivors most – but more so than that, it is a cancer which is of epidemic proportions across our Society, it must be meaningfully addressed and eradicated.

It has been South East Fermanagh Foundation's privilege to work alongside the author in approaching individuals and families and securing their involvement in the project, as well as supporting them throughout the process. SEFF's ethos is consistent with the overall message of this

Memorial quilt in honour of William Heenan, who was murdered at his farm by the IRA.
(SEFF)

publication; that the violence was futile and was wrong and that ultimately it achieved nothing other than separating people, breaking trust and ravaging lives. Over 3,700 are dead as a result of The Troubles, and tens of thousands injured with the vast majority being innocent victims/survivors who did not go out with intent to harm their fellow neighbour.

Approximately 60 per cent of those who died were murdered by Republican terrorist organisations, approximately 30 per cent of those who died were murdered by Loyalist terrorists and 10 per cent of those who died were caused by the UK State and its security forces with a small sub-section of the deaths caused through murder.

This publication is testament to the integrity and dignity which runs through the veins of innocent victims and survivors of The Troubles. Often these individuals are ordinary but in reality, they are quite extraordinary. Despite the horrific set of circumstances visited upon these individuals, they have not allowed themselves to become bitter, they are not consumed by hatred or vengeance but rather are committed to the future.

The legacy of terror and violence remains with them, and they will continue to carry that burden, and yes, many will continue to yearn for justice and accountability for the heinous and unjust actions which they were subjected to, in any democracy this should and must be afforded them. They will never forget the past, they will always honour those who were stolen away but they will not allow terrorism to dictate the future direction of their lives, and those of their families.

Enough is enough; this society needs to do better. As Ghandi once remarked: 'The true measure of any society can be found in how it treats its most vulnerable members.' How would Ghandi view our society today?

Kenny Donaldson
Director of Services
South East Fermanagh Foundation (SEFF)

Who are South East Fermanagh Foundation?

South East Fermanagh Foundation (SEFF) roots are in Lisnaskea, County Fermanagh, but the group now also has delivery offices in Rathfriland, Bessbrook, Newtownstewart, Lisburn and London (serving GB-based victims & survivors) and we also provide outreach support to victims/survivors based in Republic of Ireland.

Our ethos is clear: that in the context of 'The Northern Ireland Troubles' there was and never will be justification for terrorism and other Troubles-related criminal violence – irrespective of who carried it out. All criminal violence was wrong and unjustified.

We are proud to offer the following support services for victims, survivors and their families:

Advocacy
Befriending and SEFF calling services
Border Trails Project
Counselling
Complementary Therapies
Health and Wellbeing Caseworker's Service (Individual Needs Programme)
International-based programmes and partnerships with groups based in Spain, US and Rwanda
Social-based programmes
Welfare and Benefits Service including tribunal representation
Support with The Troubles Permanent Disablement Scheme (aka The Victims Pension)
Youth and Transgenerational programmes
Campaigning and lobbying on victim/survivor issues

In addition to the above, SEFF is also involved in a range of community outreach initiatives designed to best facilitate a confident, thriving local community:

Community Allotments
Ulster Scots Summer Schools

Festival events

Outreach work with the Churches and Schools

Cultural and good relations themed programmes

Responding to Public consultations concerning the local district

North–South and East–West orientated Projects and link ups.

'Religion and Politics have the potential to divide, it's our Values that Unite us'

South East Fermanagh Foundation

1 Manderwood Park,

1 Nutfield Road,

Lisnaskea,

County Fermanagh.

BT92 0FP

Tel: 028 6772 3884

Email: info@seff.org.uk

Website: www.seff.org.uk

Facebook: SEFF Victims and Survivors

Twitter: @SEFFLisnaskea

Abbreviations Used in this Book

Security Forces
PSNI   Police Service Northern Ireland
RUC   Royal Ulster Constabulary
RUCR   Royal Ulster Constabulary Reserve
UDR   Ulster Defence Regiment (integral part of the British Army)

Republicans
IRA/PIRA   Both refer to the Provisional Irish Republican Army
CIRA   Continuity Irish Republican Army
INLA   Irish National Liberation Army
IPLO   Irish People's Liberation Organisation
IRSP   Political wing of the IPLO
OIRA   Official Irish Republican Army
RIRA   Real Irish Republican Army

Loyalists
UDA   Ulster Defence Association (Loyalist Paramilitary)
UFF   Ulster Freedom Fighters (Paramilitary wing of UDA)
UVF   Ulster Volunteer Force (Loyalist Paramilitary)
LVF   Loyalist Volunteer Force (Loyalist Paramilitary)

Other Abbreviations
HET   Historical Enquiries team
NIO   Northern Ireland Office

Author's Personal Notes

Brian Masters, the biographer of serial killer Dennis Nielsen, wrote: 'Judge and jury (will) deal with the matter of guilt, while the writer must deal with matters of interpretation and accuracy.'* I took his words very much to heart, trying to follow these 'guidelines' when I was writing this book. I must confess that my earlier books were written with unavoidable, but deliberate, emotion; with a deep sense of anger at the people who had committed unspeakable acts of terror. However, my passion in supporting the forces of law and order, and my profound empathy for the loss of innocence among ordinary Catholic and Protestant civilians, will remain very obvious.

This book – in spite of the emotionally volatile nature of its subject – is written more dispassionately than previously, with emotive words such as evil, cowardly, cunning and back-stabbing having no place in the narrative. Difficult task though it was, I have tried to keep my opinion to that of the neutral observer. My stated objective was for balance, seeking to give equal space to the victims of Loyalist terror, as much as I gave to those who suffered at the hands of Republicans. I failed relatively to achieve this desired equilibrium for various reasons: my reputation for being a former soldier who wrote from a soldier's perspective preceded me. My undisguised contempt for the Provisional IRA/INLA, and seeing only the security force viewpoint was/is held against me. I failed

---

* *Killing for Company* (Arrow Books, 1985) revised Foreword, 2020.

also because I wasn't able to gain the trust of the Catholic/Nationalist communities, certainly not to the same extent that I have trust from their Protestant/Loyalist counterparts. And I failed because several victims of Loyalist paramilitaries retracted their statements because of family pressure, or because they had been advised by Nationalist politicians not to co-operate.

I have told the stories of those brave enough to tell them to me. I would have dearly liked to have told more of the accounts of those who suffered at the hands of Loyalist paramilitary gangs.

Introduction

'Only the dead have seen the end of war.' The most biting of all anti-war sentiments is often wrongly attributed to Plato, sometimes to other writers, but it is my belief that the words are more likely to have been those of George Santayana.* In Northern Ireland the phrase took on a distinctively sordid aspect, as people died for the most spurious of reasons, in the most squalid of circumstances. There is much of what went on in The Troubles that is still unknown; what tore the country apart over three decades is hidden to an uncomprehending and largely uncaring world. There is also much of what happened that is still nestling under the carpet, swept there by both the British and Irish Governments. In this task, they were capably assisted with alacrity by Sinn Fein, together with the great enthusiasm of their Loyalist paramilitary counterparts. This post-Troubles co-operation illustrates the need for a bloody large carpet under which to sweep the secrets of The Troubles.

It is the continuing legacy of grief for those whose loved ones were cruelly forced into premature graves. Go tell those who were condemned to painful and debilitating existences by ruthless people and organisations that their grief is merely 'a step along the road'. The boutique terror organisations – both the recrudesced as well as the tailor-made – considered the spilling of blood as but a cheap price to pay.

---

* It appears in his 1922 book *Soliloquies in England, and Later Soliloquies*, where he wrote: 'Only the dead are safe; only the dead have seen the end of war.'

Any outrage, any expedient, in their pursuit of the impossible was to them a price worth paying. Their currency was blood, just as long as it was someone else's blood. To the innocents who were killed in the lawful and morally correct pursuance of their everyday lives, they were the sacrificial lambs. To the brave, dedicated upholders of law and order, it was death rather than community respect that was to be their reward. Finally, to the children, ripped from the innocence and purity of their young lives, it was the end of their dreams and hopes. It may well be said, in this fledgling country, still a mere century old, that their citizens truly understand the statement that 'only the dead have seen the end of war'.

It was originally intended that this book would deal separately with the victims of Republican terror and of Loyalist terror. However, to have done so would be to perpetuate sectarianism beyond the grave; it would discredit the victims' memories and their monuments. Moreover, I will not segregate the victims in this book, as they have been done in Milltown Cemetery in Belfast or in burial plots the length and breadth of Ulster. The civilian, military and police dead will have their stories told together; this book will eulogise the Catholic alongside the Protestant.

It will bring together those who suffer now, and indeed will suffer for all of their lives; it will unite in grief all who lost someone, quite regardless of the church at which they pray. These are the words of the victims of terror. Their words will be treated with empathy and support; criticism will only be applied to the perpetrators of terror and to those who seek to justify and apologise for them. It will fully expose both the Republican and the Loyalist paramilitaries as they separately promote their false narratives in seeking to rewrite the history of The Troubles.

It will pull no punches about the obscene nature of sectarian murder, nor will it sugar coat or excuse the perverse logic, that killing an off-duty soldier or police officer could advance the cause of a united Ireland. Conversely, it will expose the perversion of those who killed innocent taxi drivers solely in the cause of keeping Northern Ireland inside the United Kingdom. The writer of this book holds the same opprobrium for both Loyalist and Republican murder gangs. In addition to challenging their false narratives, I will condemn the killers on both sides of the sectarian divide; I will also challenge those who seek to justify, and even glorify, these heinous crimes.

This author feels a deep abhorrence that the paramilitaries of both sides can so easily dismiss the dead in the blasé manner that characterises their claim of legitimacy. There is something quite immoral in finding justification in each and every terrible crime that they have committed; there are insufficient words in the English language to truly describe their behaviour. To the Republicans of Sinn Fein, each bombing, each shooting, each death and each maiming was a mere sacrifice to the cause. It contributed to the bigger strategy of driving the British into the sea, thus reuniting the island of Ireland.

Sinn Fein have consistently claimed to be the 'political' wing of the Provisional IRA and have persistently maintained that there is a separation between the two arms. This author is unable to detect any evidence of this claim, indeed he finds the two synonymous, or in the words of the idiom: two sides of the same coin. One former soldier told the author in a private interview: 'You couldn't get a thin sheet of paper between the two of them.' Sinn Fein are well practised in the art of distancing themselves from the bombings and the shootings, while at the same time, performing an almost contortioned body swerve as they refuse to condemn the same activities.

The same lack of separation is also very obvious between the UDA and the UFF; they are manifestly synonymous. Moreover, many of both the UDA and Sinn Fein's leading lights are the very terrorists who perpetuated the same terror over three decades. Republicans claim the moral high ground by drawing on two clauses of the freshly written Irish Constitution of 1921 to legitimise and morally justify their war of terror. It is indeed disturbing that paramilitaries, of both sides, are able to self-canonise their campaigns of misery; their insouciance beggars belief.

Nor must it be overlooked that the leaders of the Loyalist factions, hiding behind the Union flag, displayed the same callous lack of regret, providing a self-righteous justification for the murders of innocent Catholic civilians. Their consciences were apparently clear, as they claimed each and every sectarian murder as being an attack on a 'legitimate target'. The Loyalist raison d'être was plain: each death would help to punish the Catholics and turn them against the Republican paramilitaries. Every atrocity committed by the Ulster Volunteer Force (UVF), Ulster Freedom Fighters (UFF), Red hand Commandos and Loyalist

Volunteer Force (LVF) was a self-serving justification, the price of staying an integral part of the United Kingdom. The accusation of insouciance applies equally to them. Both the Loyalists and the Republican terror groups performed a psychopathic pas de deux as they claimed to be the defenders of their respective communities.

Thousands of innocents received a life sentence at the hands of the terrorists; these are their stories.

Acknowledgements

Aileen Quinton

Alan McCullough

Alan Irwin

Alex Gore

Amanda Gore

Andrea Brown

Anita Haughey

Anthony

Austin Stack

Berry Reaney

Bryan Walker

Carol Richards

Cecil Wilson

Charlie Butler

Cheryl Patton

Claire Monteith

Craig Agar

Darren Ware

David Kerrigan

Irene Kerrigan

David Temple

Dennis Maguire

Desmond Ross

Dianne Woods

Ed O'Neill

George Larmour

George McNally

Geraldine Ferguson

Ian Millar

Ivy Lambert

Jillian Burns

Julie Tipping

Lynn Anderson

Kate Carroll

Kay Burns

Ken Funston

Kevin Wright

Laura Burns

Laura Hamilton

Liam

Linda McHugh

Lucinda Thompson

Mark Olphert

Mark Rodgers

Martyn McCready	Ronnie Porter
Mary Hull	Ruth Forrest
Mary McCurrie	Ruth Patterson
Michelle Williamson	Sammy Brush
Maureen Norton	Serena Hamilton
Neil Tattershall	Sylvia Porter
Noel Downey	Tracey Magill
Peter Heathwood	Tracy Abraham
Phyllis Brett	Trevor Loughlin
Roberta McNally	Yvonne Black

And the three others who were unable for reasons of expediency to give me their real names.

To Kenny Donaldson and the good offices of SEFF.
The patience of The History Press.
The technical excellence of Stephen Wilson.

*Neil Tattershall: Manchester: 3 December 1992**

I didn't know what the hell was going on, but I was pretty relaxed, as one bomb had gone off previously and we didn't expect another. I think we all just thought that for security reasons, we would be sent home from work. What we didn't know was that the second bomb was just behind us, around 4ft away in fact, close to the wall on which we were sitting.

I jumped down off the wall on to the grass verge, then it happened. There was a huge blast and instantly, my hearing was gone and for about three minutes, I was deaf. I just felt a thump in my back, but it didn't hurt, but I do remember the split second that it happened, a terrible thought flashed into my mind: 'I am not going to see my unborn child; she is never going to know who her dad is.' I felt incredibly sad. I can't remember if there was smoke and I can't remember any specific smells, just a massive boom, the like of which, I had never experienced in my life.

Then I remember seeing people running, and I decided to join them, but my legs were locked, frozen solid and I couldn't move.

---

* From an interview with the author.

1

The Paramilitaries

For many people in Northern Ireland, 14 August 1969 was the beginning of a three-decade-long nightmare. To those who yearned for an independent and united island of Ireland, it was possibly 3 May 1921 that their own personal and political nightmare began. That was the date on which Irish Partition – críochdheighilt na hÉireann – became a reality. However, for the loved ones of John Patrick Scullion, a 28-year-old storeman from the Clonard district of Belfast, 14 August 1969 was anything but their 'hour zero'. For his grieving loved ones, their blackness began even earlier that summer day in 1969; indeed, it was even earlier: on Saturday, 11 June 1966 to be precise. The young man was shot several times, from a passing car, inside of which were three members of Gusty Spence's reformed Ulster Volunteer Force (UVF). John was attacked outside his aunt's home in Oranmore Street; it was the first sectarian murder of modern Northern Ireland. It was to herald several thousand more deaths – committed by the paramilitaries from both sides of the sectarian abyss – in which the victim's religion was the main determinant in the ending of their life.

The main proponents of sectarian murder were the aforementioned UVF, with other Loyalist organisations such as the Ulster Freedom Fighters (UFF), the Red Hand Commandos, and Loyalist Volunteer Force (LVF). On the Republican side, piously laying claim to the 'non-sectarian'* soubriquet, there was – post-1969 – the Provisional Irish Republican Army (PIRA); additionally there was the Irish National Liberation Army (INLA) and the later upstart, albeit short-lived, Irish People's Liberation Organisation (IPLO). It is worth pointing out here that the Republican paramilitary groups seemed to be an evolving system of dissension among both their own rank and file, as well as their leadership; an endless round of division. They split, reformed and regrouped, but took meticulous care in taking all of their grudges and vendettas to their new organisations. The reader might well research Gerard 'Dr Death' Steenson, whose terrorist curriculum vitae bore the initials of OIRA, INLA and the IPLO. There was, however, one constant, and that was the Provisional IRA; this organisation overcame the inter-necine warfare, remaining largely intact until the bitter end, and beyond.

The paramilitary forces had but one significant goal apiece. For the Republicans, it was to drive the British into the Irish Sea; for the Loyalists, it was to show their allegiance to the British Crown, while demonstrating their determination to remain part of the United Kingdom. Between the two sides, there was a huge gulf, an abyss even; tragically, there was never any attempt to bridge that deepening rift, as each side sought to out-do each other in vile and morbid atrocities.

The following is not intended to be either a definitive or exhaustive analysis of either side; it is merely a 'pen picture' to set the stage for the testimonies that follow.

Republicans

The Irish Republican Army (referred to throughout this book as IRA, PIRA, Provisional IRA or the Provisionals) was formed in 1919. It was

---

* Kevin Myers commented in 2010, when writing about the IRA's campaign from 1916 onwards: 'it finally destroys any claim that a non-sectarian Republic could have resulted from the violence of 1916 onwards. In a society as confessionally divided as Ireland then was, with the general Catholic-Nationalist and Protestant-Unionist divide, political violence would inevitably lead to sectarian war.' (Private communication with author)

created as a successor to the Irish Volunteers (IV), itself only formed in 1913, to continue resistance to Ireland's participation in the United Kingdom, or 'British rule'. Its role was to continue the Irish Republican Brotherhood's campaign of revolutionary warfare. The IRB proclaimed an 'Irish Republic' during the Easter Rising of 24 April 1916. The initial rebellious manifestation of this took place when the IRB's Military Council seized control of the GPO building in Dublin, aided by the IV, along with the smaller 'Citizen Army' and 200 women of Cumann na mBan: the female section.

During the Irish War of Independence (also referred to as the Anglo-Irish War of 1919–21), under the leadership of Michael Collins, the IRA carried out classic guerrilla warfare employing ambushes, hit and run raids, as well as political assassination, to force the British Government of David Lloyd George to the negotiating table. The war ended on 3 May 1921, with Ireland being granted Dominion status within the British Commonwealth – it eventually left in 1949 – and the partition of the country into the Irish Free State, which consisted of twenty-six counties under Dublin, and Northern Ireland, made up of the remaining six counties, under the leadership of Belfast.

Partition proved unacceptable to many members of the IRA, which then split into two opposing organisations: the Pro-Treaty faction under Collins, and the Anti-Treaty group led by an Irish-American, Eamon de Valera. Thus followed the Irish Civil War, which ultimately resulted in the defeat of the old IRA, heralding de Valera's departure and entry into the respectable world of Irish politics under the flag of Fianna Fáil. The defeated organisation, however, refused to surrender their arms and explosives, vowing to continue the fight to bring back the six counties of Northern Ireland into the Irish Free State.

Their campaign of insurrection continued from 1923 onwards, with peaks and troughs of activity, although it had become largely dormant by the late 1960s. However, the continued rioting, sectarian attacks and civil disobedience that led to The Troubles finally forced the IRA to reform and, in their parlance, step back into the breach. It initially declared its intention to be merely a Catholic defence force, with the respective religious communities already in an irretrievable state of polarisation by the summer of 1969. Shortly afterwards, it became more militarised, and certainly more proactive than it had been for a decade and more. It sought to take the fight to the Army and the RUC, while laying claim to the title of defenders of the Catholic communities. Even in these early stages, the inevitable signs of dissent were showing and in December 1969, following months of internal strife, the organisation split into two factions: the Official IRA (OIRA) under Cathal Goulding, and the Provisional IRA (PIRA) under Seán Mac Stíofáin. The latter faction attracted the likes of Gerry Adams, Martin McGuinness and Brendan 'Darkie' Hughes.

Following several years of conflict, which alternated between messy, internecine warfare and both sides simultaneously attacking the security forces, the OIRA went into decline in mid-1972; it became largely irrelevant thereafter. PIRA drew its moral ethos from Articles Two and Three of the Irish Constitution, which signalled the Republic's intention to bring the North under the authority of Dublin. By 1972 the Provisionals had won their battle against the OIRA and would now turn their attention to a campaign for the reunification of Ireland. To this day, Nationalists still refer to Northern Ireland as 'the north of Ireland'. They cannot accept Partition and this has been their raison d'être for over a century.

PIRA set out their campaign strategy very early on, and that was to sicken and intimidate the British public. They reasoned that this would lead to civilian pressure on the Government to withdraw from Northern Ireland. PIRA's rationale was that if they killed enough soldiers and police officers, the bloody attrition rate would somehow undermine the morale on the mainland sufficiently enough that the Prime Minister of the day would seriously contemplate pulling out of Northern Ireland. The bombing campaign from 1970 onwards was aimed at deconstructing the Northern Ireland economy, taking it back to the Stone Age and thus rendering the country ungovernable. Conversely, the shooting campaign was aimed at disgusting the English populace. Both tactics almost worked, as in time a resigned state of war-weariness began to fester amongst the British; indeed there was a very palpable feeling of 'let them get on with it; let them kill themselves, rather than our soldiers'.

Left-wing organisations such as 'Troops Out' and 'Oliver's Army' began to agitate among the working classes and their political representatives in HM's Loyal Opposition. For many years of The Troubles, notably 1970–74 and 1979–97, it was the Labour Party that held this position. This meant that the Left had a home, as well as a voice, for their campaigns to support the Provisionals in their objective of forcing a 'withdrawal' from the island of Ireland. Left-wing publications such as *Militant* and *Red Mole* consistently ran editorials and articles that were designed to undermine the morale of the soldiers on the streets, as well as recruit like-minded workers to their ideal of a socialist future. Indeed, in 1972, *Red Mole*, the mouthpiece of the International Marxist Group (IMG), ran a full front page showing the former Beatle John Lennon displaying a poster that stated 'For the IRA Against the British Empire'. Another front page showed solidarity for the Provisional IRA under a headline of 'IRA: We Will Stand and We Fight'. Sinn Fein, the political wing of the Provisionals, concentrated much effort on undermining the security forces on the streets of Ulster, sowing the seeds of both confusion and dissension. The Left's unswerving commitment to the IRA was remarkably well illustrated following the M62 coach bombing in which soldiers as well as civilian children were killed, IMG member ████ ████████* told this author in a heated conversation at the University of Warwick: 'I rejoice in the deaths of those soldiers.'

The IRA's Army Council knew that they could only win the 'long war' if they not only defeated the British Army militarily but also ensured that troops returning from tours of duty received no emotional or moral support. To achieve this, they capitalised on their ties to British trade unions, student unions, the Labour Party's grass roots and a hodgepodge of left-wing organisations. Sinn Fein targeted disparate groups such as the Socialist Labour Party and the International Marxist Group, as well as the proscribed Labour Party Young Socialist's sub group, Militant. It is arguable that Sinn Fein achieved the coup of undermining its enemies via its very own Trojan horse of the British Left.

There was to be no triumphal processions as Operation Banner personnel returned home on leave following a four-month emergency tour. When this tactic produced only moderate results, there was to be another tactic: bombing the mainland. Their rationale was that a bomb in London was, in the words of the old IRA maxim, 'worth twenty in Belfast'. They purposely avoided their Celtic cousins in Scotland and

---

* Redacted under the UK Libel Laws.

Wales, concentrating on England, their main target being London, the recognised centre of the British Crown. Nowhere was really immune in England, as attacks in Lichfield, Derby, Bradford, Manchester, Warrington and other places attest. To the 'England Team' was added the European ASU (Active Service Unit), which was responsible for the deaths of both British military personnel as well as civilians in Belgium, the Netherlands and West Germany.

Back on the streets and in rural areas of Northern Ireland, PIRA, INLA and the IPLO continued to kill soldiers and police officers in their military campaigns. They began to target off-duty personnel in their homes, in pubs, in shopping centres as well as going to and from their places of work. Their aim was two-fold: as well as the undermining of security force morale, they attempted to dissuade both Protestants and Catholics from enlisting as either full-time or part-time members. They then turned their attention to members of the Judiciary, whom they saw as 'agents of the Crown Forces', killing six as well as wounding two more. They also targeted prison officers, killing thirty – Loyalists killed a number of these HMP staff – generally at their homes or between home and work. Despite being avowedly non-sectarian, it is quite clear that this was a hollow abrogation of the truth. This author has produced numerous examples of their overtly sectarian attacks in volumes passim. The Provisionals have always argued that the death of census worker Joanne Mathers in 1981 in Londonderry's Gobnascale was 'military' but the fact that she was a Protestant is further evidence to this author at least, that it was deliberately sectarian.

Loyalists

The Protestant paramilitaries operated under the common banner of 'no surrender', and while it applies emotionally to the historical battles of 1690, at Londonderry, Aughrim, Enniskillen and the Boyne, it could be said that it applies equally to the modern idiom of 'no surrender to the IRA'. Protestants have long held the siege mentality, feeling that their country was being undermined by the Roman Catholic Church. They have long felt that in the post-Partition period, the Catholic community inside Northern Ireland has developed into a 'fifth column' of collaborators, seeking to undermine the fledgling state from within. How accurate this viewpoint was is, of course, open to interpretation. Certainly, some instances of positive discrimination towards Catholics, particularly in relation to the staffing of the Civil Service and Catholic insistence on a separate religious education system have done nothing to assuage the fears of the Protestant community. There are also the questions that the civil rights associations posed about workplace discrimination and sectarian bullying; they demanded that this be ended. Instead of helping, this agitation simply widened the gap between Protestant and Catholic. By the mid- to late 1960s, The Troubles were a catastrophe waiting to happen.

The Ulster Volunteer Force (UVF), as we will see later, had its origins in the early part of the twentieth century, formed as part-defence force and part-resistance to the growing clamour for Irish Home Rule. It also served with courageous distinction in the carnage that was France and Belgium in 1914–18. It had only a minor presence post-Partition after 1921, because of its extremely high fatality rates suffered during the Great War; it was never as numerically strong thereafter. In 1966, under the leadership of the aforementioned Gusty Spence, it commenced its dark art of sectarian murder. On 7 April of that year, a UVF gang fire-bombed the Holy Cross Girls School in Belfast, simply on the grounds that the Ulster Government had scheduled a Protestant–Catholic reconciliation conference the next day. Two months later, the same Loyalist group fire-bombed a Catholic pub in Belfast's Upper Charleville Street; the resulting blaze spread into a neighbouring house, killing Matilda Gould (77), a Catholic widow.

Following the school attack, the UVF made the following statement:

From this day, we declare war against the Irish Republican Army and its splinter groups. Known IRA men will be executed mercilessly and without hesitation. Less extreme measures will be taken against anyone sheltering or helping them, but if they persist in giving them aid, then more extreme methods will be adopted. We solemnly warn the authorities to make no more speeches of appeasement. We are heavily armed Protestants dedicated to this cause.

Loyalist paramilitaries were responsible for over 900 deaths in The Troubles. The vast majority of killings by the Loyalists were overtly sectarian in nature, but they also killed fellow Protestants; indeed, after 1994, they killed an increasing number of members of their own community. In the lead-up to the Belfast Good Friday Agreement and beyond there was much score-settling as well as an eruption of internecine feuds between the various rival gangs.

Among the worst Loyalist sectarian attacks of the 1969–98 Troubles were the bombing of McGurk's Bar in 1971, which killed fifteen people, and the Miami Showband massacre in 1976, in which several musicians were murdered in cold blood. Two members of the band were Protestants, and so there is much speculation that they combined a sectarian attack with what they probably equally viewed as a military strike. The fact that two serving members of the Ulster Defence Regiment (UDR) were killed when they planted the bomb does little to dispel the accusations of collusion between the security forces and the paramilitaries that were raised shortly afterwards. Two of those subsequently arrested for the murders were also found to have been members of the same UDR unit. The UVF were also responsible for the Dublin and Monaghan bombings in 1974, which took the lives of thirty-four people.

The Ulster Defence Association (UDA) was formed in September 1971, with The Troubles already two years old. It was created as an umbrella organisation for several paramilitary groupings, including the Ulster Freedom Fighters (UFF), which was tasked to carry out its 'military campaign'. It was responsible for around 400 deaths, again, almost exclusively sectarian. It carried out some of the worst atrocities of The Troubles, which included a mass shooting of Catholics at Castlerock in March 1993 and the Greysteel massacre in October the same year.

Such was the carnage created by the UFF, Edward Heath's vacillating Government were forced to proscribe them, having dithered for almost two years. The UDA itself, somewhat incomprehensibly, were not proscribed until John Major finally took action against them in August 1992.

The various Loyalist groupings – UVF, UFF, LVF and the rest – claimed that their attacks on the Catholic communities were aimed at that modern idiomatic obscenity, the 'legitimate target'. Their oft-repeated pronouncements of attacking Republican paramilitaries or their auxiliaries had worn extremely thin by the third decade of The Troubles. Invariably their claims that they were acting on 'high-grade intelligence' were undoubtedly mendacious, as though seeking to legitimise and exonerate their sectarianism.

A new term sprang up in the 1980s in the lexicon of the Troubles: Pan-nationalist alliance. It was a catch-all that was to encapsulate the real, as well as the supposed, enemies of Ulster. Republican paramilitaries and Sinn Fein members were naturally considered as targets, but it could also embrace the likes of people who volunteered to deliver Sinn Fein election material, those who agitated for the Irish language campaign and even members of the GAA, the Gaelic Athletic Association. Loyalist paramilitaries even went so far as to murder Gaelic footballers and members of Hurling clubs among others whom they perceived to be part of this 'Alliance'.

From being 'defenders' of the Protestant communities at places such as Woodvale in West Belfast – initially known as the Woodvale Defence Association – Loyalist paramilitaries extended their role from defence to attack. The early days saw them don mock-military uniform, armed with shields and staves, mimicking the legitimate soldiers patrolling the streets of the Shankill, Woodvale, Crumlin Road and Tiger's Bay. Their apologists attempted to put a positive yet inaccurate spin on the spectacle, reporting that the UDA was 'patrolling in conjunction' with the British Army. Photographs appearing in the *Belfast Telegraph* showed young boys copying their adults, complete with uniform and dark glasses. The UFF took to using military ranks, some as grandiose as 'brigadier' replicating the IRA's use of companies, battalions and brigades.

More often than not, it was a case of 'any Taig will do' or the obscenity of the UFF tactic 'dial a Catholic', which is covered in greater detail in this book. Robin 'the Jackal' Jackson, leader of the UVF's mid-Ulster brigade, allegedly slaughtered upwards of 100 mainly innocent Catholics in the notorious 'murder triangle' of Co. Armagh and Co. Tyrone. UFF attacks on three betting shops in Belfast were unmistakably sectarian, designed to kill and maim Catholics and nothing more. It was simply indiscriminate murder, based on their victims' choice of worship. On the rare occasions that they tried to justify this campaign of sectarian murder, they offered the weakest of explanations. They rationalised the killing of Catholics as 'punishment' for their perceived support of the Provisional

IRA, or other Republican paramilitaries. These types of Loyalist argu-
ments were centred on the 'wall of silence' that Catholic residents put up
when being questioned by the security forces about paramilitary incidents. They also claimed that PIRA/INLA had a ready-made network
of safe houses in every Nationalist area to conceal and comfort gunmen
and bombers. Perhaps the Loyalist leadership conveniently overlooked
the fact that they operated a mirror-like system themselves.

It is clear that they felt the Provisionals would surely recognise that
their campaign for reunification was dead, given the growing number
of Catholic victims filling the cemeteries of the land. If the Republicans
persisted in their campaign of violence, even more Catholics would be
cut down in cold blood. Then there was the nonsense of tit-for-tat killings, of which, in truth, both sides were equally culpable. The IRA killed a
Protestant – soldier, policeman or civilian – and the UVF/UFF would kill
a Catholic – generally a civilian – in apparent retaliation. However, after a
while, it was simply an excuse, and irrespective of the provocation, killings
were generally planned in advance. Moreover, given the plethora of sectarian murders, who knew which side was retaliating against the other and
who had instigated the deadly cycle? Chicken and egg syndrome perhaps?

The Loyalists also claimed, somewhat lamely, that they acted upon what
they termed 'high-grade' intelligence from military sources, intimating that
there was collusion with the security forces. This style of 'teasing' strength-
ened and accentuated the Republican claim of frequent plotting between
the Army/RUC, and their 'agents' inside the paramilitaries. One tragically
illustrative example was the murder of chemist worker Philomena Hanna
(26) from the New Barnsley area of West Belfast on 28 April 1992. Johnny
Adair of the UFF's 'C' Company in the Shankill allegedly ordered Steven
McKeag to the Springfield Road to shoot her. This he duly did, killing a
wonderful and compassionate human being on the mistaken grounds that
she was a sister of a PIRA intelligence officer.[*] Sectarian murders such as
this were sadly repeated far too often.

Almost thirty sectarian murders were carried out between 1975 and
1982 by UVF member Lenny Murphy in tandem with the notorious

---

[*] Stephen McKeag, Wikipedia; Lister, D. and Jordan, H., *Mad Dog* (Mainstream
Publishing, 2004).

'Shankill Butchers'. This random savagery illustrates the fickle nature of sectarian murder, without even the pretence of claiming killings as political or military. The gang would target late-night drinkers, walking in or around sectarian interfaces, reasoning that if they were walking towards the New Lodge or other Catholic areas, then ipso facto, they were Catholics. They would be hit with a blunt instrument – often a hammer – before being thrown in the back of a taxi belonging to a gang member. Once inside, their victim's fate was sealed, with there being only one documented survivor of one of their attacks. Once pinioned in the rear passenger footwell, they were beaten and stabbed, before being taken to a place of torture and, finally, violent death.

Many of the murders were based on the mere capriciousness of Loyalist leaders. Reportedly, on one occasion, UFF Commander Johnny Adair was drinking heavily with gang members in a club on the Shankill. Suddenly, one suggested, seemingly in jest: 'Let's bang a Taig.'[**] Adair allegedly immediately ordered his team to carry out a random murder. Several members drove to Rosapenna Court, in the nearby Nationalist Oldpark Road area. Sean Rafferty (44), an innocent Catholic, was sitting in his lounge with his wife and their five children. The killers kicked open the door, bursting into his lounge and immediately shooting him dead, before returning in triumph to Adair. In less than thirty minutes they had apparently decided on a killing, killed an innocent man and were back in the club finishing their drinks.

Conclusion

Both sets of paramilitaries posed a similar threat: they would strike without warning, often when it was least expected. There was only one thing predictable about their actions: that they would end in bloodshed and misery. The Loyalist groups posed a constant and very real threat among the Catholics, particularly in the sectarian interfaces, but also to those brave enough to live in a fairly mixed area. Conversely, it must also be said

---

[**] Lister, D. and Jordan, H., *Mad Dog.*

that the Protestant communities faced the very same feelings of anxiety, especially in the homes of members of the security forces, but especially more so in the remote rural areas of the border in Co. Fermanagh and Co. Tyrone. One salient difference was in the timings of these 'operations'. The Provisional IRA tended to be more meticulous in their planning, often spending weeks or even months in putting together either bombing attacks or targeted assassinations, while the Loyalist approach tended to be more spontaneous. The murder of Sean Rafferty in April 1991 (referred to later in this chapter) was a chilling example of this spontaneity. An RUC spokesman described it as: 'a naked sectarian killing.' It was a capricious and purely spur-of-the-moment attack.

Let us look first of all at the latter part of my statement about location; the Provisionals had long felt that the border area 'belonged' to them. In the mid-1970s, they launched a quite deliberate and cynical plan to de-populate the Protestant communities living and working there. Their plan involved a very real element of 'ethnic cleansing', but it was two-pronged: they also wished to make the area inoperable for the security forces. It was to be a no-go zone, controlled by their modern 'flying columns'.*

This concept was the brainchild of senior Provos Jim Lynagh and Padraig McKearney, both later killed in an SAS ambush at Loughgall on 8 May 1987. By the creation of this buffer zone, the Provisionals would be able to move arms, explosives and personnel unhindered by either the Army or the RUC. By killing off many Protestant family heads, they attempted to sever their genetic lines, as well as forcing them to move to safer areas in the country's industrial and commercial interior. As the bulk of the victims of this ethnic cleansing were farmers, the IRA's tactics would ensure that the abandoned farmland was likely to be taken over by Catholics.

It was a quite deliberate and conscious policy, somewhat contradicting their claims that they were not sectarian either in nature or practice. It wasn't subtle, but it was deadly effective, in that it created fear and

---

* Not to be confused with the concept developed by Michael Collins in the 1918–21 campaign against British troops. Collins' strategy involved actively attacking police stations and seizing territory, to establish so-called 'liberated zones' inside Ireland. Lynagh and McKearney were members of PIRA's East Tyrone Brigade. Dr William Matchett, a former RUC Special Branch officer, claimed that the unit was: 'merciless, and was responsible for at least 250 brutal killings'.

insecurity among the part-time soldiers and police reservists. This constant fear that their families' safety and livelihoods were threatened made them less effective; morale was under permanent attack. The porous border with the Irish Republic certainly gave the upper hand to the Republican groups, who were aware that sanctuary was very close by, enabling them to strike fast and disappear before the security forces could react.

Perhaps they felt safe in the knowledge that their actions would be glossed over, and quickly forgotten by the public, thanks to the articulate but mendacious comments of Sinn Fein spokespersons. Former Sinn Fein President Gerry Adams was one of several who could quite plausibly put a spin on any of their actions, backed by a powerful Irish-American lobby and also far-Left organisations in England, making the IRA almost impervious from criticism.

On the other hand, the Loyalist paramilitaries had the geography of their city communities on their side; huge Protestant areas provided them with a plethora of safe houses. They could strike with ease in Ballymurphy, New Barnsley and Turf Lodge, before fleeing to the safety of the Woodvale; they could carry out murders in the Springfield Road, Falls Road and Divis Street, with the safety of the Shankill Road being mere minutes away. Naturally, they preferred targeting the sectarian interface areas, especially in the Ardoyne and New Lodge, as well as using Lanark Way, which connected the Shankill with the Springfield Road. Like their Republican counterparts, they favoured the hours of darkness, but equally, they were not averse to striking in the daylight.

Their intel was very frequently as poor and as out of date as that of the IRA, with many Catholics killed due to faulty information that had landed at their doorsteps. Very often, their intended target had no connections with Republican paramilitaries or with Sinn Fein. If one is to condemn the Provisional IRA for targeting and killing a man who was considering signing up for the RUCR, then one must condemn with the same contempt organisations such as the UVF and UFF for killing Catholics whose only involvement was to deliver leaflets for Sinn Fein or the SDLP at election time; even to be a family member of a Republican activist was sufficient to warrant a death sentence. UVF and UFF gunmen were known to randomly knock on any door in the interface region, shooting whichever male answered. They were glibly able to claim that the victim must have been an IRA sympathiser. On many occasions, the Loyalist target had moved house, so they shot the new resident simply on the grounds of expediency, or because any Catholic would do. In their own deluded minds, they were convinced that they were sending a message to PIRA commanders. If their intended victim was not at home, that was not deemed important enough to prevent yet another murder. If it was a Catholic, walking or merely standing in a Catholic area, they were 'legitimate' targets. In the case of the Shankill Butchers, their targets were anyone entering or walking in the direction of a Catholic area; that was sufficient to warrant a terrible fate. Their rationale was that 'any *Taig* would do'.

Afterword

The deaths of almost 2,000 people at the hands of PIRA/INLA and the near destruction of Northern Ireland's economy were the end results of the Republican aim of reuniting the thirty-two counties of Ireland. It was an impossible and wretched dream, and could never have been achieved with just the gun and the bomb; this is why, eventually, and increasingly, they turned to the concept of 'the Armalite and the ballot box'.

Equally as futile were the deaths of a further 900 people at the hands of the Loyalists; this was to be the price of remaining a part of the United Kingdom. In the end, it is the British Government that will have the final say. This author's personal opinions are neither relevant, nor crucial to the telling of these stories, but one wonders how many more lives will be wasted by both sides; just how many more lives and dreams will be dashed? Loyalist and Republican terror groups performed a seemingly choreographed dance of death as they laid claim to the title of defenders of their respective communities.

This then was the modus operandi of the paramilitary groups. The stories that follow may help the reader determine if the murders contained therein are sectarian or non-sectarian; equally, who was to blame?

Quo rea?

2

1969–72

In 1921, the state of Northern Ireland was born; it was to prove an uneasy and painful birth. To continue with the childbirth analogy, its placenta proved extremely problematical to remove. Indeed, its labour pains are still being felt a century later. Partition was based on the consolidation of six of the historic kingdom of Ulster's nine counties into a separate country as an integral part of the United Kingdom. The remaining twenty-six counties would form the Irish Free State, later to be renamed the Irish Republic. Northern Ireland was to enjoy equal status with Wales, Scotland and England. The Free State remained part of the British Commonwealth, its new emblem comprising the Union flag and a golden harp on a green background. The country left the British Commonwealth on 18 April 1949, becoming the Republic of Ireland, although in truth, in the eyes of many, it had been that in all but title since Partition.

One of Northern Ireland's most pressing tasks was the establishment of its own police force. The Royal Ulster Constabulary (RUC) was formed for just this purpose. Its two-fold task was to provide a security force for the fledgling country, while replacing the long-established Royal Irish Constabulary (RIC). The new version had to be more modern, while at the same time upholding the traditions of security. The RUC's role was to police Northern Ireland during the aftermath of the Irish War of Independence, and especially during the old IRA's ad hoc militarised campaigns of 1942–44 and the later 'Border War' of 1956–62. Additionally, it had also to be a very visible deterrent to criminal behaviour.

The Irish Republican Army (IRA) shed large amounts of blood – their own as well as that of their opponents – during the short-lived but bloody War of Independence[*] and the subsequent Irish Civil War.[**] In the latter conflict, they visibly received a 'bloody nose' at the hands of the pro-treaty forces. The organisation, although severely weakened during this turbulent and chaotic period, nonetheless refused to accept the partition of Ireland. It had taken as its proof of legitimacy Articles Two and Three of the Irish Free State's Constitution. Article 3:1 stated: 'It is the firm will of the Irish nation, in harmony and friendship, to unite all the people who share the territory of the island of Ireland, in all the diversity of their identities and traditions, recognising that a united Ireland shall be brought about only by peaceful means with the consent of a majority of the people, democratically expressed, in both jurisdictions in the island.' As a consequence, the IRA claimed that the wording of the Article provided its campaign of terror and attrition with legitimacy, claiming consequently, the moral high ground. It did, however conveniently overlook the term 'peaceful means'. It was a most selective 'justification'.

The Republican paramilitary group considered the RUC as the main instrument for the enforcement and longevity of British rule. Their subsequent hit and run campaigns were aimed specifically at the undermining of police morale, as well as fighting a gradual war of attrition. This ad hoc, occasionally haphazard, warfare was designed to reduce the force's effectiveness as a militarised institution. The IRA's Army Council – based in Dublin – had vowed to make the north ungovernable, both politically and economically. The British Government, however, recognised the uniqueness of the RUC's position in facing a semi-permanent and clandestine terrorist organisation. For the Government of the day, this was uncharacteristically astute. However, it did understand that the force would be, by definition, different to the remainder of the UK's police forces. Unlike the police in England, Scotland and Wales, the RUC

---

[*] 21 January 1919–11 July 1921 with a subsequent loss of about 2,000 lives.
[**] 28 June 1922–24 May 1923 saw between 1,500 and 1,700 killed. The two periods did overlap in terms of casualties.

was to be an armed, militarised force, with officers routinely armed with sub-machine guns, assault rifles and handguns. Unlike the remainder of the UK police, they would need to travel in armoured vehicles, as well as be based in heavily fortified police stations, the like of which would horrify the 'village bobbies' of rural Yorkshire and Lancashire et al.

The period between 1921 and 1969 in Northern Ireland has often been likened to a 'long weekend' during which, when directly compared with the subsequent turmoil of The Troubles (1969–98), was almost a honeymoon for the RUC; albeit one in which danger still lurked in the border areas and caution was always advisable.

In the forty-seven years following Partition up to the onset of The Troubles on 14 August 1969, a total of fifty RUC officers lost their lives. Fourteen died after collapsing on duty, nine were killed in negligent discharges, nine perished in road traffic accidents (RTAs) and seven were killed in German air raids. Additionally, two more were killed while apprehending robbers, or 'ordinary decent criminals' as the modern vernacular would call them. However, nine officers were killed in operations carried out by the IRA. All but one of these deaths occurred on duty. On 27 January 1961, Constable Norman John C. Anderson (26) became the first member of the RUC to be ambushed and killed by the IRA while off-duty; he was shot dead at his girlfriend's house. Eleven months later, on 12 November of the same year, Constable William John Hunter (28) was shot and killed when his police vehicle was attacked by IRA gunmen. There were no further deaths as a result of terrorism until 11 October 1969, when, with The Troubles barely two months old, an RUC officer was killed by UVF gunmen near the Shankill Road in Belfast.

That officer was Constable Victor Arbuckle (29), father of a young child; he was on duty in the Shankill area following an outbreak of violence amongst Loyalists. Ironically, they were protesting at the proposed disbandment of the 'B' Specials, an RUC auxiliary force. At the time, the violence was described as 'extraordinarily severe' as UVF gunmen began firing at soldiers and police who were trying to quell the rioting. Soldiers subsequently returned fire, killing Herbert Hawe (32) – mistaken for a petrol bomber – and George Dickie (25), who was hit by a ricocheting bullet. The fatal shot was fired by a soldier in Downing Street, just off the Shankill Road. At around the same time,

Victor Arbuckle was hit by a round fired by another UVF gunman; the officer was mortally wounded. He died on the short journey to the Royal Victoria Hospital (RVH). He became the first of 306 RUC men and women to be killed at the hands of the paramilitaries of both sides during The Troubles. It must be stressed that the overwhelming number of RUC fatalities were caused by the Republicans. The Irish police also suffered, with eleven members of An Gardaí Síochána being killed by both the Provisional IRA (PIRA) and the Irish National Liberation Army (INLA) between 1970 and 1996. Additionally, two further serving officers lost their lives after The Troubles, at the hands of Dissident Republicans.

Stephen White of the RUC said, 'Constable Arbuckle was a young man in his 20s with a wife and 2-year-old child when he was brutally taken in a violent act. Our thoughts are very much with his family, but also the other RUC families. Even on that day two other officers were injured.' The dead officer's widow Dorothy was seen in press photographs at the funeral and described as: 'a beautiful young woman in a black fur pillbox hat, her face frozen in grief.' Until an interview with the *Belfast Telegraph* on the fiftieth anniversary of his death, she had never spoken publicly about her loss. They had a young son, Clive.

John Hewitt was a friend and colleague of Constable Arbuckle.

John's Story

I was 21 years old at the time and I had met Victor at Tenant Street RUC station, near the Shankill Road. He was married then and had a young son, so whilst I lived in as a single man, I didn't really get to mix socially with the married men who lived in their own homes. I had known him a couple of years and he was a pleasant type who specialised in driving, often driving the big armoured vehicles. On the night that he was killed, there had been reports of trouble at the Unity Flats near St Peter's Hill. It was heavily Republican and there was always rioting there as the Shankill residents had to go past the flats to get home. Anyway, some rumours had started that shots had been fired at Loyalists and the mob's idea was 'if the RUC won't stop these people, then we will'.

[Author's note: the Government's Hunt Report had recommended the scrapping of the RUC's auxiliary force, the B-Specials, and this too was agitating an already angry mob.]

We understood that some of the residents from the Shankill were going to advance on the Unity Flats to burn them down, and our job was to prevent that. We were dispatched from Tennent Street RUC station to block their route at Townsend Street, which was about 500 yards away, with Victor Arbuckle being one of our drivers. As was the standard operating practice at the time, we were to spread across the road, with our arms linked to stop the mob from getting through. It was a naïve and dangerous tactic as it left us exposed.

We arrived and duly spread out to stop the crowds from getting through; it was noisy and intimidating. Victor was told to stay with the vehicles, but he could see that we were being overwhelmed against heavy odds, so he came over to help us. The crowds continued to push and as I said, it was very noisy, but we noticed that Victor was on the ground; I immediately thought that he had fallen. We got to him, but as we turned him over, I could see that he was wounded in the head, and it was bleeding. Although we hadn't heard the shot, we knew that it was a bullet wound. Suddenly more shots came in and a number of officers fell, wounded; as soon as the crowd realised that shooting was going on, they began to disperse, running for their lives.

There was no time for an ambulance, so we got Victor into the back of a Land Rover and dashed off to the Royal Victoria Hospital, but before we even arrived it was realised that he was already dead. We were in a state of shock, later finding ourselves sitting outside A&E, some of us non-smokers and those who were giving up ending up with a cigarette in our mouths.

Some years later, I walked over to Townsend Street from the Crumlin Road Gaol and found the spot – a grey junction box – where Victor was hit; it was still there. Three men were later found not guilty of his murder – a charge that still carried a sentence of death at the time. They

were given jail terms ranging from six to ten years for arms offences[*]
on the night of the killing. Another of the Loyalists was found guilty of
killing a policeman on the M2 and he too was sentenced to death, but
it was commuted to a life sentence.

I was one of the escort party at Victor's funeral, which I believe was
held at Roselawn Cemetery; it was described as the biggest ever seen in
the east of the city.

At the time of his death, he was studying for his sergeant's exam and was
always reading through the training manuals. They came into my possession after I bought them from Dorothy, although I didn't look at them for
some time until I came across them in my roof space. There they were: his
name written in the front in his handwriting. She moved away to look
after their young son, Clive, and we lost touch. I tried to get in touch with
her to see if her son would like the manuals as a souvenir but I never heard
back from them.

Do I feel bitter? At the time, you had to continue. You don't have
time to dwell on things and many more things happened during The
Troubles; you have to get on with your life and with the job. I do feel
bitter about the men who shot Victor; there was never any apology from
any individual or any organisation for what they carried out.

◆

The Battle of Saint Matthews

On the evening of Saturday, 27 June 1970, in what would later become
known as that modern idiomatic obscenity: a sectarian interface, two murders took place. That particular interface was between the Catholic Short
Strand and the Protestant Newtownards Road; James 'Jimmy' McCurrie
(44) was killed by an IRA gunman – believed to be Joseph Surgenor –
as he walked home to Ardilaun Street. He was hit as he was walking in

---

[*] The *Belfast Telegraph*'s headline following the trial was: 'Arbuckle Men Get Tough
Sentences'.

the area of Beechfield School. Surgenor,[**] along with two other gunmen, including Denis Donaldson, was firing from St Matthews Chapel, into the street at purely random targets. Mr McCurrie, who had been in a club on the nearby Albertbridge Road, was an innocent victim, simply walking home in what he considered a safe area. There had previously been no major problems in the vicinity, although the previous day, a Loyalist marching band had been attacked with rocks and other missiles by a mob on the largely Nationalist[***] Springfield Road, about 3 miles across the city.

Also killed was Robert Neill (38), shot by an unnamed IRA gunman. In addition to the two dead men, a further twenty-eight people were wounded by the gunmen. This was thought to have been the fledgling Provisional IRA's first foray onto the streets of Northern Ireland, certainly into East Belfast.

The attack began when a woman out in the street chatting to neighbours was wounded by a shot fired from the nearby chapel, according to eyewitnesses. She was quickly pulled into cover by passers-by and later rescued by ambulance crews. It has been widely reported over the years that gun battles had broken out between Republican and Loyalist gunmen, but the Loyalists have always denied that this was the case. The incident has gone down in Republican folklore as 'the battle of Saint Matthews'. Sinn Fein and other Nationalist organisations have long eulogised the fighting, claiming that the chapel was under siege and that their firing was purely defensive. The fact that the victims were unarmed civilians returning home from nights out, or chatting to friends and neighbours, suggests that the firing was, in fact, indiscriminate; clearly anyone who moved was 'fair game'. Moreover, the long-held belief of the Protestants is that the Provisional IRA chose the Short Strand to 'flex its muscles' and demonstrate to the Catholics that it was ready to bring guns on to the streets of Belfast, portraying themselves as the 'protectors' of that community.

Robert 'Ginger' O'Neill, who was known to his friends and family as 'Bobby', had been out drinking on the Saturday evening but had

---

[**] Surgenor was later killed in an 'own goal' explosion in 1976 as he planted a bomb at the Gasworks on Belfast's Ormeau Road.

[***] At that stage of Belfast's history there were still a few Protestant families living on the Springfield Road; this demographic was quickly to change.

returned home to bed down for the night. He was awakened by the sounds of gunfire echoing along the Newtownards Road, going outside to investigate; shortly afterwards, on the advice of a friend, he returned home. However, he was quickly back at the scene, where he was observed smoking a cigarette with friends. At 2300 hours, very soon after his return to the scene of the commotion, a single shot rang out. He slumped to the ground, having been hit in the back by a single round. Mr O'Neill was taken to Dundonald Hospital on the Upper Newtownards Road, where he died shortly after admission. Official reports from the time state that both automatic and semi-automatic weapons were used, with about 1,500 rounds expended.

Mary McCurrie is the daughter of Jimmy McCurrie.

Mary's Story

At the time of my father's murder, there were no problems in the area at all; there was no rioting, that was a myth put out by Republicans. It is a myth that has been perpetuated by the IRA to describe what they call the battle of Saint Matthews Church.

Until then, the area was mixed and Protestants and Catholics lived together in those houses. There had been no sectarian interface in the Short Strand/Newtownards Road at the start of The Troubles, with that coming about eighteen months later after Protestants* were intimidated out of the area.

East Belfast had been relatively quiet until the incident, and although there had been some name-calling etc., older heads in the community had kept things under control. I would like to quote from the East Belfast Historical and Cultural Society's booklet,** *Murder in Ballymacarett: The*

---

* That terrible expression 'ethnic cleansing' can be applied to both sides of the sectarian divide, with Catholics being forced out of their homes by thugs from the Loyalist community and, of course, vice-versa. For further reading see *The Exodus* by Jonathan Burgess (Causeway Press, 2011).

** At that stage of Belfast's history, there were still a few Protestant families living on the Springfield Road; this demographic was quickly to change.

James 'Jimmy' McCurrie. (Mary McCurrie)

Untold Story. 'Before this current phase of The Troubles, the Short Strand population was mainly Catholic. Protestants however were living side by side with their Catholic neighbours particularly in and around Comber Street. Unlike today, in 1970 people from the whole community of the Lower Newtownards Road worked together ... socialised together and played together. Protestant and Catholic used the pubs at the bottom of the road like Lynches and McMahons alike for a pint and the craic. Children of both communities collected for each other's bonfire and defended their area's bonfire, whether it needed guarding against orange or green attackers.'

On 27 June in what I know was a pre-planned and unprovoked attack and using the grounds of the church as cover, the IRA, without warning, opened fire on unsuspecting and unarmed Protestants. It was the first time that they brought guns on to the street of Belfast, although they had been behind some bad rioting in the city. I will not tell you anything that I can't back up, but the IRA have perpetuated this myth for fifty years now.

There was no investigation by the RUC, certainly not one that involved our family, and we were never told about Surgenor and only found out when the first edition of *Lost Lives* was published. We were so angry that they made so many mistakes and things were only changed when our MP, Ian Paisley Junior, contacted the editors.

Later on, there was a memorial garden to the memory of my father and Robert Neill and my family got involved in the fiftieth anniversary remembrance. We appealed for witnesses on Facebook and over forty people came forward and their eyewitness testimony absolutely demolished the Sinn Fein/IRA myth.

I was 19 when my daddy was murdered; our family was devastated; we were numb and we could do nothing. My mum was three months pregnant at the time and my wee brother was born 6 months to the day after my father's murder. I had the travel itch at the time and had been in Switzerland in 1969 and in mid-June of 1970, I travelled to England to work as a salesgirl in Blackpool. About a week after I had arrived, I was in my hotel room on the night of the 27th/28th, when there was a knock at the door. When I opened it, there was a policeman and a policewoman standing there. I remember that one of them said: 'Are you Mary McCurrie and do you live in Belfast?' I nodded yes and one of them said: 'You have to go home because something has happened to your father.'

I was dumfounded, I just couldn't take it and I didn't know what they meant. My managers came to my room, where I packed up and followed them to their car. They drove me to Manchester Airport, but I can't remember the journey or boarding the plane or the flight. All of a sudden, I found myself at Aldergrove, just shocked. A taxi driver approached me, asking where I was going, so I told him. I remember him telling me that the Newtownards Road had been really bad the previous night but that he would take me as close as he could.

He got to Newtownards Road and I remember the absolute silence; it was like coming into an alien landscape. He drove into Ardilaun Street and I saw groups of women huddled in small groups in their doorways; one of them said: 'Oh, Mary is home.' I jumped out of the car, forgetting to pay the driver and even leaving my case behind. It was only years later that I found out that my neighbours had pooled together to pay the fare for me.

The thing which hit me the most was the empty shell which had once been my mummy, sitting in a corner.

Cecil Wilson was a friend of Jimmy McCurrie, serving in the British Army at the same time; they had been friends for over twenty years.

Cecil's Story

I met Jimmy through the Buffs and then he started drinking in the Scotch Row Pub; there were ten of us in the usual crowd. Only five of us went out on that Saturday night as five had to work the following morning. We knew that there had been stoning from Seaforde Street earlier when the Gertrude Band had come home, but it was nothing. Just a bit of a scuffle, shouting and bawling but no trouble. About eight o'clock we went to the Buff Club on the Albertbridge Road and left there about half ten/eleven o'clock. We walked round into Madrid Street … and along Beechfield Street. Just as we got to the corner with Bryson Street just where the school is … we heard this bang, bang, bang, bang.

At first we didn't know what it was and then we realised it was shooting. It was me who shouted: 'Hit the ground, all of us and don't move!' At this time, we didn't know that Jimmy had been hit. We were calling out to each other; at this point, Bobby Algie got up and ran and the burst of gunfire as he ran was unbelievable. It came from Kilmood Street because I know that area like the back of my hand. I was born and raised there all of my life and I knew the majority of the people from that area because before The Troubles, we all used to drink in the same pubs.

Anyway, we ran back down towards Thistle Street; there was a Peeler there and we says: 'There's been a shooting down there and we can't find our mate.' We went back into Beechfield Street and there's this fella we knew called Bobby Thompson standing in the street, and he says: 'Cecil, one of your mates has been hit and he's in that first house.' When we went to the first house, the Peeler says: 'Wait a minute; the man's dead and we are taking him to the morgue.' Then I had to go tell Kathleen – Jimmy's wife – and get Jimmy's eldest son and take him to the morgue to identify his father. Then we heard about the shooting on the Newtownards Road; that came from the chapel – there was definitely shooting from the chapel.

It was very hard to tell Kathleen about Jimmy. I knew he was dead, but in my heart I did not want to believe it. I was going to have to tell an expectant mother with four kids in the house that her husband had been shot. It was hard; it was very hard. I went with Jimmy's eldest son, who was 18 at the time, and walked with him into the morgue. Then we had to go back to Kathleen and confirm that Jimmy was dead. After that, I'm a blank; I can't remember anything. My mate of over twenty years was dead and I didn't want to believe it. I don't care who you are – Catholic or Protestant – it's not something any one should have to do: tell a pregnant mother her husband and your best mate is dead.

Jimmy would do anything for anybody; if somebody was short, Jimmy would be the first to put his hand in his pocket to help them out with a couple of shillings. Our wee crowd was a great bunch of lads. Hadn't a bad idea in their heads; just loved to sing, drink and a wee bet on the horses on the Saturday. Typical hard-working men. There was no trouble before that weekend, then everything changed. Even my wife couldn't go up the Grosvenor Road to see her family; it was ten years before she saw them again.

The Short Strand was part of the Newtownards Road; we never called it the Short Strand, it was always called Seaforde Street. All the streets were mixed Protestant and Catholic; as kids we played together and when I started work, I worked alongside Catholics. After that weekend, it all changed; it hardened me against the people who were leading the Catholics because the Catholics were afraid of them. That was the problem; I still spoke to Catholics I knew, but they were afraid of the IRA. I lived in the same sort of house as them; just because I was a Protestant, I didn't have a better house.

Willow Street

On 15 March 1972, Army bomb disposal experts were called to a suspect car in Willow Street close to Grosvenor Road in Belfast. They carried out a controlled explosion but were then called to another situation in the Whiterock Road, close to the Ballymurphy Estate. This second incident turned out to be a false alarm, prompting them to return to the first car in Willow Street. As they arrived back at the vehicle, the bomb, which was still active, exploded, killing both men instantly. The two men were Sergeant Anthony Stephen Butcher (24) and Staff Sergeant Christopher Robin Cracknell (29).

Tracy Abraham is the daughter of Sergeant Butcher.

Tracy's Story

Little did I know that this incident would have such an impact on my life; I remember being around 10 years old when I found out about how he had died. I came across the military funeral photos at my nan's house, but they were hastily taken away and Mum then had to explain. She told me that she was waiting for the right time to tell me, so we went home and got Dad's old Army case out and Mum went through the photos and letters explaining things in careful detail. I always knew who Dad was as there were pictures of him in nearly all the family homes, but didn't really know who he was. Everyone told me

Stephen Butcher, killed in an explosion in Belfast. (Tracy Abraham)

tales about him and told me I was very special to them; now I understand why. I spent a lot of my teenage years being paranoid, wondering would the IRA come for me, was he really on a secret mission, and the name calling at school when you tell kids how your dad was killed, they would sometimes sing, 'I'm forever blowing up daddies; ugly daddies everywhere.' That is something I try to forget. And as Mum had remarried again it was hard sometimes to ask questions because I knew it was painful for her, so I used to go to my Nan Butcher for things to do with him and would sit for hours listening to her talk about him.

I started to feel like part of my life was missing; what had happened to Dad's friends in the Army? I knew very little about him as the friend, the sportsman, and that's when I started to join different forums in search of his old friends. I did eventually find my dad's friends; his best friends in fact, and they told me tales about going out getting drunk; the usual squaddie behaviour. How he played rugby and hockey and liked to run cross country, but one thing stood out; there was not one who had a bad thing to tell me, they all said the same thing: 'He really was a true gent.' I never thought about how much my dad's death had an effect on his friends; I am still in contact with all his friends that I found and one has even been to see me and my mum. Finally my jigsaw pieces are coming together.

What I don't have is justice for my dad. He was a young man of 24, a new father, a loving husband, brother and son; cruelly taken away from us all. I still carry all those feelings from that day; I just contain them very well, but my pain will never go away. I will still long to be held in his arms, I will still wish he could tell me how proud he is of me (even though I know he is). The sad thing is I have outlived my dad instead of growing up with him; every day I see his photo: a young man eternally 24; he would have been 72 this year.

We did speak to the Historical Enquiries Team (HET); the whole process unleashed emotions and pain that I'd not addressed before and for the first time I was able to grieve for him. I've found people are like me in so many ways, and that it is OK to grieve for someone you never met but who is ultimately a part of you. I miss my dad and always will, but my heart bursts with pride when I speak about him because he saved many lives. My dad; my hero.

Bloody Friday

On 21 July 1972, the mass carnage that the Northern Ireland authorities had been waiting nervously for finally happened. The Provisional IRA had been detonating bombs for some time, with 1972 being the worst year of The Troubles for bombings and murders. Earlier in this same year, the Republican terror group had carried out attacks in several Protestant pubs – matched only in vileness by the UFF and UVF – and they had been responsible for the terrible attacks in Donegall Street as well as the Abercorn Restaurant in March. This summer Friday was to be the feared 'big one', or to be more precise: multiple big ones.

Around midday, around forty men and women, driving in twos so as not to raise suspicion, started to arrive in cars – around twenty of them – in Belfast city centre; each vehicle packed with explosives, designed to go off at separate times. Each successive blast was planned to occur only seconds or minutes following the previous one. Several of the devices were also left in suitcases, and it is worth noting that some of the twenty-plus devices did not explode. In a statement made by PIRA member Brendan 'Darkie' Hughes, the bombs were the brainchild of Gerry Adams, a leading Provisional in West Belfast* at the time; he later became the President of Sinn Fein. (Adams has always strongly refuted any involvement.)

At 1410, a car bomb exploded outside Smithfield Market. There was extensive damage, but no one was killed in the blast. It was a reprieve for the people in the area, but worse was to come. Six minutes later, a 50lb (23kg) device exploded in a suitcase planted at the Brookvale Hotel, having been planted by three armed men; the Army had already cleared the area. Just seven minutes later, a bomb planted outside York Road railway station exploded; the building was wrecked. At 1445, two bombs exploded at a Protestant garage on the Shankill Road; the 100lb (45kg) blast caused extensive damage. In the first thirty-five minutes, four blasts had caused mayhem; people were panicking, unsure of where to run to avoid the next. At 1448, a car exploded outside the Ulsterbus depot in Oxford Street, killing four employees: Robert Gibson (45), William Crothers (15), William Irvine (18) and

---

* *Voices from the Grave* (Faber & Faber, 2010).

Thomas Collops (39). All four were torn to pieces and killed instantly. Seconds before the explosion, several soldiers entered the street. Two of them, Driver Stephen Cooper (19) from the Royal Corps of Transport and Sergeant Philip Price (27) of the Welsh Guards, were unknowingly standing next to the bomb. When the timing device activated the explosion, the two soldiers simply vaporised in the blast. Within two minutes, another car bomb exploded outside a branch of the Ulster Bank on Limestone Road. While there were no fatalities, a dozen people were injured by flying glass and debris. Another bomb in a car parked outside the Botanic Avenue railway station exploded, causing massive damage, but fortunately only light casualties.

At 1502, almost simultaneously, two more explosions rocked Belfast, as a car bomb exploded at Agnes Street and a device in the Liverpool Bar at Donegal Quay caused major damage, but only light injuries. Sixty seconds later, on a bridge over the M2 Motorway, another device exploded, injuring several people. A further sixty seconds afterwards, a suitcase bomb at York Street Railway station exploded, injuring several soldiers and police officers who were searching the area, following the earlier bomb attack there. Within the space of sixty more seconds, a car bomb exploded in Ormeau Avenue, injuring several more people. At 1505, a car bomb containing 150lb (68kg) of explosives detonated outside a garage in Donegall Road but while there was much structural damage, there were no serious injuries. Almost immediately, another car bomb exploded at Stewartstown Road. A mere fifty-five minutes had elapsed since the first bomb had exploded but in that frantic period fifteen bombs had exploded, causing deaths and injury.

Shortly afterwards, at Cavehill Road, a suspicious car was spotted by a young boy scout, Stephen Parker (14), who was working in one of the shops. He revealed his suspicions to the shopkeeper and proceeded to warn the shoppers milling around. As he did so, the bomb exploded, killing him as well as Margaret O'Hare (37), a mother of seven children. Her 11-year-old daughter was badly injured in the blast. Brigid Murray (65) was also caught in the explosion; she was killed instantly.

In just eighty-one minutes, there had been twenty explosions, nine people were dead and well over 100 were injured. The *Daily Mirror* described it as a scene 'straight out of a modern Dante's smoking Inferno, at the Oxford Street bus station in Belfast yesterday after an IRA bomb exploded … one of the most bloody, horrifying disasters I have ever seen.'

The following account is from the daughter of one of those killed on Bloody Friday.

A Daughter's Story

Being the school holidays, I was eating sandwiches in the living room with my mother. I was six years old, just finished P1. I distinctly remember her standing watching the news on TV as it was unfolding. I was sitting on the rug and she was continually commenting that Daddy would probably be very late for his tea as the traffic would be at a standstill.

She may or may not have thought the worst, I will never know that, but when my uncles came to deliver the news, well words can probably not adequately depict the scene. My brother reports that the screaming was like something which will never leave him. My mother, left a widow in the blink of an eye; husband gone and our father gone. Her life was going to be hard from that moment on and all at the hands of someone else; she never asked for it and never deserved it. My mother was good, honest and true; our country upbringing was a world away from what was taking place in Belfast. For us, Belfast was simply where you went for work.

I can't say I knew much of what was going on. I was taken to a relative during the time of the funeral etc. All I knew was what I overheard growing up and the impact of Daddy's death came much later in life when I began to research news reports and subjected myself to the horrors of the explosion. The images were too graphic to bear.

Even all these years on, the trauma has left me very vigilant to the world around me. I presume people who I meet already know I am a victim of The Troubles, yet how could they? It's like you have it written all over your face. I feel cheated that I have not had the opportunity to get the education I would have been more than capable of and often sit down and think that those who did such terrible acts have actually done OK for themselves. That can be very upsetting and it seems that life can be very unfair indeed at times. As for forgiveness, I believe that a person has to seek forgiveness first and it is not for me to deliver that to them; it's for a much higher authority than me!

Kevin Wright was a friend and comrade of Stephen Cooper, one of the soldiers killed in the blasts.

Kevin's Story

After speaking to the author, I have found the strength to put my view of the events on paper. This day started the same as any other in Belfast, with people rushing off to work; loads of traffic crossing the Queen's Bridge into the city and traffic racing down from Holywood, passing us on the Sydenham bypass. I heard the radio crackle into life behind me as I was driving a Saracen towards the city; I could tell by the operator's reaction this was no ordinary shout. Little did I realise in a matter of an hour how many people would be not making the journey home from work.

As the section commander was shouting directions to me and to get my foot down, we came upon another unit at Oxford Street bus station, and we were told by them that there was a suspect car they were checking out. I looked in the direction of the car, and I saw two guys talking and realised one of them was driver Steve Cooper from my unit in Germany. He was a member of 33 Squadron (Sqn) RCT but was attached to our sister squadron for this tour. I gave him a shout and asked how he was and he replied giving me a thumbs up. I watched Steve and a Sergeant walk in the direction of the suspect car. As I turned away with the rest of my patrol to get back in our vehicle, I felt a massive blast of hot air and pressure nearly knocking me over. In an instant two lives had been taken for no reason at all. I still thought for some hours after that maybe Steve and the sergeant had got away with it and survived the blast, but sadly they had not.

On this day there were twenty bombs planted in Belfast city centre with the sole aim to kill and maim. The 'I Ran Away Army' issued a statement afterwards blaming the British Army for the bombs and loss of life, stating they gave us ample warning, and we let this happen so a week later the Government could justify Operation Motorman. They said the streets could have been cleared in time with loudhailers. Bollocks; they went out with the sole intention of killing innocent civilians. I was already in Belfast for two weeks before this event as part of the build-up of Operation Motorman, so that blows their excuse out the water.

Every 21 July I remember these events and shed a tear, not only for a friend lost but all the other innocents who never made it home from work that day. I just hope the guys responsible for these murders die screaming in pain.

The British and Irish press reacted in expected fashion:

Belfast Telegraph: 'This city has not experienced such a day of death and destruction since the German blitz of 1941. With the callous lack of remorse now so typical of the Provos, they audaciously accept responsibility for what was an operation clearly requiring considerable planning and manpower.'

The Irish Times: 'Throughout the 32 counties, Irish men and women should ponder how a virulent Nazi-style disregard for life can lodge in the hearts of our fellow countrymen; all the more virulent in that once again the innocent have been the main sufferers. Hitler in his Berlin bunker decided that the German people were no longer worthy of him and deserved not to survive. Yesterday's dead and injured add testimony to something similarly rotten in our philosophy of life.'

The Guardian: 'The wanton killing of non-combatant men, women and children – the inevitable consequence of exploding so many bombs without adequate warning – is yet another cruel act which will not be forgotten.'

Belfast Newsletter: 'On this unforgettable day, 26 bombs, borne by car and planted to take the greatest toll of life, shattered the bodies of men, women and children in a fiendish holocaust of murder and hate.'

Daily Express: 'Belfast is rocked and racked by the most ferocious blitz yet mounted by the IRA. Not even the German bombs could inflict more devastation on the capital of Ulster in the last war.'

Claudy

The village of Claudy sits to the south of the main A6 road; it is 12 short miles from the Creggan Heights area of the city of Londonderry, or Derry depending on one's political stance. The Creggan Heights is a fiercely Nationalist area and at the time the home of PIRA's senior commander Martin McGuinness in the north. Main Street, in the village of Claudy, was the IRA's target on a warm day in July 1972. On that day, they left three explosive-packed cars in the quiet streets of the hamlet. The author visited the village in November 2008, noting its quiet, run-of-the-mill nature; pleasant but unremarkable. Thirty-six years earlier, it was probably even more unremarkable, but an act of terrorism propelled it on to the world stage.

At approximately 1022 on the morning of Monday, 31 July, the same horrors that had hitherto been inflicted upon the big cities of Londonderry and Belfast paid a visit to sleepy little Claudy. One of the stolen cars – like the other two, packed with explosives – detonated outside McElhinney's public house and petrol station. Elizabeth McElhinney (59), Joseph McCluskey (39) and Kathryn Eakin, who was only 8 years old and had been cleaning the windows of her family's grocery store further down Main Street, were all killed instantly. This bomb also fatally wounded Rose McLaughlin (32), a mother of eight children, Patrick Connolly (15) and Arthur Hone (38). The three subsequently died on 3, 8 and 13 August respectively.

Some fifteen minutes later, a second bomb detonated at the front entrance of the Beaufort House hotel in Church Street. This was the road along which the survivors and uninjured from the first explosion had been directed to apparent safety by RUC officers based in the village's barracks. The evacuation was precipitated by the discovery of another suspicious-looking vehicle further down Main Street.

David Miller (60), James McClelland (65) and William Temple (16) were killed in this second blast. The last-named boy, helping on a milk delivery, had been slightly injured in the first one but he bravely continued his rounds; he died on what ironically had been his first day at work. The policemen's suspicion of the other car in Main Street was confirmed when it too disintegrated mere seconds afterwards; however, because that area had been cleared, there were no further casualties.

In all, six were killed in those fateful first minutes and the three badly wounded died over the next thirteen days. The nine dead were made up of five Catholics and four Protestants. One vital question that remains to this day is just why the Provisional IRA chose this small town in which to perpetrate one of the most bestial acts of The Troubles. It is thought likely that the attack was carried out in order to relieve the pressure on the IRA's Londonderry/Derry brigade following the recent breakdown of the ceasefire.

Another comment often made by writers and journalists alike is that, if as widely believed, Martin McGuinness was the senior PIRA commander in the north and a member of their Army Council – is it possible that he had prescience of the attack or actually gave the order? One of the bombers is thought likely to have been a Roman Catholic priest, Father James Chesney, also known as the 'Provo Priest'. His dealings with Republican paramilitaries came to light after the bombings and it is thought that the Church's decision to spirit him away to another post over the Irish border is connected with his involvement in the Claudy outrage.[*] It is also suspected that he contrived in the dispersal of his congregational collections, which were allegedly siphoned off to the Provisional IRA war chest.

David Temple is the brother of William Temple.

David's Story

On the Monday morning, as usual I was at work at a place called Donemana,[**] which is about 15 miles away from Claudy. In the late morning, I was called into the boss's office and told to go home immediately. I was only 20 at the time and was not really sure what had happened. When I arrived home, we met as a family group, but my uncle stood up to say: 'One of you is missing,' and as I looked around I could see that it was my 16-year-old brother, William, who was on his first day

---

[*] 'Claudy bombings: Father Chesney, the "Provo Priest"', *The Guardian*
[**] Also sometimes referred to Dunamanagh.

at work. I was devastated, as he was a young man who didn't deserve to die. I later learned that he was just 8ft from the blast and didn't stand a chance. In all, nine families lost loved ones.

We know that the bombers escaped across the border and even went through an RUC checkpoint at Craigavon Bridge without being stopped and searched.

1972 was the worst year for atrocities; it was a terrible year and I believe that the bombs, particularly at Claudy, was the result of the frustrations of Adams and McGuinness after their negotiations with the Heath Government in London broke down. For many years since, we asked Martin McGuinness to explain why they had targeted Claudy as it was a mainly Nationalist community, but he always refused to answer, and I don't believe that the RUC investigated it properly. We believe they knew who the bombers were and had they put some senior detectives in, they could have wrapped it up in days.

At the time, we were desperate for answers, but we were always being fobbed off and told that they were in Spain and couldn't be arrested; excuses like that were common. I knew that the Catholic Church was involved and it was no secret that a priest called Father Chesney was recruiting and indoctrinating young boys. He was sent away to avoid arrest, to the Republic and to the USA in a bid to hush things up and get him away from prosecution. Now, Martin McGuinness has always denied that he knew Chesney but why was he at the priest's death bed; tell me that?

There were no arrests and it was a major cover-up as we all knew who was responsible. They say that McGuinness did some good things but he also did many bad things and Claudy was one of them. When we confronted this conspiracy, we challenged the RUC/PSNI but we were told that some evidence was missing and some had been lost, which is why in 2013, we launched legal action against the PSNI, the Roman Catholic Church and the Northern Ireland Office. We have always maintained that there was only a half-hearted attempt at investigation because there were so many big players involved. We know that up to thirty people were involved in the manufacture, transportation and detonation of the bombs which wrecked Claudy but as some of them were informers, we believe that British Intelligence ensured the cover-up to protect their undercover sources. On a personal note, I have spoken to some former IRA men and they have confirmed that it was an IRA operation, although Sinn Fein/ IRA have always denied it.

For years, I never went back to Claudy, but later attended victims' groups and I have seen many people crying uncontrollably; my own dad died just four years later; it was just too painful. My mum died aged 91 in 2017; all those years without her younger son and without having her questions answered. This is why I fight on: I want answers.

No one wants to talk about Claudy; they won't answer any of our questions and I think that they hope that one day we will give up, but I tell you this: we will never give up the fight for justice for Claudy. It is a long road to justice and there are many setbacks, but I am determined to reach the end of that road, because too many people have too much to hide.

How do I feel now? I am still hurt and the cost in lives just drives me on. One day I will meet my brother William in Heaven; when I get there and see him again, I want to say to him: 'These are the people who know the answers and I can give them to you finally.'

✦

On 21 September 1972, the Provisional IRA targeted the homes of several part-time UDR soldiers in the border region between Co. Fermanagh and the Irish Republic. One of them, Thomas Bullock (53), lived with his wife Emily in Killynick, Co. Fermanagh. In addition to being a soldier, Thomas farmed fields at Aghalane, which is only 600m away from the border with Ireland. During the evening, the pair had settled down to watch the evening news as they always did. PIRA intel were aware of their presence, and were equally aware that in the secluded area where the couple lived there was little chance of any rapid outside rescue for them in the event of an attack. Emily Bullock (50) heard a loud commotion at their front door, leading to her going to investigate. Masked gunmen broke into the entrance hall, where they shot her in the chest; she died instantly. The gunmen then dashed into the lounge, where they shot Thomas several times; he died shortly afterwards. Witnesses heard the getaway car screech off in the direction of the border, a place that embarrassingly for the Government of the Republic was viewed by many as a 'terrorist haven'.

It was later revealed that a gang of at least nine gunmen[*] in two separate cars had made the raid on the Bullocks' house, before escaping over the Woodford River, marking the border between the two countries. The couple had known that due to the proximity of their home and farm to the crossing they were in a high-risk area. That risk could have not been higher than on that particular day, as earlier the Provisional IRA had attempted to kill all three of the UDR soldiers in the district. Hours before the fateful attack on the Bullocks, members of the same gang forced their way into the home of UDR soldier John Darling in a house close by. The part-time soldier was out of the house, working in nearby fields, the terrorists choosing instead to intimidate his wife. They eventually wrecked her furniture, stealing her husband's uniform and service weapon, before fleeing. A member of the gang also tried to locate a third UDR member, Albert Lunney, who ran a local post office. Again, he wasn't at home but the man's activities made Albert's wife extremely suspicious. Additionally, several strange cars had been observed in the small rural area.

There was a particularly unsavoury postscript that provides an important insight into the nature of Republican paramilitaries and their supporters. 'Burn House' is the local nickname of a business that burned animal carcasses; it is located in Lisburn. A member of the PIRA gang telephoned the manager of the Burn House telling him that there were: 'two Bullocks to be collected from Killynick'. On the same evening of the murders, there was a dance evening at the Catholic church hall in nearby Derrylin. A small crowd of people poured out of the hall in order to block the hearses carrying the bodies of the murdered couple. Eyewitnesses report that there was shouting and jeering as the vehicles struggled to get through. Eventually, RUC officers were called out to disperse the crowd.

Certain sections of the Provisional IRA cherished the idea of making the border area into a huge buffer zone – later developed by James 'the

---

[*] It has been suggested that John Downey may have been part of the gang. The same man – at the time of publication – was being held on charges of killing two UDR soldiers, Alfie Johnston and Jimmy Eames, at Cherrymount roundabout, Enniskillen, on 25 August 1972, and for the murder of four members of the Blues and Royals at Hyde Park, London, on 20 July 1982 (www.donegaldaily.com/2019/12/18/high-court-rules-john-downey-was-responsible-for-ira-bombing/).

executioner' Lynagh, who was himself killed along with fellow terrorists in the 1987 Loughgall ambush – in which the security forces would fear to tread. The realisation of this plan was a systematic ethnic cleansing of the area that involved driving out the Protestant residents through intimidation and murder. Shane Paul O'Doherty wrote of this campaign:

> There were a number of different reasons why the IRA decided to deliberately murder civilians, but a primary purpose was to achieve terror, shock and publicity. While the optics of these murders clearly showed a bias toward murdering Protestant Unionist civilians, murders of Catholic Nationalist civilians also occurred in order to similarly terrorise and to stem opposition in areas the IRA wished to control. [**]

Dianne Woods is the niece of Tommy and Emily Bullock.

Dianne's story

I was 20 at the time of the murders, living in Enniskillen, around 19 miles away from where my aunt and uncle lived. I remember as a child on hot sunny days going over to their house; it was exciting and full of lovely memories, particularly crossing the border into Ireland on bikes. Emily and Thomas married late in life, as she looked after her elderly mother. Thomas was what you would call a 'gentleman farmer', letting out parts of his land to tenants. He had always served his country, from Home Guard in the last war, to Customs Officer to 'B' Specials and finally to the Ulster Defence Regiment. I don't know whether he was very foolish or very courageous to be in the UDR, especially living so close to the border, surrounded by Republicans.

He was posted to the RUC station at Lisnaskea, which was about 11 miles from their house. I know that Emily was very worried about him being ambushed either on the way there or on the way home, in

[**] (irishpeaceprocess.blog/2018/01/18/ira-war-crimes-deliberate-murders-of-civilians)

Thomas and Emily Bullock, murdered by the IRA.
(Dianne Woods)

Mrs Emily Bullock,
murdered with her
husband. (Dianne Woods)

view of the fact that their house was so isolated and at the end of a very long, lonely road. I was told that when it was about the time he was expected home, she would sit on the landing, watching for my uncle's car coming up the road towards their home when he was coming off duty. She would be wrapped in a blanket, with a loaded flare pistol to hand. She always felt that one day the IRA might come calling, once prophetically saying: 'If they come for Tommy, it will be over my dead body.'

That day came on a lovely late summer's evening on 21 September. They were at home watching television when the gunmen burst in, blasting Emily straight away, before stepping over her body to enter the living room. Tommy always kept his personal protection weapon under his favourite chair, but didn't have time to even reach for it as they shot him dead. The gang escaped in several cars, straight across the nearby Aghalane Bridge, shouting and cheering, blowing the car horns as they went; celebrating the death of two lovely people. By the way, I can confirm your claim that the IRA made a sickening hoax call to the local abattoir about the Bullocks and also that several people at a local Nationalist disco came out to cheer and stop the two hearses which were taking their slain bodies away.

No one was ever arrested, although I always cherished the hope that before the last of the Bullocks passed away there would be justice for Emily and Tommy; sadly, it never happened. Even if Sinn Fein/IRA said sorry today, that wouldn't cut it for me; I want justice and I want to see them pay for the crimes that they committed. I understand that John Downey might be connected with the murders, but it has not been confirmed. I don't know too much about the RUC investigation, but I do know about the HET report in which I took part in interviews over a two-year period. It was a complete waste of time and the thirty-page report was fit only for lighting a bonfire!

How do I feel now? I would place these people below beasts; they are absolute scum. My aunt and uncle were lovely people; they were friendly, hospitable and inoffensive. Their murders were part of the IRA's ethnic cleansing campaign in this part of the border country. They were isolated and they were easy targets for the IRA's gunmen.

I joined the UDR myself and was proud to have been a 'Greenfinch'. Even today at parades and memorials, I am proud to wear that uniform. I would have probably joined up anyway, but the murders spurred me on; my ex-husband was a member of the RUCR.

You asked me about the impact of the murder on myself. I feel some distrust of Roman Catholics, not knowing who I can and cannot trust. Many of these people are supporters of the IRA. The evidence for this is the huge number of votes Sinn Fein get at elections. I feel these votes are an endorsement of terrorism. There is absolutely no way that I can forgive or forget the ones who killed Emily and Tommy; forty-eight years on and I still feel very strongly about the killers.

✦

The Ulster Defence Regiment (UDR) was formed in 1970 as an infantry regiment of the British Army in the wake of the disbanding of the RUC auxiliaries, the 'B' Specials. It was to become the largest regiment in the Army, comprising both full and part-time soldiers, male as well as female. It was disbanded in 1992, being replaced by the Royal Irish Regiment on 1 July that year. In the twenty-two years of its existence, some 368 members were killed, not only from terrorist activity, but also from a variety of other causes. Of those killed by terrorists, an absolutely overwhelming majority were killed by Republican paramilitary groups. Additionally, a further fifty-eight former members of the regiment were killed by the Provisional IRA as a consequence of their past association. Terence Maguire (23), a Catholic, was murdered by Loyalist paramilitary group the UFF some eight months after he had left the UDR.

Mr Maguire was a laboratory technician, from the Glen Road area of Belfast's Andersonstown district. He was a rarity: a Catholic serving in the UDR, and he had fallen in love with a Protestant girl who lived in Clonduff Drive in the Loyalist Castlereagh area of East Belfast. On the evening of 14 October 1972, he paid a visit to see his girlfriend, Edith, parking up his Triumph Herald in Montgomery Road. However, when he returned, he saw that his car had been badly vandalised. As he examined the damage, he was grabbed by waiting Loyalist paramilitaries from the UFF. He was bundled into a car and was taken to an area near Clandeboye Street, less than 2 miles from the scene of his abduction; it was only a short six-minute journey away. Once there, he was badly beaten, before being stripped to the waist and shot dead; his killers dragged his body to a nearby alley, where he was discovered the following day by RUC officers. On the same evening that the former soldier was murdered, a gang from the same organisation made a sectarian attack on a Catholic-owned business close to the sectarian interface with the Protestant Village area. They killed Leo Duffy (45) and Thomas Marron (59) and wounded another member of staff in Finnegan's off-licence on Tate's Avenue. It is worth noting that the distance between the attacks is only 4 miles, or a ten-minute car journey.

Denis Maguire is the older brother of the murdered former UDR man, Terence.

Denis's Story

Ballymurphy was designed as a sink estate, and the rioters turned it into a morass, tip head. Our family was appalled, as some of the rioters were known to us; no-hopers who got their kicks watching themselves on the national news. I watched a Catholic mob putting Protestant families out of New Barnsley. My younger brother, Terence, had gone to Clonard Monastery; a young priest there entreated the congregation to join the newly formed Ulster Defence Regiment, which he did. Perhaps it was the murder of three Scottish soldiers that sickened us, but I remember walking with him, in full uniform through Ballymurphy on our way to the bus stop. A year changed everything. Our cars were attacked and a mob gathered outside our house demanding 'the Brit' but luckily Terence was absent. My father managed to obtain a mortgage and we moved to a safe neighbourhood.

I was a student at Queen's University when Terence secured me a summer job working with him in the quality control office in the C&C lemonade factory. It was a happy time. I met Ethel, and Terence was courting Edith. Afterwards I set up a home with Ethel and lost contact with my brother.

After Bloody Sunday, Terence wrote a letter to the UDR resigning his position. On 13 October 1972, Terence had arranged to meet Edith at a 'safe' location. He went home first and went to bed, telling his mother to wake him. He had taken drink so she didn't. He awoke, angry, lambasting her. Despite being ordered by the UDA never to enter Edith's housing estate, he parked his car nearby and went to her house to apologise. He returned to his car to find the windscreen smashed. He was overpowered and taken elsewhere, beaten and shot through the head. He was dumped in an alleyway naked from the waist up except for his tie.

My family didn't know where I lived so I heard it from the news. My father and my young brother went to identify him; on a mortuary slab awash from Terence's blood. My father never got over it. At 62 years he suffered a brain haemorrhage and died soon afterwards. No one was ever charged with his murder.

I'd half expected Terence to be shot by the IRA, which was more traumatic. Why did he not carry a gun? The managers of C&C offered to close the factory the day of the funeral, but the workforce declined. Terence was a brave yet foolhardy person. I am happy to see the UDR remembering him in the Roll of Honour. Nearly fifty years onwards, I remember him with sadness and pride.

◆

On 28 December 1972, a Loyalist bombing team – widely believed to be from the UVF* – planted several car bombs inside the Irish Republic. One car containing 100lb (45.5kg) was left in Butler Street, Belturbet, in Co. Cavan. Sometime earlier, the car carrying the bomb was stopped at the border crossing of Aghalane by the Gardaí. However, the men inside gave the name of a local man, which was enough to convince the officers to allow the red Ford Escort and its deadly cargo to cross into the Republic; Belturbet is a very short 4 miles drive from that point.

Around 2230, without any warning, the device exploded, killing Geraldine O'Reilly (15) and Patrick Stanley (16). Geraldine was in the local fish 'n' chip shop and Patrick was in a telephone kiosk – just 15ft away – phoning his mother in Co. Offaly. The food outlet and a nearby pub were both destroyed. The attack happened just twenty-seven days after two people had been killed and 127 injured when two car bombs exploded in the centre of Dublin. The UVF didn't claim any of these bombings, although their paramilitary 'fingerprints' were all over each

---

* The Ulster Volunteer Force (UVF) was founded in 1912 as a militia designed to resist the clamour for Home Rule and Irish independence from the United Kingdom. Its aims were to fight against the British Government, as well as the Republican forces in the south, in order to prevent their traditional nine counties of Ulster from being absorbed into the proposed Irish Free State. On 4 August 1914, the British Government declared war on the German Empire; the vast majority of the UVF's paramilitaries enlisted in the 36th Ulster Division of Britain's 'New Army'. The 36th fought with bravery and great distinction in the slaughterhouses of the Somme and Verdun, and also at Gallipoli. Those left alive from the initial 36th assaults were subsequently almost wiped out in the 'Kaiser Offensive' of March 1918. The UVF was re-formed in 1919, but fell into a state of disuse after Partition. In 1966, under the leadership of 'Gusty' Spence it re-emerged as a paramilitary organisation with its main aim of stifling the Nationalist civil rights movement. It carried out several sectarian murders of random Catholics, continuing even after the jailing of Spence. Over the course of The Troubles, its ranks included sectarian killers such as Robin 'the Jackal' Jackman of the Mid-Ulster Brigade and Lenny Murphy, the leader of the notorious 'Shankill Butchers'. The UVF was affiliated with the Progressive Unionist Party (PUP) from the party's founding in 1977. There are still many moderate Protestants who are less than happy with the paramilitaries taking the name of the original UVF, which fought so gallantly in the Great War.

of the attacks. In 1993, they finally admitted that they had carried out the 1974 Dublin and Monaghan attacks that killed thirty-four people.

On the same day as the Belturbet bombing, two other bombs exploded in the Republic; the first in Clones, Co. Monaghan, which injured two people, and the second in Pettigo in Co. Donegal, which caused no deaths or injuries; all three bombs exploded within thirty minutes of each other. The cars used in the attacks had been stolen earlier on that same day in Enniskillen before being driven across the border.

Anthony O'Reilly is the brother of Geraldine O'Reilly.

Anthony's Story

Geraldine was my sister, although I didn't know Patrick before the murders. On the night of the bomb, my married sister Francis and her husband were visiting us. At around ten to ten, I offered to give them a lift to their home. Geraldine said that she would like some chips, so she jumped in the car as well. We dropped Francis and her husband off and then drove into Butler Street where there was a chipper called Slovey's. There were no parking spaces available, so I doubled-parked whilst my sister got out.

Then suddenly, there was a huge explosion as a bomb hidden in a car went off, only about 10ft from me. It was like a dream and I must have blacked out, although I remember that my car was lifted into the air. It must have only been seconds, but as I came to, I was leaning out of the open door; I could see huge holes in the car where steel and other things had been blasted through. I could see that the car in front of me and the car behind were both on fire. I managed to get to my feet and asked a passer-by – probably as shocked as me – what had happened. He managed just one word: 'Bomb.' I suddenly remembered that Geraldine had gone into the chipper, which I could see was very badly damaged, and began calling out her name.

By this time, other people, police etc. were starting to arrive, one of whom took me into a pub called The Widow's Arms, where someone made me a cup of tea. A Garda approached me and asked if Geraldine

Geraldine O'Reilly, murdered by a UVF bomb. (Anthony O'Reilly)

was in the chipper; I replied that she was, and he just told me that it was 'bad'. They took me to her to identify her body as she was in a terrible way; I was able to recognise her only because of the clothes she was wearing; it was terribly upsetting. For myself, I was bleeding and my clothes were all ripped.

I was taken to Cavan General Hospital, where my wife Marie spent a lot of time with me, as did my mother and father, who were both in a dreadful state emotionally. Geraldine was the youngest of eight children and Patrick was the youngest of seven. He was a delivery worker, only in Cavan delivering gas, but as the day had got away from them, his driver had decided to stay the night in a B&B. Patrick lived about 50 or 60 miles away, so he decided to telephone his mum in Co. Offaly to say that he wouldn't be home. I understand that the very second that she answered, the bomb went off.

Nobody ever claimed the bomb and the Gardaí interest in it, in my opinion, was very low; they didn't get any help from the RUC across the border, although the investigation such as it was seemed to go on for ages. We all believe that it was the same gang which did the 1973 and 1974 attacks on Dublin. The gang had been stopped at the border bringing the car in, but they bluffed their way through the Garda checkpoint. No one was ever arrested, but several names were mentioned over the years.

I met Patrick's family later and his heartbroken father; he never stopped looking for answers, continuing to seek the truth for over forty years until he died. I believe that the Loyalist gang never claimed it as they were embarrassed that they had killed two children. I was very lucky not to have been killed myself.

I am often asked: do I forgive? I can't forgive, no, not for them taking those young lives away. My emotions have never changed: I am still very, very sad, and what my poor mother and father went through; I can never forget their agony. At times such

Patrick Stanley, killed by a UVF bomb at Belturbet. (Anthony O'Reilly)

Geraldine O'Reilly's family. (Anthony O'Reilly)

Memorial to Geraldine and Patrick in Belturbet. (Anthony O'Reilly)

as three years ago on what would have been Geraldine's sixtieth birthday it hurts especially more. My sister Francis blamed herself as well, wrongly of course, but she has always been 'what if?' What if we hadn't gone at that particular time, what if we hadn't taken a lift; this sort of thing, playing it over and over in her mind. We have asked for justice over these last many years and received none.

In 2015, a monument to the two young people was erected close to the spot where they died. It was thanks to the efforts of Bertie Aharn, Fianna Fáil and Cavan Council. At least they are remembered.

3

1973–75

If any obscenity can be considered as 'routine' it was that of 'any Catholic will do' as Loyalist paramilitaries plumbed new depths of depravity. On Monday, 29 January 1973, it was just that: 'any Catholic will do' as UFF gunmen shot and mortally wounded Lisburn man James 'Jim' Trainor (23) at a petrol station on Kennedy Way in West Belfast. The young man, a father of two, was known as both hard-working and gifted; he worked at the Speedline Garage. During the course of the evening, a car pulled into the filling station, seemingly to purchase petrol. Mr Trainor walked across to serve what he naturally assumed were customers. He had just unhooked the pump, when it is thought that he saw a revolver in the hands of one of the men in the car. He turned to run, but the gunman opened fire, hitting him four times; the car sped off, leaving the wounded man dying on the petrol forecourt. It is thought that he clung on to life for at least an hour afterwards.

Mr Trainor left a young widow, Mary, aged 21, as well as two children aged 3 and one aged 18 months. The murder was linked to the murders of three other young Catholics. The sectarian killings were allegedly carried out by the UFF's South Belfast Brigade; some of the gang members are thought to have been from the Woodvale area, possibly under the command of Francis 'Hatchet' Smith. Over a three-day period of 29–31 January, the same unit shot and killed Peter Watterson (15) at the junction of Donegall Road and the Falls Road, Phillip Rafferty (14) and Gabriel Savage (17). Phillip was abducted from close to his home in Tullymore Gardens in the Andersonstown area; he was on his way to band practice when he was seized by the Loyalist gang. His body was found at Giant's Ring in South Belfast. Gabriel was shot and killed at the Busy Bee Shopping Centre on the Andersonstown Road. Tullymore Gardens is just 1.5 miles from the Speedline Garage, with the Falls Road and Donegall Road being a further 1.2 miles away. Including the Busy Bee Shopping centre, the murders of the Catholic boys all took place within 2 miles of each other.

One of the alleged members of the UFF gang – the aforementioned Francis Smith – strayed into Rodney Street, just off the Falls Road, during the evening of the 30th. He was picked up and shot dead by the Provisionals close to the spot where Peter Watterson was killed.

Mary Hull is the widow of James 'Jim' Trainor.

Mary's Story

Jim was the loveliest fellow I had ever seen probably in my life at the time. He had beautiful, brown curly hair and brown eyes. I thought I didn't have any chance in the world with him at all, but he came over to me and that was it; he asked me to dance with him at Glenavy dance hall. I was delighted as all my friends were after him. He was very quiet but always immaculately dressed, with a pinstripe suit and a tie, the big broad flashy ties … he just loved the style. He was a car mechanic; he just loved doing things with his hands. He loved music as well, and he loved the guitar; he had a white electric guitar. He used to go to Tech' at night and take the music classes and all. I think he had all these dreams, his own garage, but that never happened either.

We were just delighted to get this brand new house on the Old Warren estate in Lisburn. It was at first intended as a mixed housing development and in 1972 we decided to move there; it was a completely new estate. Jim was so good and so quiet, I think now, looking back, he was too good for this world; maybe that's why he was taken.

On the Sunday night, I went to bed and Jim was wakened about twelve o'clock at night; he'd had sort of a dream I thought. He said to me: 'Mary, there's an angel at the bedroom door; her hands are reaching out to me,' and I said: 'Awk, you're dreaming; get back to sleep, you've got work in the morning.' He came home that Monday afternoon, a thing he'd never done either. I can still remember his blue overalls and oil on his face. I made him a cup of tea. He had the two children in his arms, and I said: 'Put the children down; you'll see them later on.' But he wouldn't put the children down and I was kind of angry at him; and that was the last time he seen the children. When he held our boy, I think that he knew that it would be the last time he would do that. My faith tells me that.

There was a knock at the door and my daddy was there with the priest, Father Molloy from Lurgan; he said to me: 'Mary there's been an accident.' I thought he'd been in a car accident. Thinking he's alive and I would have to get ready and go to the hospital, and then my daddy, God rest him, just said: 'Mary sit down. Jim has been shot dead.' That was the Monday night and he was buried on Thursday in Milltown Cemetery.

He was shot dead by the UVF at Kennedy Way filling station, and it was a tit-for-tat murder. No one told me that he lived for an hour, I could have gone to him. I could have been with him at the end. They told me they hadn't the police staff to get me to him. I only had him for three years. It was 1973, and that particular week that Jim was killed was a horrific week; it was a nightmare at the time because every night there was a killing. There was a soldier, a policeman, a civilian; it sort of helped me a bit, because at that time, I thought, well I'm not the only one in Northern Ireland it's happening to.

I had to get a house back up in Lurgan and leave the new house in Lisburn. The people in Lisburn collected around the houses and got me money that went towards the funeral. The minister came to the door with it. I appreciated that so much, they were good people. But that was it, I was all alone.

I know in my heart today, I will never see justice, but I want it that we can be at peace and say, look, our loved ones paid a horrific price; those people were loved by other people, they belonged to people; don't let them be forgotten. My faith to me is a great help, without it, I'm nothing. I know that Jim is in Heaven; I know that from that day to this, he is still looking after me and I thank God for that. I raised his two children;

I did go off and get married again and I had another six children. I thank God for that as well, but God didn't let me go on without having more children. He knew what I was like.

A few months after Jim was killed, I was walking with the two children, and I seen a young couple ahead of me and they were kissing and cuddling. I just thought: my life was over and that was it, but God had other plans for me and He heard my prayers. I do believe that it was God's help which gave me my life back. I believe that He looks after all of us and he saw that I had carried it well.

I attended Crumlin Road courthouse with my father, to be awarded compensation. The judge presiding over the case was Maurice Gibson.[*] It was horrific, I was told by the solicitor to dress down like I was going in to beg. My daddy said: 'She's not going in to beg, she's always immaculate and that's how it's going to be.' I went and got my hair done, that was the one thing I always allowed myself. Judge Gibson made me stand up in the court. He awarded me £6,000 for the loss of a life, but didn't ask what had happened. He looked down on me from the bench and said: 'Quite an attractive young lady, prospects of remarriage.' Looking back I wish I'd said something, I didn't ask to be there. I shouldn't be still fighting, but part of me remembers that young girl that I was then and I feel sorry for her. No one ever asked, 'Mary will you be all right? How are you doing today?' So she's who I fight for.

I am not a bitter person; people have all lost their lives: civilians, soldiers, policemen. When I was in court, there was the young widow of a dead soldier there at the same time, and our stories were the same.

---

[*] On 27 May 1987, Senior High Court Judge Maurice Gibson (73) and his wife, Lady Cecily (67), were killed by a PIRA bombing unit at Killeen, Co. Armagh, as they crossed the Irish border into Northern Ireland. The gang, which gained much notoriety in the border area, is believed to have been under the command of Sean 'The Surgeon' Hughes. Hughes was nicknamed 'The Surgeon' by the Army, who blamed him for carrying out strikes against soldiers with surgical precision. The judge and his wife had been on holiday in North Wales. They had taken the ferry to Dublin, where a Gardaí escort accompanied them as far as the border at Co. Louth. Shortly after the couple crossed into Northern Ireland, a 500lb (227kg) landmine in a culvert exploded as their car passed over it. The blast totally wrecked their car, killing them both instantly and leaving a massive crater in the road.

There is no difference at all in a broken heart; it is still broken, whoever you are.

[Author's note: Part of Mary's testimony was taken from an interview with Allison Morris from the *Irish News*. I am indebted to both women for their permission to allow me to supplement her testimony with selected text from the August 2020 interview.]

✦

On 5 May 1973, a routine foot patrol of the Parachute Regiment was passing through Moybane, Co. Armagh. A Provisional IRA bombing unit had planted a large device close to their route, linking it with a command wire inside the Irish Republic. As the patrol reached the location of the bomb, it was detonated; Warrant Officer II William Vines (36) was killed by the massive blast. Unknown to the rescuers, the IRA bombers, fully aware that a follow-up unit would set up an ICP (incident command post), had planted a secondary device. This was a ploy that they used very successfully over the years, although none with as much devastation as that which killed eighteen soldiers within an hour at Narrow Water, Warrenpoint in Co. Down, on 27 August 1979. In the 1973 incident, the command wire for the device was concealed along the ground leading into the Republic and was fired by the terrorists, who were hidden within their 'safe sanctum'. A 'blind eye' was often shown by the Gardaí, thus allowing them to operate with impunity.

Follow-up units quickly arrived a little under three hours after the first blast. Whilst a unit from the 17/21 Lancers was close to the seat of the original device, a second bomb exploded. Corporal Terence Williams (35), a father of three from Canterbury in Kent, and Trooper John Gibbons (22), father of a newborn son, from Edinburgh, were killed instantly. The two men became respectively the fiftieth and fifty-first soldiers killed in Northern Ireland in 1973.

Linda McHugh is the widow of John Gibbons.

Linda's Story

My husband, Trooper John Gibbons, 17/21 Lancers, was brutally murdered by the IRA on 5 May 1973. John was born in Edinburgh and was a much-loved son of Annie and Jim; he was the third born in a loving family of seven children. He was known as 'Jock' to his friends and was stationed in Wolfenbüttel, Germany, at the time; we lived in a comfortable home a few miles from camp.

Weeks before John left for his tour in Northern Ireland we had the joy and happiness of bringing our newborn son Christopher home. We made every moment count, knowing it wouldn't be long before he had to leave. Together we decided that I would stay in Germany whilst he was away. We wanted to keep life as normal as possible. It was challenging and I missed him terribly but military wives do cope and I was no different. After two long months away John came home on his R&R. We had a wonderful four days together.

Christopher had grown so much and John loved every moment he spent with him. We talked constantly about the holiday we had been saving up for on his return. This was going to be such a special time for us as we would be able to introduce Christopher to his grandparents and relatives in Edinburgh and Yorkshire. Mostly John kept quiet about his tour in Northern Ireland. When I did mention the subject he would make light of any danger. However, he did say if anything should happen I was to remarry as long as I chose someone who would love Christopher as much as he does. I did worry but never doubted that he would come home.

On Saturday, 5 May 1973, not long after lunchtime, I had a knock on my door; my world was about to collapse. Uniformed Army officers and the chaplin, as well as an officer's wife, were standing there, along with my sister who was working on camp. I was holding my son and the chaplin kindly took him from me. Someone gave me a tablet and glass of water. We sat down and holding my hand, the officer's wife started to tell me what I already knew in my heart. I could only hear the clock ticking, I was numb. I don't recall the following hours.

John was killed instantly by a booby trap bomb whilst on duty with the squadron checking the area of an earlier explosion and death of a

Trooper John Gibbons, killed in an IRA blast. (Linda McHugh)

Linda McHugh is the widow of John Gibbons, here pictured with Kenny Donaldson. (Linda McHugh)

soldier. This was a cold and cowardly plan with the intention of killing any soldier or police officer sent to the incident. The explosion was brutal and devastating. John stood no chance. This was two weeks before his 22nd birthday.

Broken and traumatised, within forty-eight hours Christopher and I were put on a flight back to the UK and my mum's home. Our belongings were packed by someone else and sent on later. I never had the chance to share my grief with our friends before I left. Before John was returned I was advised not to view his body as his injuries were so horrific. The coffin was sealed. This led to many months of denial and dreams that he was still alive. My mind could not accept the truth. These were very dark, lonely days.

After about six months I received no more contact from the regiment; no one asked how we were managing. Without Christopher, my saving grace, I would never have found the strength to move forward. Thankfully my mum was there to help and support me and John's family were always in close contact. Periodically I had to endure an inspection, which was to check that whilst I was receiving a war widow's pension I wasn't living with another man. In the early years I was very vulnerable and found this extremely distressing as the pension for me was an acknowledgement of John's sacrifice and a link to the military life we shared.

Slowly and gradually I was able to move forward building a new life for Christopher and myself. Life was becoming more normal. Eventually I was blessed with love and happiness again and remarried. At this point my compensation pension was stopped. To me this felt like there was no longer a Government acknowledgement of the sacrifice John gave for his country, which left me feeling deeply saddened.

When I remarried it gave us the family life we so tragically had taken from us. With great joy our daughter was born and completed our family. The support and love of my husband and children gives me the strength to deal with recurring emotions that on occasions break my heart.

John has always been a part of our family and the pain of his loss is never far away. Our lives were shattered by the perpetrators of his murder but I would not allow them to determine my future.

✦

Sergeant John Haughey (32), a father of three young children, from Didsbury, Manchester, was posted to Northern Ireland in 1973. One of his duties included commanding a foot patrol in the Brandywell area of Londonderry; he was a very popular NCO, and well-liked by his men. His unit – 94 Locating Regiment, Royal Artillery – was based in an old factory close to Lone Moor Road and Stanley's Walk in the Brandywell district, a notorious, hard-line Nationalist area. The west side of the Foyle, comprising the Bogside, Brandywell and the Creggan, was an extremely dangerous area for both the RUC and the British Army.

On 21 January 1974, a foot patrol under Sergeant Haughey left the base to do a security check of their TAOR (Tactical Area of Responsibility). It was normal SOP (standing operating procedure) that when a foot patrol left the factory, one soldier would dash out, immediately taking cover; in this instance, it was John Haughey. The tactic was designed to make him a 'hard target', giving him a measure of protection, while allowing him to shepherd the rest of the patrol through. In this instance, the cover was behind a telephone junction box. Sadly, this type of 'hard targeting', 'going firm' etc. had been witnessed far too often by the IRA's legion of 'dickers'. * Under cover of darkness, a bombing team had placed an explosive device in the same junction box behind which several patrols had been seen to take cover. As the NCO crouched down, the device exploded, mortally wounding the Didsbury boy, as well as injuring several others. He was rushed to Altnagelvin Hospital, where he died shortly after arrival. Witnesses have advised the author that, despite his grievous wounds, John Haughey was concerned about his boys and asked repeatedly if they were all uninjured.

Anita Haughey is the daughter of Sergeant Haughey.

Anita's story

My dad was my personal hero. He loved Army life and enjoyed every opportunity that went with it. We had a wonderful life as a family stationed in Celle, Germany. We travelled over the Continent during the summer holidays, camping and discovering new places. Dad was very loving, patient and great fun. He always had time for us kids and I still

---

* A dicker is generally a paramilitary sympathiser, or is on the fringes of the organisation; their job is to provide local intelligence relating to the movements and tactics of the security forces. Hence: dicking or to be dicked.

On right: Sergeant John Haughey, killed in an IRA blast, Londonderry. (Anita Haughey)

miss him. 21 January 1974 was the day my life changed. I was 7 years old, and the ripples in the pond that were created by my father's death still continue to this day. I will never forget it. I don't remember the first call, maybe we were still at school, but I knew my mother was preparing to visit my father in Londonderry, as he had been injured in a bomb blast but was expected to survive.

There was a knock at the door, as nobody had a home phone in married quarters in those days. I remember standing with my two brothers, Martin and Andrew, to see an officer in his number 1 uniform, his polished Sam Browne belt shining in the light from the hallway. He was accompanied by another person, whom I don't remember. I think somehow I had expected to see my dad magically returned from Northern Ireland as he had recently done at the Christmas just passed; it wasn't to be.

The officer was invited in, and we were ushered into my bedroom to amuse ourselves. My mother already had a friend with her, Sheila Jackson, who I think was going to be looking after us while my mother was away. Sheila was a very supportive and close friend; she was a person we could trust and knew well amongst the army personnel. Myself and my two brothers had no idea about what was happening. We already knew our dad had been injured, and that our mother would be travelling to Northern Ireland to visit him, but we had no clue his life was in danger.

We were called in to the living room after the officers had left. I looked at my mum. Her face looked strange; swollen and puffy from the tears. I didn't understand why my mother looked so different. Mum falteringly told us, 'I've got something to tell you ... Your Daddy's dead kids'... and then collapsed into tears. I was scooped into the arms of Sheila Jackson, whilst my mother hugged the boys. I didn't want to cry but felt I should. I felt numb and very strange as I had not witnessed this kind of emotion in adults before. I remember also feeling angry that nobody had warned me that my daddy might lose his life in Northern Ireland. Within twenty-four hours we were on a plane heading back to the UK. We had lost everything. Along with my father we lost our home, schools, friends, a support network within the regiment, and a wonderful life. It was all changed.

I learnt from later reports that my father had, in a semi-conscious state, tried to enquire about the other men in his troop whilst being driven to hospital in the ambulance. Fortunately there were no other fatalities on that occasion. The irony for our family was that my dad's own family were Irish Catholics and my grandfather was born in Londonderry, but as a young child he had been burnt out of his house by the Black and Tans. The family then fled to the relative safety of Donegal, which is where he had grown up. I still find it so hard to fathom how my dad had been killed on the streets, and by the hands of the people that his own father had been born amongst in that bloody civil war.

My dad's body was flown back to Manchester, where he had been born, and he was given a military funeral at St Catherine's RC Church, where my parents had married ten years earlier. Eight members of 94 Locating Regiment, including Major Tom Hughes, also came over. The coffin was carried through the streets of Didsbury on a 25-pounder gun carriage draped with the Union flag. The sudden death of my beloved grandparents fifteen months later can be attributed to the stress they endured during the previous year. They were still young and vibrant, but died within ten days of each other. We also lost my younger brother

Andrew at the age of 18 in a car accident. I know things would have been different had my father lived.

I lived with my mum, Christine, and my brothers Martin and Andrew in married quarters in Celle and I have some great memories as a child there. I was conscious that Daddy was away, but I knew that, because he was a soldier, he was often away. On Christmas Eve, he suddenly appeared at our house, dirty, grimy and smelling like a soldier; a smell I loved and have always loved; the best daddy in the world was home for Christmas. I remember with a startling clarity that he was carrying his rifle – an SLR – and although many people have told me that I must have imagined it, it is enough for me that I remember the wooden stock and the elliptical holes along the wooden stock; it is also enough for me that the author of this book believes me, too.

I remember that the rifle was quickly secreted away, but that wasn't important, because my daddy, my soldier, my hero, was home for Christmas. He went back to Northern Ireland on Boxing Day and straight to his unit in Londonderry after a couple of wonderful days with us all. Just twenty-six days later, on 21 January, he was on patrol on Lonemoor Road when an IRA bomb exploded right next to him. He was fatally injured and died shortly afterwards; I had lost the best daddy in the world. Afterwards I learned that the Coroner had described his murder as: 'a horrible, brutal murder in which a man doing his duty was blown into eternity' but at 7, I was unaware of what a man in Londonderry had said about my soldier, my hero.

I try not to entertain bitterness, as it destroys people's lives even more than loss, but sometimes it is difficult. I often think about the many thousands of human beings whose lives have been blighted by the senseless murders in Northern Ireland, and it helps to realise I am not alone, and I live in hope that one day I can get some kind of acceptance and peace.

I remember as a child, the anger I felt about not knowing how dangerous it was for my father out there. Naturally we were protected from that worry, but I felt I had been cheated of the truth. I know that one individual arrested for my father's murder some years later was not prosecuted down to his confession being under the influence of sedatives due to alcoholic withdrawal symptoms! Can't have been as bad as bleeding to death due to wounds inflicted by terrorists, I say.

✦

On 4 February 1974, a coach chartered for use by soldiers and their families set off from Manchester headed for Catterick in North Yorkshire. A member of the IRA placed a large explosive device in the luggage hold of the coach. When the device detonated as the coach drove along the M62 close to Huddersfield, eleven people were killed and a twelfth died three days later.

Paul Reid (17) and Leslie Walsh (19) of the Royal Signals; Leonard Godden (22) and Terence Griffin (24) of the Royal Artillery; Michael Waugh (22) Guards; and John Hines (22), James McShane (29) and Stephen Walley (19) of the Royal Regiment of Fusiliers were all killed. The dead included 23-year-old Clifford Houghton along with his family, Linda Houghton (23) and their two young children Lee (5) and Robert (2).

Mo Norton is the sister of Bombardier Terence Griffin.

Mo's Story

Terence (Griff as he was known by his friends) spent his last weekend on leave at our family home in Bolton with his friend Len. They had a happy weekend together with us all.

Just after midnight my father heard a newsflash on the radio that there had been an explosion on a coach but very little information was forthcoming at this stage. We waited all day for news; we kept listening to the news bulletins on the television hoping and praying that he would be safe. We were continuously ringing the telephone number that was given out but they could not tell us if Terence had survived.

After waiting over seventeen long and arduous hours we were finally told that Terence had died. Twelve people in total, two of them little children, a whole family were killed and many more injured. To say we were devastated would be an understatement. We were all totally heartbroken. My lovely mum and dad and my two sisters were so completely overwhelmed and distraught with grief. We each have had to deal with our grief in our own personal way, but I will never, ever forget 4 February 1974 and what effect it has had personally on my life.

Time goes by and it is now forty-six years since we lost Terence. It is still painful to think about the circumstances of how he was cruelly taken from us and the devastating effect it had on my parents and sisters. The circumstances of how he died in such a violent way were incredibly heart-breaking. You do get to a point of acceptance; you know

Terence Griffin, murdered along with ten others in the M62 coach bomb. (Maureen Mo Norton)

he will not be coming back, and life has not been the same without him.

The perpetrators were never brought to justice, nor are they likely to. I do think justice is important for us to live in a civilised society. I, however, do not live my life dwelling on the injustice of it all as that would be fruitless, not just for myself but for the rest of my family and friends. Sometimes I am asked if I have forgiven and I must be honest and say that I do not feel the need to forgive, neither do I spend my life hating the perpetrators. I do not think it is my place to forgive what happened. War is ugly and ugly things happen. If I were to apportion blame, it would be towards the terrorists but also a large part would be towards the politicians that allowed a terrible situation to flourish for so many decades.

It has been more beneficial for me to get involved with others who have been affected by terrorism and try to do something positive. I was involved as a participant in the Johnathan Ball Foundation for Peace in Warrington from 2005 until 2020. I went on many courses and travelled to Northern Ireland and the Republic many times, meeting with others who had been affected by terrorism. I found this to be a very therapeutic way of dealing with any negative emotions I had regarding what had happened to Terence. For the last two years, I have been a Citizen's Educator for WAVE Trauma Centre in Belfast and talk to trainee doctors, nurses, counsellors at Queen's University Belfast on the trauma I had experienced and what happened to our family. The feedback has been positive. I along with my family will always miss Terence and we talk fondly of him. I regard myself lucky to have for twenty-one years of my life a big brother so funny, so amusing, so kind and loyal. I know I will miss him forever.

✦

On Friday, 17 May 1974, in Dublin city centre, the Ulster Volunteer Force (UVF) – which had been, somewhat incredibly, legalised by British Secretary of State for Northern Ireland Merlyn Rees some two weeks earlier – took the terror war to Dublin, the capital of the Irish Republic. It should be noted that it took them almost two decades before they admitted responsibility for the terror attacks in the city. In a series of blasts, twenty-six people were killed, with the death toll tragically including a nine months pregnant woman and a baby in arms. No warnings were given before the bombs exploded, three of which occurred in Dublin during rush hour. An hour and a half later, a further device exploded in Monaghan, which killed five people and fatally wounded two more; they would later die of their injuries. Most of the victims were young women, although the ages of the dead ranged from five months to eighty years. No one has ever been charged with the attacks, which have been described by the Oireachtas Committee on Justice[*] as an act of international terrorism.

The list of those murdered in Dublin by Loyalist paramilitaries that day is as follows: Breda Turner (21); Antonio Magliocco (37) an Italian; Anna Massey (21), who was due to be married in June that year; Edward O'Neill (29), whose son was badly injured and whose wife gave birth later to a stillborn baby; Marie Phelan (20); Anne Byrne (25); Colette O'Doherty (21), who was nine months pregnant and due to have her baby induced in hospital that very night; Christina O'Loughlin (51); Maureen Shields (51); Anne Marren (20) and her friend Josephine Bradley (21);

---

[*] The Oireachtas, sometimes referred to as Oireachtas Éireann, is the National parliament or Legislature of Ireland.

Marie Butler (21); Simone Chetrit (31), a French citizen in Dublin to learn English; John Dargle; Patrick Fay (47); Breda Grace (35); Mary McKenna (55); Dorothy Morris (57); John O'Brien (23), his wife Anna (22) and their baby children, Jacqueline (17 months) and Anne-Marie (5 months); Siobhan Rice (19); John Walsh (27); Elizabeth Fitzgerald (59).

The following anonymous contribution is from a survivor of one of the Dublin bombs.

A Survivor's Story

I have had extensive therapy and memory reconstruction over the past few years and what I am going to tell you is partly what I can remember of that terrible day and partly through my treatment as well as access to medical records.

I remember being in the barber's and we stepped outside into Parnell Street; there was a crack, a flash of white light followed by flames. The next that I can remember is that the blast blew across the road from one side to the other. I was on the ground; I could see legs running and people were screaming; I was kicked as someone tripped over my body. Then I saw some boots; lady's boots, but the legs were on fire. She fell down in the street right next to me, but at that moment I went out like a light. Some of what happened to me next is as a result of therapy as well as medical records. The building next to me collapsed right on top of me; I received crush injuries to my head, sternum and pelvis. Someone grabbed me by the legs to pull me clear and I could hear voices shouting. I had nightmares for years which I called my 'hooded man' dream; he has no face, only a hood with a tattoo of a spider on his hands.

I could see a substantial wound in my upper leg and groin which had blood pouring from it; I tried to put my hand inside this deep gap in my body. At that moment, a man's voice called out: 'That child has to go to hospital,' but someone responded: 'That child is dead!' I was put into a car in which there was another injured boy who was crying. The next bit is weird, because I had an out of body experience. It happened at a time when the records show that I was in the operating theatre at

Jervis Street Hospital under anaesthetic. I could see myself standing in the hospital car park; my T-shirt was torn, I was bleeding, all my clothes were ripped. I could see cars and ambulances queuing to get into the hospital. There was a church over the road with rows of coffins all laid out, with porters bringing the bodies out of the hospital and putting them straight into the coffins.

We lived in inner-city Dublin in a rough neighbourhood where it was tough for a single mother with kids and I was constantly fighting, always getting into scraps. It was an unforgiving place where you had to fight your corner or go under. PTSD was unknown in those days, but I was so traumatised, so lacking in understanding that I became uncontrollable. The first evidence of this I suppose was when we walked into Parnell Street to watch a St Paddy's Day parade. The banging of the drums shocked me as I associated it with the sound of the bomb. It was my first flashback; the first of many over the years. They would take the form of a slow motion nightmare; I would see the flames coming towards me, but as they reached my face, they stop, but then the face of a monster comes out of the flames, screaming at me.

Do I forgive them? I feel cheated, robbed of my life. In 1993, I tracked down one of the UVF bombers, a man called James Mitchell, to his home. To be honest, I just wanted to kill the bastard. When he opened the door, I saw an old man; that was him, now aged well into his 70s. I told him who I was and challenged him. He admitted to me that he had been one of the bombers but he was so blasé and tried to justify it with 'What about Kingsmill then?' He was referring to the IRA massacre of ten Protestant workers in 1976. Just then, Lily Shields, another gang member, turned up behind him. The police had put out a story that she was dead. I remember saying something like: 'Jesus, Lily but you look good for a dead woman!'

Mitchell said to me: 'Are you here to kill me?' I told him that I wasn't but I just said: 'Just before you die, I hope that you see all the faces of the people that you have killed and they scream at you.' I walked away into my future and am trying to get my life back.

[Author's note: James Mitchell was a former RUC Reserve Officer as well as a member of the UVF's Glennane gang, responsible for over

100 sectarian slayings. He died in 2008; Lily Shields was nominally his housekeeper, but is now known to have been a UVF member.]*

✦

In the late summer of 1974, Belfast, always a dangerous place to be at virtually any stage of The Troubles, became even more dangerous as both the UVF and UFF stepped up their sectarian attacks on the Catholic community. Between July and October, the two separate Loyalist paramilitaries killed eighteen people in the Province; seventeen of the dead were civilians. The thirteenth victim was an OIRA member, Patrick McGreevy (16); his shooting took place in Clifton Street, Belfast. Sixteen of the murders were committed in Belfast. This was also a time when massive in-fighting took place between the two main sets of Loyalist paramilitaries. The UFF were much bigger than their rival UVF, particularly in East Belfast. Cusack and McDonald described: 'systematic harassing of UVF men in pubs, developed into attacks on UVF men's homes', with on one occasion a hand grenade being thrown through the window of a leading UVF member. Retaliation was swift, with the UVF detonating a bomb at the Bunch of Grapes pub on the Beersbridge Road, a UDA/UFF stronghold in the Ballymacarret area of East Belfast. Retaliation followed retaliation, eventually spilling out into a monstrous brawl in the Loyalist wing at Long Kesh, which injured almost sixty men, including eleven soldiers. This then was the background to an attempt by the UFF at mass murder.

Macrete's was a concrete company, based in Duncrue Street, Belfast; it employed Catholic as well as Protestant workers, but was perceived as a Roman Catholic company by Loyalist paramilitaries. On the morning of 19 September 1974, a minibus containing some of the company's workforce approached the factory. As it slowed to await the opening of a security barrier, a waiting gunman armed with an automatic weapon opened fire on the stationary vehicle. Several shots hit the van, wounding Desmond X, who was 19 at the time, and two of the other passengers. It is not known if the weapon had a stoppage, but the firing ceased as

---

* www.irishtimes.com/opinion/families-of-the-troubles-victims-must-learn-the-truth-1.1218615

the gunman then escaped in a stolen blue Ford Escort, found later in the Shore Road area close to the Loyalist Shankill; it had been stolen earlier in the York Road area. Only one man was ever charged: Michael Atcheson, who was the driver, was jailed in 1976. Informed opinion feels that it was likely a gang from the UFF, probably from the Shankill area.

Desmond X spent some time in hospital; these are his words.

Desmond's Story

I lived, and still do, in Castlewellan, but worked in Belfast, which was a fair journey twice a day. On the morning of 19 September 1974, I was in the firm's red Transit van, picking up workers from all over to get them to work. I was sitting on the second row, immediately behind the driver. I remember that we had picked up two boys from the Grosvenor Road, and we had just arrived at the security barrier at the factory. As the barrier was lifting, two things caught my eye: I saw a car with the engine running, the exhaust snaking into the cold air – it was around 0700 hours – and then the sight of a man in a black balaclava, with a machine gun in his hand.

He opened fire instantly, it was more of a spraying, with the bullets crashing in through the glass. I was hit twice in the chest, with the two lads either side of me being hit in their legs. I was shaking with fear; there was pandemonium, coupled with fear and shock. I had been hit in the chest, but I was in too much shock to register the pain; only the fear. The man then dashed back to the waiting car, which then screeched away. I remember that the ambulances were there quickly, and I was moving with shock and just wanted to stand up, but the medics made me lie down. It was only afterwards that one of the two other wounded men told me that my elbow flew back into his ribs in that moment that I was hit. They both had blood gushing out of their wounded legs.

I was taken to the Royal Victoria, and as soon as the shock began to wear off, I had this very quick feeling that I wanted to put everything behind me. Whilst I was there, there was a terrible screaming and moaning coming from the next ward; a nurse told me that a soldier had received a really bad wound, and that he was in absolute agony. After a while, the crying out ended as he was moved to another ward; I don't know what happened to him, but I really hope that he recovered.

The two bullets had penetrated my skin, before ricocheting off my ribs and emerging from another part of my body. I was deeply blackened with bruising, my ribs were incredibly sore. The surgeon told me that I must have had ribs like steel, which caused the bullets to bounce off them! The staff in the hospital were brilliant – one even offered to give me a haircut – and they really looked after me. I was there for a week, before I was taken back home to Castlewellan.

It was two years before I went back to work, but I never returned to Macrete's, instead choosing to work for the DOE in their historic buildings section, working as a scaffolder. It was less money, but at least it was local and I didn't have that long journey into Belfast and back every day; there was also the bonus of it being less risky!

I don't recall much of an investigation, although a couple of years later, two RUC detectives came to the house to inform me that a man from the gang had been arrested. I did turn up at court in Belfast to give evidence, but the man pleaded guilty and I was sent home.

I never suffered too much physical pain, but there was a lot of emotional trauma. I met my wife about eight years afterwards, and it took her a while to understand what I was going through. We bought a house in Castlewellan in 1983, and ironically enough, it was one which had been rebuilt after an IRA bomb explosion. There were lots of IRA bombs in Castlewellan, I can tell you.

You asked me what I felt about the gunmen, the men who did this to me; well, I can tell you that I feel sorry for them. It was their background, their environment that caused their actions. I could never understand how they could go out to kill and harm people that they didn't even know. I must tell you that we were brought up to like and respect people, and as a result, I never entertained any thoughts about joining the paramilitaries. You asked me what I would do if I could meet the gunmen today; I can say this: I would hold no hatred for them or the people who planned it.

The van contained Protestants – like myself – as well as Catholics, and the workforce at Macrete's was the same: mixed. I suppose that the Loyalist gang perceived that it was a purely Roman Catholic workforce and that is why they chose to try and kill the people on board.

✦

Tullyvallen Guiding Star Temperance Orange Lodge is situated just off the Blaney Road, near Newtownhamilton in Co. Armagh. The local Orange Order had arranged one of their regular meeting there on that fateful night of 1 September 1975; they opened their meeting with prayer, and were having a general discussion. At this point, several masked gunmen burst into the hall through the kitchen at the back. Armed with at least two machine guns, they sprayed the inside of the room with bullets, attempting to massacre all the seventeen men sitting in the hall. While this was happening, another gunman fired through a window from outside. Three men were killed immediately, while several others were wounded. One of the wounded died in the back of the ambulance that had arrived to try to save his life. A fifth man died two days later in Craigavon Area Hospital.

An off-duty member of the security forces – known to be RUC – attending the meeting was able to use a personal protection weapon to fire back. He shot and wounded one of the gunmen, who escaped with the others. The medical services and an Army patrol arrived very quickly afterwards; a routine search by the soldiers discovered a metal container with 2Ib (just under 1kg) of explosive inside; this was defused.

Four of the Orange Lodge members died that night. The murders were later claimed by the Republican Action Force, thought to have been either an expedient flag of convenience used by the Provisional IRA's Army Council, or more likely an attempt to distance the Republican movement from what was an undeniably sectarian attack; possibly by an out of control local unit. The Provisionals have always claimed that when they killed – which as posterity has recorded was with great frequency – it was never carried out on sectarian lines. This author has unearthed countless examples that easily contradict their protestations of innocence. The murder gang were aware of the identities of the men who would be in the hall, although they would not have known that an off-duty policeman would also be in attendance. It is also worth noting that at the time PIRA was supposedly observing a ceasefire, which made the sectarian attack even more embarrassing to the movement.

The dead were: James McKee (73) and his son William Rowland, known as 'Ronnie' (40), Nevin McConnell (48), John Johnston (80) and Willie Herron (68). Berry Reaney was one of six others wounded in the attack, as was his brother, Archie, and his dad, Jack.

Berry's Story

The meeting at the Orange Hall that night was just one of several regular ones which we held there. There was a sense of fear in the area at that time, locally three Protestants and two Catholics had been murdered in the previous two weeks; living only 2 miles from the border with the Republic and closer to the Nationalist Cullyhanna made you feel uneasy every time you went out. It was right in the heart of 'bandit country'. There was always the fear of kidnapping, shooting or getting caught up in crossfire or a bombing incident.

We were about half an hour into the meeting, when there was a huge crash as the side door to the hall was rammed in, and two men clad in balaclavas, armed with machine guns[*] burst in from the kitchen. There was no hesitation; they just opened fire, spraying everywhere. James was close to the door at the end of the table; he stood up and was cut down immediately from less than 3m. I was at the opposite end of the table and I just threw myself to the floor as the shooting continued. During the shooting I felt a thud on my left forearm; I realised that I had been hit. The shooting went on for about twenty to thirty seconds, but it seemed a lot longer; it seemed an eternity. What I didn't realise though was that one of the people at the meeting who was an off-duty RUC officer had opened fire on the attackers with his personal protection weapon, wounding one of the gunmen.

When the shooting stopped, I was clinging to the ground, but thinking that those boys were going to come round and finish us off with

---

[*] Author's note: some of these weapons were also used in the PIRA ambush at the Kingsmill massacre in January 1976; eleven Protestant workmen were shot, with ten killed, and another severely wounded.

Scene of the Tullyvallen massacre. (Berry Reaney)

shots to the head. Nothing happened, and soon people were moving around, with some moaning with pain. My brother, Archie, had been hit on the back between the shoulders, whilst another brother, William, was lying motionless; later we found that he had fainted with shock. There was an awful stench of cordite with the air being full of blue-grey smoke; the smell was very pungent.

Then we saw Dad, lying and bleeding badly; he was obviously badly injured. We managed to get him to his feet, and placed him gently on a raised platform so that we could see how hurt he was. As I said, he was bleeding severely, blood was running from several wounds in his right arm out of his coat sleeve, but we managed to get his arm raised and tied up to stop further blood loss; he was also wounded in the foot where a bullet passed through just below his ankle bone. Just looking around, we could see that James and his son, Ronnie, were dead; it was already too late to help them. John Johnston was also dead, Nevin was still alive, but was severely injured – blood could be seen coming from several wounds on his body. Despite medical efforts to save him, he died shortly afterwards in

Willie Herron, killed in the Tullyvallen
massacre. (Berry Reaney)

Nevin McConnell, killed in the Tullyvallen
massacre. (Berry Reaney)

the ambulance. Willie Herron was able to walk around, but commented about having been hit in the stomach; however, he insisted that the medics on the scene attend to the other wounded and the young men first. Sadly he died two days later in Craigavon Area Hospital. I mentioned my middle brother, William, earlier; we rolled him on to his back, but fortunately there were no bullet holes; it was just the shock which caused him to faint.

I was in hospital for under two weeks, but it took a lot longer than that to get over the terrible shock, and the memories of that night have never left. Each survivor remembers a different angle of the shooting, and our different stories are needed like a jigsaw puzzle to form an over-all picture of the attack as we remember it. Four of the men were buried on the one day, with one service in Clarkesbridge Presbyterian Church for James, Ronnie and Nevin; James and Ronnie are buried side by side in the adjoining graveyard, Nevin was buried approximately a quarter of a mile away in the 'Hill Church' graveyard. John Johnston was buried in Freeduff graveyard, just over 2 miles from Crossmaglen; it really was a terrible time for the families and those in hospital.

The IRA never admitted that they had carried out this overtly sectarian attack, instead it was claimed by the Republican Action Force. One man was arrested for the murder of a UDR man sometime later and

'Ronnie' McKee, killed in the Tullyvallen massacre. (Berry Reaney)

James McKee, killed in the Tullyvallen massacre. (Berry Reaney)

John Johnston, killed in the Tullyvallen massacre. (Berry Reaney)

The funeral procession of Nevin McConnell and James McKee, Tullyvallen massacre.
(Berry Reaney)

he admitted that he had driven the getaway van on the night that we were attacked.

We all made statements to the RUC, of course, but in many ways the investigation was poor due to the circumstances of the time. Murders were almost daily and they didn't have the manpower or the modern forensic science to help them. They were overstretched; we never heard back from them; there was no follow-up. One thing which angered all of us came later at the Inquest, where the RUC inspector gave an inaccurate account of what had happened. There was no retaliation against the local Catholics; it didn't enter our heads. The local Protestant clergymen organised a United Service of Worship for all the local Protestant Churches the following Sunday, where a large congregation stood in silence to endorse a resolution calling for 'no retaliation'. We acted with restraint, but the Government and police lack of action and attitude upset everybody.

How do I feel now? I will never forgive those men who carried out this dreadful deed, because I can never understand how these young men and their not so young masters can just take up a gun or plant a bomb and take someone's life. The Catholics preach about the preservation of life, so how can these men go to church on a Sunday, being taught this, and then go out the next day and kill? I can't square how they can worship in church, then appear to be quite happy to commit murder. What happened was a form of ethnic cleansing; the IRA knew that the adults from several families would be there that night; killing them would wipe out several Protestant households; that's why they did it. The gunmen planned it well; they knew exactly who they were going to kill.

I see some of the survivors at least once a month; they all feel the same as I do; some will discuss it, others won't. Some won't even discuss it with their family. So to repeat: I will never forgive them.

4

1976–80

On 27 January 1976, John McCready (56), a North Belfast business-man, part-time fireman and member of the Orange Order,* was walking home from a Masonic club meeting. He was intending to walk home to help his wife celebrate her birthday. However, as he reached the junction with Charnwood Junction and the Cavehill Road, a car that was later shown to have been stolen in a Catholic area pulled alongside him. One man got out, immediately confronting Mr McCready; he asked him his name and the area in which he lived. Tragically for the father of one, he gave the 'wrong answer'. One of the gunmen opened fire, hitting him five times, mortally wounding the businessman. He died in the Royal Victoria Hospital on 6 February.

His killers had identified him as a Protestant by virtue of the fact that his address was in a Protestant area; in their extraordinary rationale, that alone signed his 'death warrant'. It is highly likely that he was killed by PIRA, in what was an overtly sectarian murder. The Provisional IRA contained many 'hot heads' as well as those who simply would not follow orders; others simply selected their own agendas. There was an element of both criminal and psychotic behaviour in the Republican organisation, and it is often felt that The Troubles gave them an outlet

---

* It is a most sobering thought that almost 10 per cent of all those killed during The Troubles were members of the Orange Order; this statistic includes both civilians and members of the security forces. The total number of Orange Order members killed by terrorists is a quite staggering 339.

for these traits. The Provisionals made a series of hollow claims during this period of turbulence, to the effect that they were not a sectarian organisation. However, many of their killings bore the hallmarks of sectarianism; moreover, they were carried out under the 'all-embracing Irish cloak of patriotism', to borrow a phrase from Irish writer John Dorney. The history of The Troubles is suffused in the blood of people who were simply in the wrong place at the proverbial wrong time.

Martyn McCready is the son and only child of the murdered man.

Martyn's Story

I was aged about 30 at the time of the murder of my dad; I was living about 10 miles away at the time. At around 2245 on the evening of 27 January, I received a phone call from the police. They informed me that my dad had been knocked down in an accident on Cavehill Road, and that I should come straight away. As I drove up the Cavehill Road towards my dad's house there were UDR, RUC as well as Regular Army on the Cavehill Road at the junction of Charnwood Avenue; it was chaos. I was stopped at a checkpoint and told that I wasn't allowed to go any further. After I had explained who I was, they waved me to my parents' house, where a policeman met me at the door; he told me that my father had not been knocked down, but that he had been shot. He asked me to tell my mother the sad news, adding that I should get to the Victoria [Royal Victoria Hospital].

I drove straight there and was greeted at the side ward in which my father was, but told that I could only see him for two minutes. My dad was in a bad way, only able to turn his head to the right; there was blood in his lungs which made a gargling noise, so it was extremely difficult to understand what he was saying. From later reports and trying to decipher what he was saying to me, it transpired he was walking along the road to his house, intending to post some letters on the way. However, before he even reached the pillar box, a car pulled up alongside him and a young man of about 16 or 17 shot him at point-blank range five times, hitting him in the heart, lungs and stomach. As

Mr and Mrs John McCready. (Martyn McCready)

*John McCready, murdered
in Belfast by the IRA.
(Martyn McCready)*

I said, I could barely understand him, but he kept saying: 'Look after your mum.'

He underwent emergency surgery, during which they had to remove his spleen, and there were tears in his heart from the bullet. They also discovered that he had put his hands up to protect himself, but one of the bullets went through his watch and into his chest. His younger brother offered one of his lungs if it would save Dad's life, but the wounds were far too severe and he passed away at 1255 on Friday, 6 February 1976.

Some years later, SEFF introduced me to a female UDR soldier – a 'Greenfinch' – called Margaret Melville. She had sat with dad and comforted him in a way only a woman can do, holding his hand as neighbours, alerted by the shootings, brought out blankets to keep him warm. She bandaged his wounds as best she could, going in the ambulance with him. Margaret kept trying to reassure him, encourage him, but he knew that he was dying and just wanted to make sure that Mum was going to be all right. She told me that he was unable to finish many of his sentences.

There was an investigation by the RUC, but I am not convinced how thorough it was. The gun used to kill Dad was found in the Sinn Fein offices in the New Lodge. It transpired that the car used by the gunmen had been parked at Carr's Lane, just off the York Road, and stolen whilst the owner was in a nearby club. False plates from a stolen motorbike were then fitted to the car. All we know for certain is that Dad had been at a Masonic Lodge meeting in Arthur's Square and decided to have a couple of drinks at the Belfast Royal Academy Social Club with friends. He declined a lift, setting off to walk the 500 yards home when he was shot down.

There were some arrests over the years, including a known IRA man; he died in prison of natural causes. The actual gunman was known to be a member of the IRA's youth wing, living in the Old Park area. He was arrested but said not a word over several days of investigation before they eventually released him without charge. From what I know, another of the gang was arrested for taking part in terrorist activities; he got six years in 1977. There was a HET report into the case and it highlighted several discrepancies and mistakes. Apparently, when the suspects were arrested, because they were known to the RUC, their fingerprints were never taken and used in comparison; had they done so, they might have been arrested for shooting Dad. I should also mention that thanks to diligent work by an inspector at York Street police station, fingerprints were found on the back of the false number plates which the killers had put on the stolen car which they used in the murder.

The following is a section taken from the Historical Enquiries Team (HET) report:

Suspect 1 was arrested again on June 7 1976 on his own, under terrorism legislation. He was questioned about terrorist activity and membership of the Provisional IRA. The record does not show whether he was questioned about John's murder. He was released without charge on June 9, 1976.

He was arrested again on February 10, 1977 under terrorism legislation after his name had been supplied anonymously, as a suspect in the murder of a soldier in January 1977. He was released without charge on 12 February. He was re-arrested for this murder on 3 May and in May 1977 he was charged with the murders of two police officers, three soldiers and two civilians, (one an infant killed by a bomb) all in North Belfast and all attributed to the Provisional IRA. He was convicted of the murders and in 1990, while serving a series of life sentences in the Maze prison, he died of natural causes.

Suspect 2 was also a member of the Provisional IRA from the same street in the Bone area as Suspect 1. Records show that Suspect 2 was arrested several times on suspicion of terrorist offences during the mid-1970s. In April 1977 he was convicted of possessing explosives with intent to endanger life and with membership of a proscribed organisation and sentenced to six years in prison. The offences occurred in June 1976, just a few months after John's murder.

Suspect 2 had a substantial criminal record for involvement in car theft and driving offences, before and after his terrorism convictions in 1977.

It was normal practice to fingerprint all suspect terrorist prisoners as part of the reception process at Castlereagh police office. There is no record that Suspects 1 and 2 were fingerprinted on February 3. If they had been their fingerprints would have been sent to the fingerprint

BANGORIAN DIES OF GUNSHOT WOUNDS

Victim of terrorist attack in Belfast

distance to his home that the cold-blooded shooting took place.

THE DEATH OF Mr. John Edward McCready ten days after being shot near his home in Belfast has caused sorrow in his native Bangor. He received severe chest injuries, and died in hospital on Friday. The funeral, which took place to Clandeboye Cemetery on Tuesday, reflected the high esteem in which he was held.

A popular member of an old Bangor family, John was born in the Mill House, Windmill Road, fifty-six years ago. Shortly afterwards the family moved to Hayford, Upper Balloo, and he attended the little Primacy School nearby for a time, later going to Rowandene School, Hamilton Road.

He followed his father to embarking on a career in building. After serving his apprenticeship with a local firm and working for a time at Ballyholme Shipyard, he joined the local contracting business - the Loopland Building Works, Belfast. They acquired and converted the former police station in Victoria Road, Bangor, into flats, and are engaged in several contracts in and around Belfast.

Although living in Old Westland Road, Belfast, John retained strong ties with his native town - mainly through the Orange and Masonic Orders. Cleland Pipe Band, in which he played as a boy, had in John a generous benefactor. He loved pageantry, and was a familiar figure at local "Twelfth" demonstrations and highland gatherings.

Those who knew this genial, kindly man - he helped people of all creeds and classes - find it inconceivable thaat he had any enemies. It is thought that the bullets which killed him were fired indiscriminately from a car. He had been given a lift from a meeting in the city centre, and had insisted that the driver leave him off on Cavehill Road. It was while he was walking the short

Mr. JOHN McCREADY

Mr. McCready is survived by his wife Renee (nee Rainey, of Bangor) son Martyn, who lives in Grahamsbridge Road, Dundonald; his parents, Mr. Mrs. John McCready, brothers Nat and Tom, who all live in Belfast; and sister, Mrs. Margaret White, Dundalk. To them, and little granddaughter Karen, sympathy is tendered in their tragic bereavement.

St. Barnabas Parish Church (to which Mr. McCready belonged) was filled for the funeral service on Tuesday. The Rector, Rev. J. Clyde, gave a moving address, in which he paid tribute to Mr. McCready's qualities of heart and head. At the graveside in Clandeboye Cemetery Mr. Clyde was joined by the Rector of Bangor Abbey, Rev. Canon James Hamilton, and by the Bishop of Down, Right Rev. George A. Quin, who gave the blessing.

Many local friends of the family, as well as Orange and Masonic brethren, joined the cortege at the cemetery. Cleland Memorial Pipe Band paraded

John McCready press cutting. (Martyn McCready, Belfast Telegraph)

bureau the same day to confirm their identity. It is likely they were not fingerprinted on this occasion because they were already on record, having been arrested on previous occasions.

The pain never goes away, you know? Mum came to live with us, staying with us for several months before getting a house next to her sister in Bangor. At one point, she did go home for two or three days but had to come back to us. She often had nightmares, sometimes waking up and calling out: 'John, John.' It was so distressing and so hard to watch.

I do have some things which I would like to add: my father was taken away from us, and never saw his grandson. Because his granddaughter was only 3 at the time, she never got to know him; she only knows him through the photos which we have of him. He helped me to build my own house, which we still live in today.

The men who shot my father did two things: they took a man's life away and they shot my best friend. He was a person who I loved so much. He taught me everything that I know; he taught me so much, we worked together in the building trade – and we socialised together. He was a man who was loved and cherished by everyone he knew. It has been horrific without him over the years.

Dad once told me that no one has a right to take a life; there is only one person who can take a life and that is our Lord.

✦

In the previous chapter, we spoke of the five murders at the Tullyvallen Guiding Star Temperance Orange Lodge; in total seven* members of the Lodge were killed by Republican terrorists. On the evening of 25 February 1976, almost six months after the massacre there, the Provisional IRA killed Joseph McCullough, a part-time soldier in the UDR. Private McCullough lived on a very remote farm at Blaney Road, Newtownhamilton in Co. Armagh. Because of its isolated position, it was extremely vulnerable to attack by cross-border terrorists. For reasons of security, the soldier only visited once a week to feed his animals. On the evening in question, three members of the local PIRA unit – believed to include at least two brothers – knocked at the door of the farmhouse, having observed their victim enter. As he opened the door, one of the men immediately stabbed him in the throat; in all, he was stabbed a total of five times, including two fatal wounds to his throat. His body was left where it fell; unknowingly to the killers, Private McCullough was still alive although barely. In an effort to kill or maim follow-up security forces, a booby-trapped explosive device was planted on the dying man's body.

One man was later arrested and convicted for his role in this murder. He was also convicted of the five murders at Tullyvallen and the murder of another soldier, Corporal Robert McConnell (32), on 5 April, less than six weeks after the killing of Joseph McCullough. The subsequent HET report stated that one of the suspects was: 'an active terrorist who belonged to the Cullyhanna Unit of the 3rd Battalion of

---

* The seventh was William Meaklim (29), a former RUCR officer who was kidnapped and tortured by the Provisional IRA on or about 16 August 1975. A Republican source chillingly told the *Sunday Times* in 1999: 'he was given an awful death to try and make him talk'.

the South Armagh Provisional IRA'. The report also shows numerous arrests for two other members of the gang, although no formal charges were ever laid.

Alan McCullough is the nephew of the murdered man.

Alan's Story

Uncle Joe was a member of the Tullyvallen Lodge and the only reason that he wasn't there on the night of the attack was because he was attending the wake of a fellow UDR Soldier, Joseph Reid, who had been murdered by IRA terrorists near Keady two days previous. My Uncle Joe was a member of the UDR and he was also a former 'B' Special. He was the seventh member of the Lodge to be murdered by IRA terrorists in just 7 months. He was a labourer who did a bit of work on the family farm where he had been born and raised. At the time of the killing, he was staying with friends, returning on

UDR soldier Joseph McCullough, murdered by the IRA. (Alan McCullough)

occasions to feed his dog and his few pigs. The farm was less than 2 miles from the border which made it very easy for terrorists to quickly cross over into the Republic. The farm was about a mile away from where the Tullyvallen massacre had taken place.

From what we know, he was attacked at his door by a well-known local Republican who stabbed him in the throat using a bayonet, giving him no chance to draw his personal protection weapon. He was stabbed again, before being booby-trapped with explosives and left for dead. We think that he tried to crawl for help but shortly afterwards an explosion was heard in the area; this would not have been an unusual occurrence. The next morning, his neighbour's son came looking for him and found his dead body. As normal this instigated a huge RUC and Army follow-up immediately afterwards. It would appear that the terrorists had been waiting for him, hidden in one of his outbuildings.

I can tell you this: he was killed by local men including two brothers who were never convicted of his murder. One of the other members of the gang was John Anthony McCooey, who was convicted of being a get-away driver in the Tullyvallen killings.* It is thought that the killers went to the Republic and were mixed up with terrorism and other criminal activities whilst they were there. As I said earlier, they were pure evil. The facts are that McCooey was the driver. He drove the two Hearty brothers to my uncle's farm. He let them out at the end of his lane (approximately half a mile long). They walked to the house to commit murder while McCooey remained in car until their return. When they returned, they were laughing about how they had just killed that UDR ★★★★★★! The Heartys were not as far as I know related to McCooey.

I joined the RUC the month after my uncle's murder and I was proud to do so. I am still angry about the murder and I cannot ever forgive the killers. I knew who they were, but I could never in cold blood take the law into my own hands. I worked in the area, occasionally in uniform. On one occasion, I had to stop the daughter of one of the families involved; she was as nice as pie, butter wouldn't melt, but you should have seen her face when I told her that I knew all about her and her murdering brothers.

There is one thing which I have to raise; Toby Harnden in his book *Bandit Country* reports a claim from a Republican source that my uncle was a member of the Glennane Murder Gang. I know that he received

---

* Author's note: John Anthony McCooey from Cullyhanna was convicted of driving the gunmen to and from the scene and of IRA membership. He was also convicted of involvement in the killings of UDR soldier Joseph McCullough – chaplain of Tullyvallen Orange lodge – in February 1976, and UDR soldier Robert McConnell in April 1976. McCooey was named in a subsequent HET report. The convicted man received seven life sentences for seven murders, with four periods of five to fourteen years for other terrorist offences, including the murders of five men in the Tullyvallen massacre.

this story from a Republican, but I can tell you that it wasn't true; he never was involved with them and he wasn't sectarian. That claim from a member of the IRA caused the family a great deal of hurt and offence. It angered us because it took away his good name. The family realise that the words were not from Toby Harnden. My uncle was a friend to everybody, Catholic and Protestant, and he hated the Loyalist sectarian murder gangs. He warned that the antics of the Shankill Butchers would eventually bring out the same sectarian hatred down here. He didn't have a single ounce of hatred in his body. The murderers didn't even try to take him a fair fight; they ambushed him in cowardly fashion.

[The author, Toby Harnden, told me the following in a private conversation: 'The problem is that I didn't make that comment, as I mentioned in the email correspondence we had. It's on page 184 of *Bandit Country*; it's a quote from a Real IRA member, not a statement from me.]

I was living in Belfast at the time and Uncle Joe was scared to come up there to see us because he thought it too dangerous, though he was living in a remote border area. In the end, I don't fault the RUC investigation; they didn't have the resources and they were literally going from murder to murder. It is unfair that the killers weren't caught, but I understand why. The Army and the RUC were so stretched.

So, his killers are still walking around free; I know that even if they are arrested and convicted, they will serve only two years at most. But I know that one day they will have to meet their maker and answer for their crimes. They are pure, pure evil, all three of them, all involved in terrorism. I can't reveal their names and you can't print them, but it was common knowledge in the area that they did it. In the HET report, McCooey named them during his interviews, but no charges were ever brought.

Chlorane Bar Attack

On a trip to Belfast in 2012, the author walked down Gresham Street close to the Nationalist Smithfield Market area where the Chlorane

Bar had once been located. In its place is now a large car park and diagonally opposite is a new pub that trades as The Hudson Bar. Back in 1976, the Chlorane's drinkers were from both sides of the sectarian divide; an unusual and by no means widespread feature of The Troubles. It had been the subject of a firebomb attack some three years prior to the Loyalist attack of 5 June, during a ceasefire. That attack was made by the UFF, but the UVF clearly wanted to show their fellow Loyalists how to do the job 'correctly'. One unanswered question at the time was, why the decision was taken to break the ceasefire, which at this stage had only existed for fourteen days.

On the evening of 5 June 1976, two UVF units that both operated from the Brown Bear and Windsor Bar in the Shankill Road carried out the attack, which was designed to cause maximum casualties. The combined gang, comprising five men, hijacked a taxi outside another bar, holding the driver as well as his unfortunate passenger hostage, under the supervision of armed men. The taxi was driven eastwards towards the city centre; it attracted no attention from either the RUC or soldiers; even during The Troubles, men from both communities still continued their social drinking habits. Upon arrival at the Chlorane Bar at 2200 hours, four of the gunmen donned their masks and jumped out of the taxi with the driver remaining inside; the engine was left running in the manner of a normal waiting taxi.

As usual for a Saturday night, the bar was packed with drinkers; it was still only dusk, as the long evenings of the British summer kicked in. The four masked men burst through the front doors, charging inside. One of the four gunmen was Robert 'Basher' Bates, a member of the Shankill Butchers gang. Once inside, they ordered everybody to stand up, before demanding to know if there were any Protestants there. One such person, convinced that it was the IRA, ran from the room to barricade himself into a toilet. The frightened customers were then forcibly separated into two separate groups, based on their respective religions.

Edward Farrell (45), a Catholic, also tried to run towards the toilet but was shot twice in the back and head, dying almost instantly. The owner of the Chlorane, James Coyle (64), known by the UVF team to be a Catholic, was still standing behind the bar when a gunman shot him in the heart at point-blank range; he also died almost instantly. At that stage, the other gunmen began firing indiscriminately; two Protestants were struck by the hail of bullets. Daniel McNeil (47), a father of five, was hit, killed instantly, and a friend, Samuel Corr (53), was mortally wounded, dying minutes later. He was attended to by a member of the RUC after the gunmen had fled, but he died before medical assistance could reach him.

Another Catholic, John Martin (59), was fatally wounded; he died eighteen days later. Several other customers were also hit and wounded, some badly, in the indiscriminate shooting. One customer pretended to be dead but one of the gunmen stood over him, firing several shots into his lower body, badly wounding him. One of the gunmen then went into the toilets where a Protestant – a Mr William Greer – was hiding; unable to force the door open, the gunman fired several shots through the door, badly wounding the man, who survived. Several other drink-ers in the upstairs bar were left untouched; with no obvious means of escape, they were clearly terrified, thinking that they would be next. However, one of the murder gang called out the simple words: 'That's it!' With that, with the air thick with smoke, they left the bar. Once outside, they climbed into the waiting taxi, removing their masks once they felt that they were safe from recognition.

The hijacked taxi then drove up North Street in the direction of the Shankill, but paused outside the Catholic Unity flats. One of the gunmen fired several shots at a group of youths standing outside the Nationalist flats. Shortly afterwards, they abandoned the taxi in Beresford Street, before releasing the driver and his fellow hostage. They then went inside the Long Bar to celebrate the deaths of four innocent men and the fatal wounding of a fifth. Less than two weeks later, the UVF returned to the Chlorane to totally destroy it with a large explosive device.

The following account was given to the author by the son of one of those in the bar at the time. He advised the author that he would only relate the story of his dad provided that neither name was revealed, a measure of the fear still generated by Loyalist paramilitaries.

A Son's Story

Daddy is gone now and has been gone these past few years; the attack at Chlorane left him a broken man, and although not wounded, what he saw in those terrifying seconds scarred him for life. I was in my final year at school, so I was 16 at the time, still a young lad but old enough to realise what was going on around me and inside my own home.

We lived not far from the Shankill and there were plenty of pubs but Daddy had mates who, like him, had no ties with the paras and he liked to go over to the Markets for a quiet drink with people he trusted. I had grown up with the shenanigans going on all over Belfast and the rest of the country. I was about 12 on 'Bloody Friday' and like the others we heard the bombs going off all over the city and I well remember the one which went off at Star Taxis, on the Crumlin Road as it wasn't far from us. I do know that many of the IRA's supporters in the Markets – close by the Chlorane – were clapping and cheering every time a bomb went off. Mummy was very scared that Daddy went down there drinking, and it is ironic that she was afeared of the IRA when in the end, it was the UVF who came close to killing him.

He didn't come until the Sunday morning in the early hours after the shooting, but I was awake when he came home. He looked wrecked, tired and he looked scared and he seemed years older. He wouldn't talk about the things that he had witnessed; he only talked to Mummy about it and the Peelers who came to take statements and the like. He always looked nervous, like he was scared of his own shadow, and he lost interest in lots of his pleasures. He rarely went out drinking and when he did, it was somewhere close by, always avoiding places that the UVF and the UFF drank in. I went with him a few times, generally drinking clubs in and around the Shankill Road, but he avoided places when they were busy and always sat watching the door. Every time someone came in, he reacted and it was no pleasure being with him because no sooner had we started a conversation, someone would walk in and he would be following him with his eyes. He was a real 'nervous Nellie' but at the time, I couldn't really understand why.

One of his loves was Linfield FC and he loved going down to Windsor Park to watch them play of a Saturday; I remember on Boxing

Day when I was about 12 or 13 going down with him to watch Linfield play Glentoran. He really hated them; would never mention their name and would spit when they were mentioned. Before every home game, he was 'high do' about the game; that's how much he loved them. After the Chlorane shooting, I can only remember him going once or twice, usually with my uncle – his little brother – and he would never take me. I went on my own and once saw an international match there against the English where we all sang 'The Sash' and the English fans joined in too, not that there were many of them.

Daddy was never interested in politics and, although he never made this public, he hated the Loyalist paras as much as the IRA, and he had good reason to hate the IRA. Around Christmas time in 1971 – I was about 11 or so – he saw the aftermath of the Balmoral bombing on Shankill Road.* He saw them bringing the bodies out and never forgot the two wains who were killed in their prams. It was naturally popular to hate the Republicans, but it wasn't popular at that time, especially being of the Shankill, to hate 'our lot' as well. As I say, he never advertised it as there was always UVF or UFF supporters, and one of my older cousins was in the UFF. I would not wish to name him for obvious reasons, even though I am now living in Scotland. These people have long memories and they hold grudges for generations, not just years.

Daddy worked near the Markets, but he spent most of the post-shooting on the sick until his bosses got sick of it and sacked him, about two years after the shooting. He was happy to collect his 'brew' and stay at home where he felt safe, but it wore us down. He never was the 'life and soul of the party' before the attack, but he was normal, at least normal to us, but he changed and he never got over the things that he saw that night. I suppose that you would have called it 'shell shock' or PTSD.

I don't want to tell you the exact year that he passed, as that would reveal too much information, but I was in my 20s, and it was shortly before I got married and moved away from Belfast. Mummy died a few

---

* The bombing of Balmoral's Furniture showroom on the Shankill Road occurred on 11 December 1971. A PIRA bombing team carried out a no-warning bomb attack, killing four people, including two babies in the street. It came just a week after the massacre of customers in McGurk's Bar in the New Lodge that killed eighteen people.

years later and I used to come over on the Larne Ferry every couple of months to see her. I came over to her wake and for the funeral, but I have not been back since. Belfast was my hometown, it was a place of great childhood memories and until the Chlorane it was the place where I wanted to stay.

The UVF gunmen didn't shoot my daddy, but they killed him as surely as if they had done. They destroyed his life and Mummy's and they destroyed all our lives. I would love to get all of the IRA and all of the UVF and the UFF and all of the others and put them on a desert island and drop a huge fucking bomb on them. They are gangsters and scum and they don't care. They just go on breathing good oxygen, but I hate them all; they are all the same, no difference between them at all.

✦

During the tortuously long course of The Troubles, the Ulster Defence Regiment lost 368 men and women to various causes in the twenty-two years of its existence (1970–92) and a further fifty-eight former members were killed because of their past association. The vast bulk of those who lost their lives at the hands of terrorists were killed either at their full-time jobs or at home. On 9 November 1976, the Provisional IRA murdered Lance Corporal James 'Jimmy' Speer (46), a father of three, at his place of work. The UDR soldier was from Desertmartin, Co. Londonderry; he ran a car repair garage in the same village, opposite his home.

He was at work on the day of his murder, when three men pulled up in a car. They asked Mr Speer to look at their car as they suspected that the radiator was leaking. He very obligingly agreed to help, but first went to talk to his secretary, a Mrs Pitts. As he turned his back on them, one of the men produced a weapon, immediately opening fire on Mr Speer. He fell to the ground, mortally wounded, at which point a second man also opened fire, hitting him again, multiple times; he died very shortly afterwards.

Deirdre Speer-White, his eldest daughter, was 16 at the time. In 2016, she told the *Belfast Newsletter:*[*]

I was 16. My sister Cheryl was 14 and my brother Dermot was 10. It was coming up to my 17th birthday. We were there. We didn't see the actual seconds when it happened but his garage was only a few feet across the road from our home so we heard the shots. He was in the office in the garage, talking across the desk to the secretary. She phoned across, I think she tried phoning the police when the gunman was still there. She phoned across to my mother and we all ran out and we saw him taking his last breaths; I saw him. It is not something that ever leaves you. It is something you never forget – the sight of his dead body lying there, all the blood.

It has been alleged that the killer was Ian Milne,[**] former PIRA member, now a member of Sinn Fein and former representative of the Legislative Assembly (MLA), although he has always protested his innocence. Another man – Hugh Joseph Corey – was questioned about the murder of Lance Corporal Speer. He was not convicted, but he and Michael John McVey were found guilty of the murder of another UDR soldier, Robert Scott, who was killed in an IRA bomb attack four months earlier. They are thought to have been the officer commanding and quartermaster respectively of the local PIRA unit.

Cheryl Patton is the middle daughter of the murdered soldier.

---

[*] Source: www.newsletter.co.uk/news/ill–never–forget–sight–my–father–lying–there–blood-1194208

[**] Milne was sentenced to life in 1977 for the murder of a UDR soldier, Robert Scott; he served fifteen years before being released from HMP Maze in 1992. He was once dubbed one of the three most wanted men by the security forces on both sides of the border; he had achieved an earlier notoriety following his escape from Portlaoise Prison in 1974. He was charged with murders of both the aforementioned UDR soldiers, with the attempted murder of RUC officer, William McLernon and with causing a bomb blast at Castledawson. However, he was not convicted of the murder of Jimmy Speer.

Cheryl's Story

On the day of his murder, three men arrived by car and went to his office, where he was talking to his secretary, Mrs Pitts, and asked him to look at their radiator. He said he'd be out in a minute and turned to finish speaking to Mrs Pitts. The first gunman then shot him followed by the second gunman. He was shot eight times to the side of his head, neck and chest; six times by the first gunman and twice by the second.

We lived opposite Daddy's workshop, and we heard the shots, although I said to Mummy that it was just a car backfiring, as it happened regularly. Very shortly afterwards, Mrs Pitts phoned over to tell us what had happened. We all ran over the road and he was

Jimmy Speer, killed at his garage by the IRA. (Cheryl Patton)

lying there covered in blood. Mrs Pitts was cradling his head. There were a few struggled gasps followed by a horrible guttural sound and Mrs Pitts said: 'It's over, he's dead.'

He was buried on Remembrance Day, which was Deirdre's birthday. We were back at school a few days later, really as a sign of defiance. The Secretary of State had sent Mummy a wreath, but Mummy took it back to Stormont to return it. He wasn't there, so she spoke to Lord Melchett.[***] She said everything that she had to. All he did was to ask if we all wanted a cup of tea.

As my sister said, she was 16, I was 14 and my brother was 9, almost 10, when the murder happened. The days around that time are very blurred

---

[***]   Peter Mond.

Jimmy Speer and family. (Cheryl Patton)

and I don't remember very much at home. Some things are completely blocked out and I am still numbed to that time. I do remember the day I went back to school (a mixed religion school), a boy in my class sitting across from me, laughing at me. Ian Milne – now a Sinn Fein Councillor – was arrested, along with Hugh Corey, but they were never convicted. In the end, because a line-up wasn't conducted properly by the police, the court therefore ruled the evidence as inadmissible.

A number of years ago, the Historical Enquiries Team (HET) produced their report on Daddy's murder, but it was a meaningless document. It tells the story of where he was born, it quotes newspaper articles and other useless information that we, as his family, obviously know already; apart from naming Ian Milne, it was a pointless, expensive exercise.

Daddy's murderers have ruined the life that we could have expected; should have deserved. They destroyed my mother's life, she never had a healthy day again; they destroyed our happy childhood and robbed us of many special times. Certain dates were always bad for us as a family:

Deirdre's birthday was Daddy's funeral, Mummy's birthday was their wedding anniversary and Christmas Day was Daddy's birthday. I still find it very difficult to talk about, especially if someone mentions him when I'm not prepared.

I would say however, that with age we think and see things through in different ways. I think that maybe if Daddy's killer had asked for forgiveness at the time and been genuinely repentant, then through the years I may have thought: 'He was young, groomed by older, evil men etc. and may have come to terms with incidents in a way.' However, the man who we suspect has said publicly in more recent years that he regrets nothing. He is an unrepentant murderer; he is a would-be serial killer/mass murderer. I do not and will not forgive this unrepentant excuse for a human being.

✦

On 10 March 1977, the Provisional IRA attacked a part-time soldier as he arrived for work at Masstock Cement factory in Gortgonis, Coalisland. Masked men had earlier forced several members of staff at gunpoint into a room, where they were trussed up. They then lay in wait for the UDR man, Corporal Davy Graham (38). Armed with a pistol and a shotgun, they came up behind him in the work's canteen, shooting him in the back; they continued to shoot at him as he lay helpless on the floor. The part-time soldier, a father of three, died of those wounds on the 25th of the month.

There has been much speculation over the years that some of his Catholic workmates may have known in advance about the attack, with several calling in sick that day, including a man to whom Corporal Graham regularly gave a lift. There has also been further speculation that the Army may have had advance information about the planned killing, but failed to pass on this information to the murdered man. It is considered likely that this was in order to protect the identity of a possible informant inside the PIRA unit. As this author has stated on occasions *passim*, this was a dirty war, with both the IRA and British Intelligence trying to outdo each other's dirty tactics. Several other observers have made the same speculation, with numerous examples in other publications by myself.

Serena Hamilton is the youngest daughter of the murdered UDR man.

Serena's Story

I was 7½ at the time, and I want to emphasise the 'half' because that's all the time that I had my daddy before they murdered him. On the morning that he was shot, we woke up and immediately realised that my brother was late for his first day at his new school. My other brother and myself were OK though, as our wee school was just over the road. Daddy was looking out of the window at his garden, as though he was mentally planning out where he was going to put things. Anyway, he left for work as normal and we all got ready to go to school. Sometime later, there was a knock at the door and one of our neighbours came in and asked for Mummy. She said that that there had been an accident at Daddy's work and that she should go straight away to Dungannon Hospital. When she arrived, she was informed that Daddy had been shot and was now in emergency surgery. Not long afterwards, he was transferred to the Royal Victoria Hospital (RVH) in Belfast for more complicated treatment.

Over the years, we were able to piece together what had happened. Every day, Daddy picked up one of his Catholic workmates to give him a lift, but he had called in sick, as indeed a couple of others had also done so. I began to get a little suspicious, as on the day of the shooting there were so many absentees. There are more questions than answers as to why this happened; was it a coincidence? Had there been a warning to them from the IRA telling them not to go into work that day?

There is another matter which has bothered me over the years. Daddy worked with a fellow member of the UDR at the factory, a Sergeant Beatie; interestingly enough, he also wasn't in that day either. The IRA had tried to kill him a few months earlier. Another thing was that when the shooting took place, there were lots of Army patrols in the area and they were there very quickly afterwards. In fact, a soldier found one of the weapons only about half a mile away from the factory. I have always believed that the Army knew in advance about the intended hit, but did and said nothing. A couple of months later, Mummy met the Undersecretary of State for Northern Ireland. She was told that two gunmen had been seen at the back of the factory, some weeks earlier; they were very likely carrying out a

Davy Graham and his wife, Eileen. (Serena Hamilton)

'dummy run' for the attack. It is diabolical that they knew in advance and didn't warn him of the danger.

Mummy was at the RVH for the next eight days, whilst we stayed with relatives; most of what had happened was kept from us, but we were aware that Daddy had been shot. We were only very young, but we often talked amongst ourselves about if he might die. On the eighth day, with some signs of recovery – Daddy had lost his spleen, his liver and kidneys were damaged, but he was responding well on dialysis – Mummy came back home. However, that evening, the telephone rang; it was the call which she had been dreading. It was the RVH asking her to return urgently as Daddy had deteriorated. She went straight there, where she held his hand, cuddled him and prayed with him; she was even convinced that he had called out her name. Shortly afterwards, she was ushered out of the room and told to wait outside, but as she stepped into the corridor, Daddy passed away. He was a strong man who fought hard to stay alive.

She came back over to Granny's where we were staying; her first words were: 'Davy's gone; Davy's gone.' Everyone was crying, there were so many people crying, but I just put my head into the pillow and cried myself, not really understanding that I would never see my daddy again. I remember that Mummy was sedated, drugged up, not really knowing what was going on. Soon afterwards, his body was brought home, with his coffin being taken to lie in rest in my bedroom. I wanted to see him, but I wasn't allowed to; it wasn't to be. The day of his funeral came – it was held with full military honours – and although I was allowed to go there, I had to stay in the car whilst my two brothers who were 9 and 11 were allowed to stand at the graveside. I suppose that was the way that families protected their young in those days.

Later on we moved to Dungannon where, over my childhood, I heard lots of bombs, shootings, that sort of thing. There was a large Army presence in the town; we saw lots of patrols. They were just young men, far away from home and their families, but they looked after us; we always felt protected. Over time, the investigations just tapered off; the politicians who came to our house made lots of promises, such as 'no stone will be left unturned' and we trusted them, but in the end, nothing happened. When I got older, I served in the Medical section of the Territorial Army (TA) whilst Mummy served for eleven years in the UDR. Even though we were TA, we were under the same threat from the Provisional IRA; every time our Land Rovers passed through Nationalist areas, rocks would be thrown at us.

Over the years, the names of Daddy's killers were revealed to us, but I cannot reveal them publicly; I can tell you this, one of the names mentioned was the Tyrone Brigade's quartermaster at the time. Sadly, there was never enough evidence to convict them for the murder. All of the bombings, like Enniskillen etc., were terrible, but to the terrorists, they were just designed to kill as many people as possible; they didn't care who they killed. In Daddy's case it was different; the IRA singled him out, planned it, right down to knowing where he lived and worked. What was revealed was that about half an hour before he was due to arrive – the IRA knew to the minute all of his routines – gunmen arrived, taking two of the workers as hostage, trussing them up. Daddy clocked in, before walking to the canteen to put his sandwiches away; as he did so, the gunmen came up behind him and then shot him in the back, causing him to fall to the floor. As he lay there, the killers

Davy Graham's family at his memorial service. (Serena Hamilton)

continued to fire into his helpless body. I know that as he lay there, he called out 'Eileen, Eileen, Eileen.' One of the killers was a boy of 16 or 17, being 'blooded' on his first kill.

How do I feel today? I have everyday thoughts about what happened, but it has been a roller coaster forty-odd years, with some thoughts being blanked out. One thing which hurts is that his killers live very close by, only a short distance away; they still have their lives, but my daddy lost his. I have no forgiveness because in our society there is no justice; in our society, murderers can just get away with it. We have been let down by our government and I can't understand why they have done the dirt on people who served and gave up their lives for their country. I know this, one day, the Devil will take them and they will suffer in the same way that we have.

Serena very kindly agreed to the inclusion of the following, previously private thoughts, which she directs at her father's murderers:

On the Eve of the Murder.

You sit around the fireside with your family, your cold heart planning the murder you are going to commit the next day. It will leave a family without their loved one, yet you think nothing of it.

You meet your accomplices in the early hours of the morning, again thinking nothing of the weapons you have loaded, to gun the man down, taking away his life, but still you think nothing of it.

The innocent man arrives at his work ... you shoot, shoot and keep shooting ... murdering the man who will always be in my heart ... taking my daddy away and yet you still think nothing of it.

✦

On Sunday, 20 May 1979, RUCR Constable David Stanley Wray (50), father of two children, attended Claremont Presbyterian Church in Northland Road, Londonderry.* The part-time policeman and former UDR soldier had once lived in the Glen Estate on the west bank of the Foyle. The estate had once been predominantly Protestant, although many had moved away over the years as a consequence of relentless Republican

---

* During the Northern Ireland Troubles there were a number of occasions when people were murdered whilst they attended church. The following is taken from the *Belfast Telegraph*, 28 July 2016:

Norman Duddy was an inspector in the RUC, and had been stationed in Londonderry for 22 years. He served on the committee of Strand Presbyterian Church and also sang in the choir. On the morning of Sunday, 28 March 1982, he was murdered by two masked IRA gunmen as he was leaving the church with his young sons after the morning service.

Karen McKeown was a Sunday school teacher in Albertbridge Congregational Church in East Belfast and was also active in the Girls' Brigade and the church youth group. The 20-year-old student was murdered on 17 October 1982, by an INLA gunman. He came up behind Karen and shot her in the back of the head as she was standing outside the church.

Judge William Doyle, meanwhile, was murdered on Sunday, 16 January 1983, as he left midday Mass at St Brigid's Roman Catholic Church at Derryvolgie Avenue in South Belfast. He had just got into his car to drive away when two IRA gunmen approached the vehicle and opened fire, hitting him five times and seriously injuring a 72-year-old woman sitting beside him.

intimidation. Additionally, the Provisional IRA had tried to kill the reserve police officer on the estate some three years earlier. He was ambushed and badly wounded outside his home, and not expected to live; however, he returned to duty at the RUC base in Rosemount a year later. Consequently, the family moved to Seven Tree Road in the Waterside area of the city.

The church was a mere 1.3 miles from the border with the Irish Republic, marking it an area vulnerable to the 'shoot and scoot' type of attack favoured by Republican paramilitaries. On the Sunday morning, as Constable Wray got out of his car, waiting PIRA gunmen shot him twice in the back; he died at the scene. At least ten men from Londonderry were questioned by the RUC, of whom Anthony Kelly, Peter Griffin, Kevin Anthony Deehan and William Anthony Doherty were tried and convicted for their parts in the murder. Three of them received life sentences for the murder, whilst a fourth escaped the same punishment as he was under age at the time of the killing. Anthony Kelly – he later escaped along with thirty-seven other convicted Republican terrorists from Long Kesh in 1983 – was 17 at the time of the murder. Kevin Deehan had already been jailed in 1975 for possession of nail bombs, ammunition and explosives. However, he had been released, thus leaving him free to kill the off-duty RUCR man.

---

continued

Mountain Lodge Pentecostal Church in south Armagh was the scene of a multiple murder on Sunday, 20 November 1983. The evening service was under way and the congregation were singing the old gospel hymn, Are You Washed in the Blood of the Lamb? Suddenly, republican gunmen entered the building and killed three of the elders — John Victor Cunningham, David Wilson and William Harold Brown. Seven other people in the little church were wounded by the attackers.

Mary Travers was shot dead on Sunday, April 8, 1984, as she was leaving St Brigid's Roman Catholic Church with her family. Her father was a judge. Later, Senior Sinn Member Danny Morrison described the murder as 'regrettable, but understandable.'

The IRA also murdered Patrick Thomas Kerr, a Roman Catholic prison officer, on February 17, 1985, as he was leaving a service in St Patrick's Cathedral in Armagh. Two of his children were with him and witnessed the killing of their father, who was shot. RUC Sergeant Hugh McCormac was killed by the IRA on Sunday, March 3, 1985. Mr McCormac sang in the choir at St Gabriel's Retreat at the Graan, near Enniskillen, and had just arrived with his family when he was shot by two terrorist gunmen.

Constable Wray's two teenage children were horrified onlookers to their father's murder; Lucinda Thompson is the daughter of the murdered policeman.

Lucinda's Story

At the time of my daddy's murder, I was 19 and my brother John was 17. On Sunday, 20 May 1979, we set off for church as usual, picking up the organist's wife in order to drop her off at the church. We were a wee bit early, so we popped down to put petrol in the car on the Strand Road; I remember that it was raining heavily. We stopped; myself and Daddy got out, with John being last out to grab our hymn books. I noticed that Daddy had parked at a bus stop. I jokingly told him that the police would give him a ticket but he laughed back that it would take a brave policeman to do that to him.

RUC Officer David Wray, murdered in Londonderry. (Lucinda Thompson)

Daddy walked around to the pavement, but suddenly I heard him shout: 'Get …' followed by several very loud bangs. I looked at him and I could see that he was dead; the colour had drained completely out of his face. Daddy was shot by both men, neither of whom wore a mask. I was very defiant and screamed at one of the gunmen: 'I will remember you until the day I die!' He responded: 'I'll shoot you!' He did fire at me, but the shots kept hitting the ground; one of them ricocheted into my ankle with a sting – the metal is still there today and always sets off the metal detectors at Heathrow Airport.

Then I saw John; he had a very strange mark on the bridge of his nose. I asked him why he hadn't warned Daddy, but he told me that one of the men had a pressed a gun right into his face. There was a woman close by, lifting a toddler out of her car, and I screamed at her for help. She just said: 'No, I'm getting out of here.' She just bundled the child back into the car before driving away; I could tell that she was absolutely terrified. I told John to run into the church for help, but he was too scared, so I ran for help; I just remember that the street was empty and silent. Just then one of my uncles came running over to me shouting: 'What's happened?' but I just pushed him away and headed for the church entrance. Ronnie Struthers*was there and I said: 'Daddy has been shot!' He looked at me in an odd way, because I think that he thought that I was confused, as Daddy had been shot three years earlier.

Anyway, we all went over to the car where people had started gathering; someone had put a blanket over Daddy's body just as the police and an ambulance arrived. I should add that my handbag had been wedged under Daddy as he fell; sometime that afternoon, it was brought to our house. Daddy was taken away, so we phoned Mummy's sister-in-law to ask her to break the news for us and stay with her until we got there. As soon as I saw Mummy, she began reaching for her coat in a real state of confusion. She told us that she would need to go to the hospital to sign a consent form for an operation as she had done three years earlier, not realising that this time he was dead.

We had to visit Strand Road RUC station, where John and I were separated; later they took us home, where lots of people, relatives as well as neighbours had gathered to comfort us. Our doctor wanted to give me a sedative, but my then boyfriend said to him: 'No, because when she wakes up, she'll have to face it all over again.' Daddy's body was brought home later that evening.

Over the next day or two, I had to visit the police station again to take part in photofits, identity parades; that sort of thing. I picked out Daddy's murderer four separate times, leading to the arrest of five men, several of

---

* Ronnie Struthers' son, Robert (19), was a member of the RUCR; he was murdered by the IRA on 16 June 1978, at Lorne Electrics, Londonderry, where he worked as an apprentice electrician.

whom were found guilty, including Kevin Deacon and Anthony Kelly, who was only 17; the latter escaped from the Maze Prison in 1983.

On the day before the funeral, I answered the phone to a man who kept on insisting that he speak to Daddy, and he persisted until I explained that Daddy was dead. I will never forget what the caller said next: 'Ha, ha; this is the IRA; it took us twice to get him!' Our number was changed within minutes. The funeral was held on the Tuesday. As we were about to go out, we saw that there were scrums of media, TV, the lot, outside. Mummy said to us: 'Go and be brave and respectful; don't give in to them; tears are for private.'

The trial was the following year, at Crumlin Road courthouse in Belfast. We had to sit in the courtroom, facing the very men who had killed Daddy. It emerged during the trial that the IRA had paid the men £500 each for shooting Daddy. I was too upset to speak, so a police-woman read my evidence on my behalf. Later on that day, I was in the toilets of our hotel, where a radio was playing. Sure enough, news of the trial came on and I was mentioned as having been too distressed to give evidence. At that, I just threw up; I couldn't help it. A member of the hotel staff showed great sympathy, especially when I told her that I was the one who had just been mentioned on the radio; this lovely lady brought me a drink.

During the sentencing, we had to walk past the killers' families; one of them spat at me. I think that it was Kelly who shouted: 'We'll be better fed than you over the next fifteen years!' It was unfortunately probably correct as well. Three years later, Kelly escaped in a mob of thirty-eight IRA prisoners from Long Kesh, which led to the police coming to warn us that he was loose. A few years later, we were invited to take part in a BBC programme with Archbishop Tutu on the subject of reconciliation. Kevin Deehan had wanted to apologise, but we said no, although in any case, the IRA refused to allow him to say sorry. Kelly was later caught in the Republic and sent to Portlaoise jail, but the Irish courts refused to extradite him to Northern Ireland to finish his sentence for murder. It also later emerged that Martin McGuinness sanctioned the murder of my daddy, and even disciplined a young IRA member who was sent to hijack a car for the attack but lost his nerve. All that came out in court.

One thing which I would like to clear up with you is a lie which was published in *Lost Lives* and some of the newspapers; it was reported that we accepted a wreath from the 'Mothers of the Bogside'. It is not true; they came to our house, but we refused to accept anything from them, which caused them to argue and abuse us. We wanted nothing from them, especially their pious, insincere words: 'It wasn't personal; it was just the uniform.'

I definitely do not forgive them; they got fifteen years – Kelly escaped after just three years – but we got a life sentence. Daddy wasn't there to give me away at my wedding; he wasn't at John's wedding; there were no milestone moments for us and he never got to see his grandchildren or great-grandchildren grow up; I can never forgive that.

On 6 June 1979, the Provisionals attacked a full-time UDR barracks located in the Malone Road area of Belfast. Sometime on the previous day, armed men had hijacked a red open-back tipper lorry in the Nationalist Andersonstown Road area. At around 11.15 on the morning of the sixth, the vehicle stopped outside the barracks, which was situated in a leafy suburb to the south of the city. Two gunmen on the back of the lorry fired almost forty shots into the camp, hitting four soldiers. One of the rounds hit and mortally wounded Alex Gore (23), who had been standing near a flagpole. The attackers knew that a portable building, visible from the firing point, would contain military personnel. As a consequence, their fire was concentrated on this point. Shots also hit the company office, although there were no reported casualties in this location. Finally, as the lorry began to move off, a home-made hand grenade was thrown towards the wounded men. Fortunately, it failed to cause any further damage, but Private Gore died at the scene. One of the soldiers, who had suffered a head wound, ignored his injuries to help drag the dying man to cover, helped by another comrade.

The gunmen raced off, but on recognising an off-duty RUC officer at a petrol station on Tate's Avenue, began firing shots in his direction. The quick-reacting policeman returned fire, but was unable to claim any hits on the terror gang; the lorry drove off, to be later abandoned near

Milltown Cemetery. Only one member of the gang was ever caught: Brendan Patrick Mead. On Friday 29, 1980, Mead was convicted of Alex's murder and sentenced to life imprisonment. He was also convicted of other crimes connected with the attack, for which he received prison sentences ranging from three to fifteen years, all to run concurrently with the life sentence. He was also convicted of the attempted murder of two UDR privates, of causing an explosion, possession of firearms, possession of explosives, hijacking of a lorry, and membership of PIRA. He was sentenced to a further seventy-five years in prison, to run concurrently. He was one of the escapees from HMP Maze in 1983. During the escape, one prison officer died of a heart attack after being stabbed, another prison officer received a non-fatal gunshot wound to the head and a third was shot in the leg. He was later recaptured but was granted amnesty following the Good Friday Agreement. He was released from custody on life licence on 15 August 1994, having served fifteen years and two months' imprisonment.

Amanda Gore is the widow of Alex Gore Senior, who was killed in the attack at Malone Barracks; she was over seven months pregnant at the time.

Amanda's Story

On the day that Alex was killed, I was at work with the Northern Ireland Electricity Service, just a five- or ten-minute drive away from the barracks on Malone Road. I was just returning to my office when I heard gunfire followed by an explosion, but I thought that it was an attack on the RUC Station on the Lisburn Road; I didn't at first even think that it was at the barracks. I am not sure why I thought that, but I just never thought for a second that the place where my husband was stationed was the subject of the loud noises which I could hear. Not long afterwards, a member of staff informed us all that the radio had just announced that shots had been fired at the barracks. I must confess that I felt immediately sick, but put that down to being heavily pregnant; it was surreal, and something about it just didn't feel right. Later on, I discovered that a friend had actually witnessed the attack by men on the back of a tipper lorry.

Not very long afterwards, my boss came out of his office asking for Amanda; now, as I am known as Mandy, I didn't at first respond. Then I realised that it was me and went over to him. He told me that his boss – two above me – wanted to have a chat, which I didn't really understand. We walked down this corridor when a door opened on my left; out came a man I knew – Colin who was part-time UDR – but as soon as he saw me, he quickly turned on his heels, closing the door behind him. It was strange, but I didn't know what to think. Then my boss told me that we were going to the main interview room, which puzzled me.

I entered with my head down; the first thing I saw was two pairs of black boots and khaki trousers. At that moment, I knew that was it; I knew that something had happened to Alex. As I looked up, I could see a doctor, a nurse, the big boss, UDR Captain Brennan and a colour sergeant, all there waiting for me. Someone said: 'There's been an incident,' but before they could tell me more, I very calmly said: 'He's dead?' A voice told me that he was; everything fell silent after that; there was nothing more to be said. One of my female colleagues took me home to the house which Alex and I shared with his mum. She had a heart condition and a UDR Greenfinch was sitting with her as they didn't want to leave her alone after two UDR men had called at the house first as they didn't know that I was still working.

My GP came not long afterwards, prescribing me sleeping pills and tranquilisers; for a while, I was so out of it, everything was going on around me, although I knew what was going on. The UDR arranged for everything for me so that I didn't have to raise a hand; they sorted out the undertakers, the funeral, everything. They really had no experiences to fall back on, even having to borrow number two dress uniforms from another unit. There was one officer in particular – Captain Harry Hutton – to whom I am indebted; he knew what he was doing; he was lovely, a true gentleman. Early on the day of the funeral – held at Carnmoney in North Belfast – he was there, standing with me all day; he never left my side.

Our son – Alex Junior – was born on 26 July without a dad, but he had plenty of people and plenty of love around him. We lived with my parents and they spoiled him rotten; in fact, everyone did.

Forty-one years later, how do I feel? It still hurts; it is as if it were just yesterday, and remember, I was just 18 at the time. One of the gang who killed my husband was called Mead; he tried to contact me through a Dutch journalist as he wanted to apologise to me; I said no! About a year later, the journalist turned up at my door and I was too polite to send him packing, so I gave an interview, during which he told me that Mead wanted to apologise. I remember my reply as though it was yesterday: 'It will be a cold day in Hell before I accept an apology from him.' Honestly, he can take his apologies to Hell with him! I remember that he was one of the Maze escapers in 1983; it brought it all home to me when I saw his photo staring back at me in the newspapers!

There's no forgiveness to be had from me, whatsoever; he was part of the murder and I have no sympathy for him. I am proud of my husband and I am proud of my son; they were both soldiers. I will just end by saying that the family of the UDR and Royal Irish could not have been any better for me and my son.

Private Gore left behind a young child as well as a pregnant widow; Alex Gore Junior is the son of the murdered soldier.

Alex's Story

Mum was pregnant with me when dad was murdered; I was born six or seven weeks afterwards, so I never even got to know him. As a kid growing up, I didn't really understand what was happening, why I hadn't got a dad and why we always seemed to be visiting a cemetery. As I got older, I began to understand more and started developing a deep hatred for the Provisionals and for all Catholics as well. I was a bit of a teenage tearaway, always in the courts, but fortunately two uncles who were in the UDR helped me a lot and steered me in the right direction; eventually, I joined the Army.

I was brought up in the Loyalist heartland of Sandy Row, and what with all that had happened to me, I could so easily have become involved with the paramilitaries and many of the people who lived near me did end up joining them. I served with the Queen's Royal Irish Hussars, seeing action in Kosovo and Iraq (twice) before finally sent out to Afghanistan on Op Telic. I was injured in a roadside bomb in Basra as well as having a few hairy moments fighting the Taliban. I served with Roman Catholics out there and I had no problems with them at all, although I knew that if it was back in Northern Ireland, things between us might have been very different. As I say, I had settled down by then in terms of the sectarian thing and was calmer. I later transferred to the Royal Irish.

When I was a teenager, I discovered that one of the gang involved in the killing of my dad was called Brendan Mead. I know that he escaped from the Maze in 1983 when I was about 4 years old and that he only served fourteen years before the Good Friday Agreement. That's not an awful long time to serve when you consider that he was involved in murder. It would be about 2007, before his name turned up again, when the Orange Order and UDR Home Service informed us that he had become a 'born again Christian' and wanted to talk to Mum, presumably to apologise. A journalist actually came to the house one day whilst I was home on leave but out with friends. My mum told him in no uncertain terms that she would never accept any apologies from Mead.

When I returned home, I was very angry, but also worried that she may have told him that I was serving in the Army; thankfully, she hadn't told him anything other than to clear off. I was pleased as we were on the eve of departure for Afghanistan and I didn't want any additional pressure. I am pleased to say that Mum is still alive; she never remarried. She later helped with the HET enquiry but I am not too sure if they came up with any new evidence; the other members of the IRA gang who killed Dad are still out there enjoying life.

Do I forgive them? To put it politely: no! They took away my dad and as a result, I was never able to meet him. Losing him had a great impact on my life. They took away someone who would have been a great influence to me; they robbed me of that. They took away Mum's husband and made her life so much more difficult. My dad was only doing his job, making a living for his family. As far as I am concerned, they can go and rot in hell!

✦

During the course of The Troubles, Loyalist paramilitaries were responsible for about 900 deaths. In the main, ordinary Catholics who were chosen either purely at random, or on the basis of highly flawed intelligence. The following story is from an intended victim of the UFF; this man survived a terrible sectarian murder attempt. On 27 September 1979, UFF gunmen arrived outside a small block of flats in Cooke Street, just off the Ormeau Road in South Belfast. They have always maintained that the objective of the attack that followed that night was the death of a 'known Republican'. However, their intel proved unreliable and instead they attacked and severely injured an innocent Catholic, Peter Heathwood. I am truly thankful that Peter survived; the gunmen, however, were never caught. Like so many Catholic and Protestant victims, Peter was never involved with Republican paramilitaries.

In interviewing Peter, the issue of collusion was raised, and whilst I am happy to include his uncensored comments, I need to stress that collusion – from either side – was never proven in a court of law. Republicans have made claims that the RUC and Army fed information to Loyalist paramilitaries, and even ensured a 'clear run' at their Sinn Fein and PIRA targets. It is certainly true that the UDR contained rogue members who were secretly feeding information to the UVF, as witnessed by the involvement of four UDR soldiers in the UVF gang that carried out the Miami Showband massacre in 1976. There was also the case of former RUC officer John Oliver Weir, who betrayed secrets to the UVF; he was convicted of a sectarian murder in 1977.

Conversely, there is much suspicion among the security forces that elements of the Irish Defence Force and the Republic's police, An Gardaí Síochána, colluded with the Provisional IRA. Indeed, the Smithwick Tribunal raised many questions about Gardaí conduct in the killing of senior RUC officers Superintendents Harry Breen and Bob Buchanan at Jonesborough on 20 March 1989. It was alleged that a Gardaí contact betrayed the cross-border route of the unarmed police officers, following a joint RUC–Garda conference at Dundalk. Similarly, the same tribunal raised questions of Gardaí collusion with the PIRA bombing team at Narrow Water on 27–28 August 1979 following the deaths of eighteen British soldiers. The accusations were centred on the wilful destruction of forensic evidence by a Gardaí sergeant and the denying of access to the bombing point for Northern Irish investigators.

If collusion existed at all, it was on a minor, purely local level, not the major scale that some unfounded accusations would have us believe; it may well have occurred at a local level, possibly some illegal co-operation between paramilitaries and security forces, but it was never on a grand scale and it was never institutionalised.

Peter's Story

I was born on 13 May 1953 and reared in Fitzroy Avenue, Lower Ormeau Road. I went to school, grew up there and married an Ormeau Road girl called Anne Daly. I was 20 and she was 18 when we married. I was a student teacher at St Joseph's College and Anne was a waitress. She worked to help put me through college and I qualified in 1975.

For the first couple of years after qualifying, I couldn't get a permanent job. There were very few subbing jobs about and even less permanent teaching jobs. I was disillusioned and left the teaching profession to take up work as a sales rep with an insurance company. I excelled in this role and within six months I was a team manager and doing extremely well. We bought a bigger house on the other side of town in Clifton Park Avenue in North Belfast, which we divided into three apartments to let out to tenants. My father had advised me not to move to North Belfast as he always considered that it was the most dangerous place in Northern Ireland. To my regret, I didn't listen to him.

On Thursday, 27 September 1979, I was working and doing calls in the Lisburn area. I phoned Anne and told her I would be working late and would not be home for dinner. She told me she was making shepherd's pie and chips. This was my favourite meal and so I changed my mind and came home for dinner.

I was sitting in the back room watching the six o'clock news and bouncing our baby daughter in her chair when the doorbell rang. Patrick, who was 7, was playing in the hall and Annemarie, who was 5, was upstairs. Anne opened the door and I heard her scream 'gunmen, gunmen'. I jumped up and the door was open, a gunman had Anne by the hair and was frogmarching her up the hall. I stood behind the door, reached out to pull Anne in and slammed the door against the gunman. He fell into the hall, knocking pictures off the wall as he landed. I put the bar across the door, as the second gunman ran up the hall and fired shots through the door.

The first bullet hit me in the right arm, broke my ribs and travelled along my spine and down into my back. The second bullet hit me in the right nipple, taking it off, scorching my chest and coming out the other side. The third bullet missed me and also missed the baby Louise sitting in her bouncy chair by 6in. During this time they were shouting 'Fenian bastards', Anne and the kids were screaming. The second gunman then took his mate out of the hall, got into a car and drove off.

I remember falling back towards the hearth and Anne putting her hand under my head to save me from hitting it. I tried to crawl behind the sofa but my legs wouldn't work. I do not remember this but before I lost consciousness Anne said I asked for a priest and asked her to tell my father – Herbert Heathwood who was 64 – that I was OK. I remember nothing else until I woke up in the Royal Victoria Hospital about ten days later, having initially been taken to the Mater.

This part of my story is told through my family and my wife's account of what happened. The police and ambulance crew arrived followed by two CID, who walked into the room as if they were going to a party, looked down at me and said: 'Who the fuck is he?' A young man who was renting an apartment upstairs came down to see what all the commotion was about and the CID men went to him in the hall and said: 'That was meant for you, we have champagne waiting in North Queen Street, you're a dead man.'

My mother, father and sister arrived and the medics were working on me on the living room floor. As they could not get a stretcher in, they brought a body bag to lift me out to the ambulance. My father saw this and thought I was dead, his last words were: 'Oh my poor Peter.' He clutched his chest and dropped to the floor beside me. My sister, who was a nurse, gave him CPR and someone phoned for a second ambulance. There was some confusion at the ambulance station as they knew an ambulance for Heathwood had already been dispatched to that address. The police used their flak jackets to lay him on and carried him out to a jeep to take him to hospital. He was dead on arrival.

I was fifty weeks in hospital and dropped from 15st to 7st. Some of this time was spent at Musgrave Park Hospital for rehabilitation. The first bullet that broke my ribs had bounced off my spine, causing paralysis, and although I had some feeling and movement in my legs, a doctor at the hospital said: 'See that chair, you may get used to it because you are going to be using it for the rest of your life.'

About a year later I began to think about the incident, who did shoot me and what exactly happened? Other things started to happen, too. A woman who worked in a Social Services office across from my house had witnessed the gunmen pulling up and entering my house. She was phoned later and told to withdraw her statement. The one bullet I had taken out of me was sent to Foster Green [Hospital]. They held on to it for a while but no one ever came to pick it up for forensics and so it was discarded. The police told me the Provisional IRA shot me, but I received a criminal injuries claim because it was the Loyalists who shot me. Of the two CID men who came to the house on that night, one was later revealed to have been a member of the RUC's E4A unit, which was later involved in 'shoot to kill' incidents in Armagh.

I know that you won't agree with me, but it is my belief that when Margaret Thatcher came to power that year, she allowed the Intelligence agencies to encourage Loyalist attacks on known Republicans. My family and I believe that there was collusion between RUC Special Branch and the UFF and that we were caught in a dirty war between the State and PIRA. I believe that the man in the top flat was the target that night, and I never knew that he was a 'shinner' or PIRA member. I rented the room to him in good faith, even taking out bank references etc. He had a good job, seemed quite inoffensive, and as I had lived my life in the south of the city, I had no idea of who was who in the north of the city.

As I said, the top-floor tenant was almost certainly the intended target, but that the killers were inexperienced, and started shooting at the first male whom they saw – me! I do not believe that fingerprints were taken, and no forensics were carried out on the bullets taken from my body. I also believe that the eyewitnesses were intimidated via phone calls to their places of employment etc. The later HET follow-up was half-hearted, and they refused to investigate thoroughly because I didn't die. The other thing that I wish to raise is that when they had the big 'Supergrass' trials in the 1980s, many convictions for several murders were made, for killings before and after the attack on me, but never for my own attackers.

I was never a Shinner and I was never involved with the IRA or anything like that. My wife's brother was a member of the Royal Marines, who left the service following 'Bloody Sunday' in January 1972. There is no way that I would have had anything to do with Sinn Fein/PIRA: then or now!

As time passed I tried to return to work but was not successful in getting either a job within the teaching profession, or indeed with the insurance company because I was in a wheelchair. I used to hate when I would be out with Anne in a cafe or restaurant and the waitress would ask, 'Does he take sugar in his tea?' I returned to Queen's University Belfast in 1986 and completed an IT course but have never been in paid employment again and believe this was a great loss of opportunity.

The impact the shooting had on my wife Anne was immense. She was a very happy-go-lucky, good-looking girl with long red hair and it changed her completely. She had moved back to her mother's while I was in hospital and when I got out I lived at my mother's house. I took the compensation to keep the family together and we bought a house up near Dunmurray, but she was haunted by the memories and would repeat time and time again, 'I shouldn't have opened the door.' She blamed herself. Her physical and mental health deteriorated and in October 2006 she died of heart problems, which was caused by years of depression, alcoholism and PTSD brought on by the attack, aged 51 years. For me losing Anne was far worse than losing the use of my legs. She too was a victim of the 1979 attack on our home, which highlights the ripple effect this violence has on both victims and survivors.

✦

On 30 October 1979, Corporal Fred Irwin (43), a father of five and a part-time soldier in the UDR, was murdered by the PIRA. Corporal

Irwin worked full-time 'on the dust', as Britain's invaluable army of dustbin men and council cleansing department employees have referred to themselves. He lived in Moy, Co. Tyrone, and was known to drive to his place of employment in Dungannon every morning at around 0800. Like all good security-minded UDR men, he did vary his route, but it was impossible to do so on the last leg of his journey. On this particular morning, a PIRA murder gang was lying in wait for him. As he reached Oaks Road, close to his place of work, masked gunmen opened fire from behind a nearby wall with US-supplied Armalites. His car was hit thirty times and he died almost immediately. In addition to his own five children, the dead soldier and his wife also fostered three other children, following the death of his brother.

Alan Irwin is a Church of Ireland Rector in Fermanagh. His uncle Frederick and his father, Thomas Irwin, were murdered in separate incidents by the Provisional IRA in 1979 and 1986. I have chosen to put the two separate incidents into different chapters.

Alan's Story about Fred

My uncle Fred was a part-time soldier in the UDR, working in his full-time job at Dungannon. He always gave one of his neighbours – a Roman Catholic – a lift into Dungannon, but on this particular morning, the man was not going, so my uncle travelled alone. As you know, he was ambushed by the PIRA and he was hit so many times that his body was almost unrecognisable. My dad – later also killed by the PIRA – had to go see the body of his brother and he often cried himself to sleep with the memory of it all. I do recall that at his wake, my uncle's coffin was closed due to the terrible nature of his injuries.

I was at school on the day of the murder, being just 14 at the time, when my dad just called in to take us home; I recall that he didn't say a word to us at the time, so I just assumed that something had happened at home. He eventually broke the news to us that uncle Fred had been murdered by the PIRA. At the house there was pandemonium and tears; we were so close as a family and it was just so difficult to make any sense of this; my aunt was inconsolable, as were my cousins.

My father made the funeral arrangements, but we were warned by the RUC that the route which he had chosen from Moy to Sixmilecross would take us through a heavily Nationalist area, and given that it would be a military funeral might stir some things up with the local players. Dad insisted and it was a full military funeral.

It was afterwards that we struggled; the family lost some of its vibrancy. Financial compensation was very little and often my uncle's family struggled to make ends meet. His widow remarried

UDR soldier Fred Irwin, ambushed on his way to work. (Alan Irwin)

and as soon as she did, the Government took away her widow's pension. We missed the get-togethers, the banter and I imagine that many, many other families went through their own losses. My brother took his own life at 17, as our grief just built up.

Thinking back, it is hard to say how I felt; numbed, angry, hate and revulsion. I kept asking myself why and wondering what it was all about. The PIRA seemed to get away with everything; they seemed to have a free rein with everything. Every terrorist atrocity just made us relive the horror of Fred's death over and over again. No one was ever caught; Fred's killers were never brought to justice. My aunt died of cancer in 2019, but at least we were able to have the closure, which was denied to us by the nature of Fred's terrible death. What I didn't know on the day of his murder was my own father would meet the same fate, just over six years later.

If I am to forgive, then the question still exists, whom do I forgive for the hurt and pain I have received through their violent murderous actions towards my father and my uncle? As I have said, I do not know who they are. I have yet to receive the answers; truth and justice were sacrificed on the altar of peace in an agreement that led to terrorists being equated with their innocent victims. Terrorism is still terrorism and murder is still murder. Forgiveness is a process. Whether many are on that journey is known unto God, as are those for whom the words and actions of others have hindered that journey from beginning.

✦

During the long and violent period of Northern Irish history known somewhat euphemistically as The Troubles, almost thirty members of Her Majesty's Prison Service were killed by paramilitaries of both sides. Their deaths were claimed as legitimate and justified for the most spurious of reasons. Some of the murders were supposedly carried out following accusations of the intimidation, bullying and discrimination towards paramilitary prisoners. To date, there has not been one single shred of evidence produced by any paramilitaries that would in any way justify the murder of any of these prison staff. The most senior officers[*] to be killed were: Governor Albert Miles, Assistant Governor, HMP Maze, killed by the IRA on 26 November 1978; Governor Edward Donald Jones, BEM, HMP Crumlin Road Gaol, killed by the IRA on 19 September 1979; and the Assistant Governor of HMP Maze, William McConnell; he was shot by PIRA gunmen outside his home in the Belmont area of Belfast on 6 March 1984. One of the murdered officers was retired from the service and two were female officers: Agnes Jean Wallace, killed by the INLA on 19 April 1979, and Elizabeth Matilda Chambers, killed when she became caught up in a INLA terrorist attack on a member of the UDR on 7 October 1982.

At approximately 0700 on the morning of Tuesday, 30 December 1980, prison officer William Burns (45) was leaving his home in Knocknagoney Park, Belfast, en route to his job at Crumlin Road Gaol. As he prepared to depart, UVF gunmen who had waited outside shot

---

[*] The chief officer of Portlaoise Prison in the Irish Republic, Brian Stack, was shot outside the national boxing stadium in Dublin by PIRA gunmen on 25 March 1983; he died from his injuries eighteen months later.

him several times; he died shortly afterwards. Within a quarter of an hour, a second UVF gang shot and wounded another prison officer at Castlereagh in South Belfast, ambushing him at traffic lights. The murder was claimed by a group calling themselves Loyalist Prisoners Action Force; this was a flag of convenience used by the UVF. The attacks were believed to have been ordered by the UVF leadership inside Crumlin Road Gaol. They claimed that they had acted as a result of the 'maltreatment of Loyalist prisoners'. He was the nineteenth PO to be killed during The Troubles and had served for fewer than three years.

PO Burns left a widow and four children; Kay Burns is one of his daughters.

Kay's Story

I remember the day so well; I was 21 at the time, Mummy and Daddy were both 45. It was about 7.30 in the morning, and I was in bed when he set off for work. I was over from Birmingham and the bedroom I had faced the road, so I heard every sound. I heard all of the shots. It was right outside the front door, and I remember lots of the neighbours rushing over to see if they could help, and an ambulance was called. I rushed over to Dad and he was still alive; I held his hand and he was able to speak, telling me that he felt really cold. He was rushed to Dundonald Hospital but we received a phone call within the hour telling us that he had passed away.

It seems that the gunmen were waiting for him in a car, but at the angle of our house, their car must have really stuck out, so it is strange that no one noticed them. As I said, it was 7.30 a.m., so we don't know how long they had been waiting or if they had waited all night. Dad and all of the other prison officers had been advised to vary their routes and the times they set off and the times that they returned home; they were all very security conscious. It is horrible to think that we were being watched so they could potentially kill him; it was frightening. We also found out that a few minutes after my dad was shot another prison officer was ambushed and shot at traffic lights at Castlereagh. I am

Prison Officer William Burns, murdered by the IRA.
(Kay Burns)

not sure, but I think that this was the second time that the officer was ambushed; I am pleased to say that he did survive.

The day of his funeral came; it was held in Knocknagoney Presbyterian Church. It was the church we had attended when we were younger. It was the first funeral that I had ever attended and it was my dad's. I remember the overwhelming smell of flowers as I walked in; there were so many wreathes and it was a wonderful tribute to Daddy. I remember also that there was a sea of colours as there were so many prison officers – colleagues of his – and lots of soldiers from the UDR. As I said, there was a sea of colours and there were mourners there from every generation.

The day was pleasant, weather-wise, and I do remember that there were some photos of the funeral in the *Belfast Telegraph*. There were some of his colleagues as well as my brother carrying his coffin. I also remember that in those unenlightened days, women weren't always welcome and I have this memory that my mum had to get permission to go to the graveside. I also want to pay tribute to my cousin, James, who was a great help.

PO Burns' memorial. (Kay Burns)

There was an investigation by the RUC, but as I was back in Birmingham, I didn't get too much information. I know that on at least a couple of occasions, people were arrested and questioned, but no one was ever charged. It was a terrible time for the family as ten months later my brother Trevor, who was 20 at the time, was killed in a very suspicious road traffic accident. Several eyewitnesses later stated that his car was being chased at the time of the crash, but we never learned any more. The UVF claimed the killing of Daddy.

You asked me if I forgive Dad's killers; no, definitely not! I always knew that I would never forgive them. I didn't want to sit in the same room as them, like some other bereaved people have done. I hope that they have had horrible lives; I don't know them, but I do hope that their lives have been horrible. Murder doesn't get you anywhere; they will get their just deserts, at least that is what I like to think.

✦

It was inside Her Majesty's Prison, the Maze, that UFF prisoners once displayed a sign designed, it was said, to raise morale. The hand-painted sign, made by the inmates read: 'Better to die on your feet, than to live on your knees in an Irish Republic.' Mark Simpson, of BBC Northern Ireland, wrote: 'To them, it was the reason for their militant loyalism. To many others, it was simply an excuse for 25 years of sectarian killings.'

Loyalist paramilitaries killed over 900 innocent Catholics, the vast majority of them in sectarian attacks, taking lives in a most random, ad-hoc fashion. For some of these Loyalists, it was considered the only way to hit back at the IRA's campaign of violence, whilst for others it was surely an outlet for psychopathic tendencies. There can be no excusing nor condoning the killings of so many members of the Roman Catholic community; there can be no rationalising of the years of terror. UFF and UVF gangs caused heartbreak and misery in North and West Belfast, as well as in mid-Ulster, the notorious 'murder triangle'. Sectarian murders by Loyalists will receive the same short thrift from this author as do those committed by their counterparts in the Nationalist communities. What follows is the story of a Catholic man who was a teenager when his dad was shot dead as he returned from a Friday night out in West Belfast. He demanded anonymity as he was equally fearful of both sets of what he described to me as 'sectarian gangsters'.

Liam's Story

I don't wish to name my father, nor in anyway identify my family, because the men who I am sure killed him live fairly close by and I want no recriminations against my brothers and sisters and their children. For the first time that I can remember, I finally have a sort of peace, and if I betray any information about names and places, then they can get to all of us. In Northern Ireland today it is better to be a shadow; that way, no one hurts you.

My da was an ordinary, hard-working Catholic man; he was married and he had half a dozen kids. He worked most of his life at Shorts in Belfast; he worked with Catholics and Protestants alike and he got on well with them all, because they talked about football and the dogs and never at all about politics. They laughed and joked and shared flasks of tea, and they did all of the things which working men always did. He worked hard to put food in our bellies, clothes on our backs – even if the younger ones had to use those which the older ones had grown out of – and there was an annual trip to Co. Down in the sunshine. He was a good man with never a bad word about anyone; a good dad to us all and a good man to our mother.

When it happened, you have to remember that Northern Ireland had gone mad; the RA were killing Protestants and the UDA were killing Catholics; neither side had a viable reason, they just did! I was in my last few years at school; things were tough but like all of us, we managed and we were happy and uninvolved. Da's only 'vice', as he called it, was to go out to the pubs on a Friday night for a jar or two; that was what got him killed in the end. Come Friday, Ma would give him his beer money and off he would go to meet his mates around the Falls and Springfield Road areas. This Friday night was different; he didn't come home, didn't come back at all. The Peelers came knocking the next morning; two of them in their dark uniforms – most called them 'black bastards' – with several soldiers with their blackened faces and their rifles, giving them protection. The soldiers looked tough and very serious, but at the same time, there was a scared, wary look about their faces.

An old sergeant told Ma that there had been an accident and that Da was very badly hurt. This gave us hope that he was still alive, but as we were getting our coats on, he admitted that Da was dead. My world just went numb and I felt sick, really sick; I was in a total state of shock. I went with her to the mortuary at the Royal Vic' but we were advised not to go in, but we both had to see him; after all, I was the oldest; I was now the man of the house.

I will never forget the sight of him lying there. I will never forget that sight as long as I live. They covered him up to his throat with a white sheet, but they couldn't keep the bloodstains off it. He had a sort of cap on, but you could see a tiny hole on one side of his head and then a big wadge of bandage under the cap, where the bullet had come out. His head was so bruised and swollen, but the hole was as big as a house; I will never be able to put that sight out of my mind. There was an awful stink of chemicals, which made me want to throw up.

I am going to fast forward a few months, because the funeral, the closed casket, everything, took such an emotional toll of me. I can't discuss this without tears and I have shed enough of those.

There had been eight of us in our family unit; suddenly there was one less; Da was gone and there was a huge hole where he had once been. Ma was 40-odd, but looked more like 70, with her grey, unkempt hair and tired face. She had six mouths to feed and was reliant on state handouts, plus a few quid from Criminal Injuries. But she managed, and kept us all in clothes and school uniform and food and, of course, the Catholic Fathers helped. Most of all, she kept us decent and she kept us free from hatred and thoughts of revenge. One of my sisters wanted to join Cumann na mBan* but Ma soon put a stop to that and kept her out of trouble. Living in the area around the Falls Road, Springfield Road and Divis Street, several of my muckers got involved with the RA, and one that I am aware of was killed by the Peelers .I will come to him in a moment. One boy I knew was green-booked** and offered to introduce me to the local commanders, but Ma made it clear that we were not to go down that route and, thank God, kept me out of all that.

No one was ever caught for Dad's murder, but the UDA admitted to the killing and there was some nonsense about him being a member of Sinn Fein; it was untrue, as he had no time at all for politics. All the RUC told us was he was walking back from a club in the Falls when he was shot at random by paramilitary killers. We never really found out any more and I have never bothered with the HET, as I have been told so many stories from others about how useless they are. Ma died in her seventies, having struggled all of her life, and having to struggle even more when Da was taken from us. She never knew peace, but, God bless her, she kept us out of the paramilitaries.

---

* Literally the Women's IRA Council, but applied to the women's section of the IRA.
** The Green Book is the IRA's operating manual; it is their rule book, laying out conduct and behaviour.

I mentioned earlier that one of my muckers joined the RA – I won't name him – moving weapons and bombs around for them. He was killed in a shoot-out with the Peelers, very close to where we were living. I didn't go to his funeral, which was at Milltown but left from his house a few streets away. It was the full military affair, with tricolours, black gloves, berets and everything. His death was another unnecessary death of a young, impressionable life, caused by the Godfathers of Nationalism, just as young Protestants were killed by the leaders of the Loyalists; just a waste.

I was brought up a very strict Catholic with Mass, Confession, everything, but neither Da or Ma taught us hatred; I had nothing against the Protestants. Of course, there were rivalries between schools and clubs; there was piss-taking, insults and some scraps; plenty of them in fact, but it was part of growing up in Belfast. What I could never, and can never, understand is why those men killed my father for nothing, other than he was a Catholic man in a Catholic area.

The men who took his life showed no mercy, no pity, no hesitation; they killed him without conscience, without a second thought, and probably not even a second glance at his lifeless body in the street. I wonder if they could ever have imagined my mother, or my brothers and sisters, sat around Da's coffin, crying their eyes out. Would they have given a thought to her frail body, out in all hours, cleaning and ironing for a few pence just so that we wouldn't go without food? She had no man to provide a wage for the family; would they have still shot him in the head had they known? I think that they still would have, because the Loyalists were like the RA: no conscience, no pity; they just killed for the sake of it. For all of those thousands of deaths, it didn't achieve a united Ireland and it won't make Boris Johnson any keener to keep the North in the UK. He and the English will do what suits them.

The Loyalist paramilitaries took my da, they took my mother's husband and they took away his chance of being a grandfather and walking his girls down the aisle. But one thing which they never took from me was my soul; they never got inside my head, filling it up with the same hatred which drove them on. Although I have a sort of peace, I still fear them because of the harm they can still cause, but I don't hate them and I don't hate the Protestants either.

5

1981–85

During The Troubles it is believed that a total of twelve postmen, some of whom were part-time UDR or RUCR personnel, even some who had the most tenuous of connections to the security forces, were killed by the Provisional IRA. The following men were the subject of fatal attacks by the Provisionals:

Ivan Vennard was shot by IRA gunmen while collecting mail on the Republican Kilwilkie Estate in Lurgan on 3 October 1973; he was a former member of the UDR, having left the regiment nine months earlier.

Robert 'Bobby' Lennox was a part-time soldier in the UDR. He was shot dead by IRA gunmen as he delivered mail to a remote cottage at Drumard, Knockloughrim in Co. Londonderry on 2 April 1976.

Gordon Liddle was collecting mail close to his home in Drumgole, Lisnaskea, when an IRA bombing unit triggered a roadside bomb between Lisnaskea and Newtownbutler on 17 July 1976; their real target was an RUC mobile patrol, which they expected along the same road. There is some speculation that the Provisionals might have been targeting his two brothers, who were serving members of the RUC.

Stanley Adams, a UDR soldier, was delivering a letter – posted by the IRA to lure him to a remote spot – to a house near Pomeroy in Co. Tyrone on 28 October 1976. He was ambushed by waiting IRA gunmen and shot dead.

James 'Jimmy' McFaul, a UDR soldier, had just returned home from work, delivering mail in West Belfast, on 27 July 1977. He opened the door of his house in Cuan Avenue on the Woodvale Estate and was shot dead by IRA gunmen.

Jack 'Jock' Eaglesham was a part-time soldier in the UDR whose main job was as a postal delivery worker. On 7 February 1978, IRA gunmen ambushed his Post Office van, spraying it with automatic gunfire as he drove out of Rock Primary School, Cookstown in Co. Tyrone.

Patrick McEntee was a retired postman whom the IRA claimed was a former soldier in the British Army. There is no evidence to back up this claim. Mr McEntee was attacked five years earlier, in 1973, by an IRA punishment squad as they *suspected* [author's italics] him of being an informer. He was kneecapped and left permanently disabled. On 24 June 1978, while driving with his wife at Drumuckavall, Co. Armagh, they were forced to stop by IRA gunmen. Mrs McEntee was ordered out of the car as the gunmen forced him into the back, before driving across the nearby border into the Irish Republic. The gunmen shot him dead, before unceremoniously driving back into Northern Ireland, abandoning the car in Ballsmills, near Crossmaglen.

Noel McKay was a Post Office engineer who lived in Finaghy, West Belfast; he had just returned home to his pregnant wife on the evening of 26 July 1978. Masked PIRA gunmen had waited for his return, calmly walking up to him as he parked his distinctive Post Office van. He was shot ten times at point-blank range, dying at the scene. It is thought that it was a case of faulty intel on the part of the Republican paramilitaries as Mr McKay had no connection whatsoever with the security forces.

Howard Donaghy was a part-time policeman in the RUCR; his full-time job was with the Post Office. On 11 September 1978, as he was working on his new bungalow near Omagh, Co. Tyrone, he was hit with a rifle shot from an IRA gunman before several others ran across and fired several shots into him as he lay on the ground.

Robert Batchelor worked for the Post Office as well as being a part-time soldier in the UDR. On 27 November 1978, he parked up in Hammill Street, close to the Divis Street flats where he worked. He was shot dead by IRA gunmen from the Falls Road in Belfast. He was hit in the head several times, dying almost instantly.

Alan Price was a postman and not a member of the security forces, past or present. However, on the morning of 19 February 1983, he agreed to swap shifts with another postman who was also a part-time soldier in the UDR. As he delivered mail to a remote farmhouse in Sessiagh, Co. Fermanagh, he was shot dead by waiting IRA gunmen.

Nathaniel 'Nat' Cush was a former UDR soldier, having left the regiment in March 1987. He was working at Tomb Street Post Office in Belfast. Whilst he was at work on 15 June 1987, an IRA bombing team had placed a bomb underneath his car. The device exploded as he turned on the engine and he died instantly. He had also served with the Regular Army until 1967.

✦

In this book, we have in the main dealt with the 'silent victims', the loved ones of those left behind following paramilitary violence. The next story involves a man who personally survived a terrorist attack. Like fellow UDR man Noel Downey (see Chapter Six: 1986–90), part-time soldier and postman Sammy Brush survived his encounter with the Provisional IRA.

At approximately 0600 hours on Saturday, 13 June 1981, two men arrived at the home of Mrs Mary McGarvey in Armaghlughey Road, Ballygawley; she was in the house with her sister at the time. One of the men announced that they were members of the Provisional IRA, instructing them to be quiet. They informed the women that they would not be harmed, provided that they co-operated. Both men were armed with handguns; they informed Mrs McGarvey that they would need the house until about 1 p.m. She was asked for her permission, but at the same time, warned her of the consequences if she chose not to acquiesce. Both women later told the police that the two gunmen were very quiet, but that they were not allowed to be on their own.

At about 10.30 a.m. William Hall, a neighbour, came to the house, followed shortly afterwards by a Michael Russell; they were both let into the house, but were detained by the gunmen.

Sergeant Sammy Brush of 8 UDR was working in his full-time role as a postman for the Royal Mail. He had a delivery to make in the remote rural area of Cravney Irish, some 1½ miles from Ballygawley in Co. Tyrone. He was attacked by the two gunmen, who had lain in wait for him. One of them – Terrence 'Gerry' McGeough[*]– was later convicted over the attack; the other man was alleged to be Vincent McAnespie. The latter was tried for attempted murder but acquitted.[**]

The UDR man was hit four times, but although wounded, and with his right arm – his shooting arm – disabled, he managed to return their fire. He was able to get off three shots, one of which hit one of the gunmen; the pair then fled to a waiting car. Sergeant Brush managed to drive to the nearest RUC station and safety; he spent eleven months recovering from his very bad wounds, with a further two years as a physiotherapy outpatient in the military wing of Musgrave Park Hospital in Belfast. He was a former 'B' Special who had joined the Ulster Defence Regiment in May 1970. He was eventually able to resume his duties with 8 UDR. Ten of his colleagues were killed by Republican paramilitaries; Sammy Brush would have been the 'eleventh man'.

---

[*] McGeough was arrested in 2007, some twenty-six years after the attack, the day after he had stood as an Independent Nationalist candidate at Omagh in the Northern Ireland Assembly Elections. He was convicted in 2011 and sentenced to a total of twenty years for four separate offences. He had previously been a member of Sinn Fein. He was released under the Good Friday Agreement in 2013, having served only two years. He was a member of PIRA's East Tyrone Brigade. He was also charged with attacks on the British Army in West Germany and detained by the West German Polizei. During his trial in Germany, he was extradited to the USA to face charges of attempting to buy surface-to-air-missiles in 1983. He served in US prisons until his release in 1996, at which point, he was deported to the Republic of Ireland. [Gerry McGeough guilty of 1981 Samuel Brush murder bid, BBC News]

[**] McAnespie's case was dismissed on technical grounds; he was identified by two witnesses hiding the weapons used in the attack. However, at the start of his trial one of the witnesses died and his elderly wife was too ill to give evidence. The case, dismissed as 'hearsay evidence', is not considered substantial enough to gain a safe conviction. [www.bbc.com/news/uk-northern-ireland-11713249]

Sammy's Story

It was Saturday, 13 June, and I was working. Around 1245 hours, I had almost completed my rounds, with only four more houses to deliver to. I recall that I had one particular letter for a Mrs Mary McGarvey and set off in her direction. I must point out that, owing to the dangerous times in which we all lived, I was wearing light body armour and a .38 Special Smith & Wesson revolver, which I carried in a shoulder holster. I carried five rounds of .38 ammunition in each trouser pocket.

I drove along the Tullyvar Road from Ballygawley, then turned left into the Armaghlughey Road, and then left again into 'McGarvey's laneway'. I arrived there at about 1 p.m.. I stopped the van, put on the handbrake but although it was sunny, it was a cold day, so I left the engine running; for some reason, I left the driver's door open. I recognised a VW motor vehicle which I knew belonged to Michael Russell. I could see through the window of the house that there were people inside. I also noticed that the front door was closed, which I thought was strange as it was normally open on a good sunny day and the weather on this occasion was fine.

Anyway, I posted the letter through the letterbox in the front door of the house, but as I was turning to get back into the van a gunman appeared from the lean-to at the side of the house. He was about 10–12ft away, and he started to fire at me with a revolver. I could see that the gunman was wearing a black/dark-coloured anorak, with something covering the lower part of his face. As I was being fired at, I felt a thump in the left side of my chest, 6 to 8in below my shoulder blade; I then felt a sting in my right shoulder. I turned and ran from the parking area, onto the laneway in a direction further up the laneway away from the Armaghlughey Road. Shots were still being fired at me, and I was hit twice in the back above my waist.

As I ran up the laneway I was trying to draw my Smith & Wesson with my right hand, but each time my hand came away without the revolver. I realised later that was because of the severe injuries in my right shoulder. I managed to draw the weapon with my left hand. I had worked out that there was more than one gunman in view of the number of shots being fired at me. I could hear different footsteps. At this stage, shots were still being fired at me, and I was feeling quite breathless; breathing was very difficult. I knew that I had been badly injured, as I could taste blood in my mouth. I didn't know at that time, the bullet that hit me in the right shoulder had cut the nerves going to my hand, before passing through my right lung. It exited in the centre of my back, just missing my spine.

I knew that if I stayed there, I was going to die, so I turned around to head back to my van, which had been fitted with a steel plate behind the driver's seat. As I did so, I saw the second gunman on the laneway adjacent to the parking area. This gunman had a lighter-coloured anorak; he was pointing a revolver at me, holding the revolver with two hands. I fired two shots at this gunman, who then moved onto the parking area out of my line of sight. I then heard rustling in the hedge; I believed that the other gunman had tried to get around behind me, so I fired two shots into the hedge. I had now expended four out of my five rounds, so I reloaded my pistol, and was able to get back to the van and drove to Ballygawley Police Station. From there Constable George Gilliland[*] took me in a police car to South Tyrone Hospital in Dungannon.

I know that Terence Gerard McGeough was one of the two gunmen on the basis that, on the same day that I was shot, he was admitted to hospital with a wound[**] received from a .38. He crossed the border to be treated in Monaghan. He also applied for asylum in Sweden and in his asylum application he made unequivocal admissions in respect of the charges. To compound that, he wrote a book in which he described the shooting incident!

Since the ambush on 13 June 1981, there has been a chill in the relationship with my Roman Catholic neighbours, almost as if I was somehow to blame for returning fire. This was fairly passive at first, in that it was no more than ignoring me, or making some snide comment, right up until the 1998 Belfast agreement, when it became more aggressive.

I believe it then became a concerted effort to drive me from my home by attacking my property. There were several acts of vandalism on

---

[*] Constable Gilliland was murdered by PIRA along with Constable William Clements at Ballygawley RUC station on 7 December 1985.

[**] McGeough was later transferred for treatment to a gunshot wound in his chest at St Vincent's Hospital, Dublin.

my cars, such as smashed windscreens, slashed tyres, IRA slogans scored on doors and bonnet, panels dented, windows smashed, and several door mirrors broken. There were also attacks on my home, with windows broken on many occasions; additionally, the shed at the rear of the house which contained the oil tank was burned. Altogether there were over forty separate occasions when the attacks resulted in costing hundreds of pounds, and least three which amounted to thousands of pounds, some of which was covered by insurance.

Both my late wife and I were regularly subjected to verbal abuse by Republican youths. However, we were both determined to remain in our home in spite of all the damages and abuse. My wife passed away on 25 September 2017, and I am still living in the same house; things are fairly quiet at present, which is due more to the Covid-19 restrictions than goodwill from Republicans.

[Author's notes: Prior to Sergeant Brush's shooting, 8 UDR had lost nineteen members, all killed by Republican paramilitaries; most of them were murdered while off duty. Many more had been attacked and received serious injuries, again most attacks had taken place while the victims were off duty. Altogether, 8 UDR had thirty-four members murdered between 1971 and 1990, including two members of 8 RIR in 1993 and 1994. Additionally, nine former members of the battalion were killed by Republicans after they had left the regiment.]

✦

The RUC had several divisions, including undercover units as well as uniformed officers. One such section was the Headquarters Mobile Support Unit (HMSU). It was an elite unit, intended to be the police force's own equivalent of the British Army's Special Air Service (SAS) and as such was trained by them. It was designed to confront terrorists with 'firepower, speed and aggression'. It was the RUC's very own version of 'shock and awe'. It began life as the Special Patrol Group in 1977, being replaced by the HMSU – or SSU as it was also known – in 1981.

In early January 1983, the HMSU received intelligence that the Provisionals were planning to kill a part-time UDR soldier in either

Rostrevor or Warrenpoint; the intelligence reports were extremely hazy. As the crow flies, the straight distance between Warrenpoint and Rostrevor is 1.97 miles, with a driving distance of 2.11 miles. As a consequence of the lack of specific information, the operation was an extremely difficult one for the officers involved.

The soldier concerned was known to make a weekly trip with his elderly father in order to collect his pension; it was known by the terrorists that the trips generally alternated between the post office branches in both locations. On 6 January, three of the RUC elite unit's officers were dispatched to the area. As they passed through Rostrevor, they became aware of a suspiciously parked vehicle, very close to the local Post Office. One officer approached the car and was shot immediately; he was badly wounded. The other two officers were also hit as the gunmen pressed the attack; they were mortally wounded. The first officer survived his wounds after receiving emergency medical treatment. The unit's first fatalities were Sergeant Eric Brown (41), a father of three from Moira, Co. Down, and Constable Brian Quinn (23) from Bangor, Co. Down. The killers were not apprehended until 1985 when a Warrenpoint man was charged with the murders.

Andrea Brown is in a tragically unique position in that not only did she lose a family member to terrorist activity, but she was also injured herself at the hands of the same organisation several years later.

Andrea's Story: Her Dad

My daddy was a sergeant in the HMSU. He and his colleagues had been briefed that there was going to be a hit on a part-time soldier who took his father on a weekly trip to collect his state pension. Just to let you know, this is covered also in Eamon Collins' book *Killing Rage*. Daddy was very tall – he was 6ft 4in – and was squeezed into the passenger seat, with Percy Scott driving and Brian Quinn was in the back. As they drove through Rostrevor, they noticed a car with the windows all steamed up, parked outside the post office. Percy did a U-turn, stopping near the suspicious car; he got out alone, before walking over to what he could see were three men. As the window was rolled down, he could see that the driver had a newspaper on his knee, but there was a gun underneath it.

Percy shouted a warning to Dad, but at that instant, the gunman raised the gun and fired at him, hitting him in the shoulder. My daddy was a big man and struggled to get his big frame out of the car. As he got out, one of the other gunmen hit him in the heart, causing him to collapse to the ground badly wounded; Brian Quinn was also hit. Both men died at the scene within a few minutes. Percy, who I have

Eric Brown. (Andrea Brown)

told you was wounded, managed to get a few shots into the fleeing car, which was later abandoned at Warrenpoint.

What hurts me to this day is that Percy saw the killer and recognised him but he refuses to give his name. I know that he has suffered mentally as he was the only survivor, but believe me, I know what survivor's guilt feels like and in the same circumstances I would have revealed the name.

I was 12 at the time, living in Moira with my two sisters then aged 13 and 17. Daddy's murder really impacted on the whole family. He was very well known in the community; the life and soul of the church, all the events; everything. Part of Mummy died also. I have some vague memories of the funeral; Moira came to a standstill because my daddy was known to everyone in that small community. There was one thing which did sour things and it displays the difference between decent people and some of these Republicans. On the day of the murder, a local man went into one of the shops in Moira, praising the IRA, telling the shopkeeper: 'They got a good one when they got Eric Brown.' I was sickened; it was disgusting. Later on, we brought some carnations, three of them, carefully laying them on his grave. We went back later, but some local Republicans had desecrated our touching little display, turning the carnations upside down. It really brought it home to me that there was a difference between the local communities.

The thing is, they get away with it time after time; they preach conciliation and respect and then they display all this hatred. If I allowed it to, it would make me very, very bitter. Not towards ordinary Catholics, but towards the paramilitaries. It is not about what you are, it is about who you are; if you are decent with me, I'll be decent with you. In time, someone was arrested, but during interrogation over a whole seven-day period he refused to speak and under the law the RUC had to release him. The getaway driver was later arrested and convicted, but he refused to incriminate the other killers.

You asked me how I felt today; well to be honest, the day that my daddy was killed, was the day that my family as I knew it died as well. Life changed drastically for all of us. It wasn't long after Christmas; I recall that I had saved my pocket money and bought Daddy a pen with a digital clock on it. I was so proud of it; one school morning, without seeking permission, I took it out of the study to show my friends at school. Because I never asked anyone if I could take it, I believed for years that losing him was God's punishment to me. I know different today. Had he not died, I don't think that I would have been involved in the Lisburn bomb five years later. I will explain more later.

At around 1310 hours, on Tuesday, 18 January 1983, PIRA gunmen hijacked a Ford Cortina from a house in Robert Street, close to the River Foyle in Londonderry. One of the gunmen held the family of the house hostage as three more drove the car 2 miles (3.2km) to Seymour Gardens in Nelson Street, in the Nelson Drive Estate; the journey was short, taking about five minutes. They stopped outside a shop belonging to a former RUCR officer, John Olphert (39), a father of two. He was in the process of serving customers in the grocery and post office when he saw two masked gunmen approaching the front door. He managed to block the entrance, but one of the men opened fire, hitting him and causing him to collapse. The gunmen then pushed the wounded man aside, barging their way through the wrecked door. Mrs Olphert had dashed to her wounded husband's side, cradling him in her arms, but the gunman fired several more shots into the man's defenceless body, hitting him in the head. He died very shortly afterwards. The car was found abandoned and burned out at Rossdowney Road, some 1.7 miles (3km) away. The gunmen were then collected by another car before speeding away to the Gobnascale area of the city.

John Olphert, murdered at his shop in Londonderry by the IRA. (Mark Olphert)

Mr Olphert had resigned from the RUCR the previous July, intending to devote his time to the development of his business; in short, he had not been a serving officer in the police force for some six months, but was still singled out for murder by the Provisional IRA.

It is thought that one of the gunmen was William Fleming from the Creggan Estate in Londonderry; he was himself killed, when he and Daniel Doherty – from PIRA's Gobnascale unit – were shot dead in an ambush by undercover soldiers on 6 December 1984. The two men arrived on a stolen motorcycle at the city's Gransha Hospital, with the intention of killing a part-time UDR soldier who worked there as a male nurse. One of the soldiers had spotted that Fleming was carrying a pistol and so took the decision to ram the gunmen's motorbike. It was stated that Fleming made a movement towards his weapon, at which point the plain-clothed troops opened fire, killing both men.

At Mr Olphert's funeral, Bishop James McHaffey told the mourners, referring to the murderers: 'If such people are the so-called liberators of the Irish people, then God help Ireland.' His revulsion was shared by a group of Roman Catholic priests in the city, which issued the following statement:

People often seek to justify their evil deeds by attempting to portray their victims as enemies of some noble cause, and on that account, as somehow deserving of their fate. Catholics should not leave themselves open to such deception. They must always remember that each of us will one day have to render an unaided and strict account of our lives on earth to God.

Mr Olphert was just one of twenty-six members of the Orange Order to be murdered in Londonderry between 1972 and 1994. No one was ever brought to justice for his particular murder, but it is known that at least two known PIRA members from the Gobnascale unit had been seen in the shop in the days before the killing. Mark Olphert is the son of the murdered former RUCR officer.

Mark's Story

18 January 1983 started off a normal day. Up at 7.30 for breakfast and to wave my dad off as he went to open his shop. As a boy, my father worked in a greengrocers and his lifetime's ambition was to own a shop. He got his wish and in July 1982, while still a serving RUC GC reservist, my dad opened Caw Supermarket in Nelson Drive, Londonderry. He resigned from the RUC and he never did do another shift after he opened his shop. I was 12, and I have very good memories of those times. Helping my dad out in the shop was great. In fact, the summer of 1982 was one of the happiest of my life, but back to 18 January 1983. Dad left for work and we got ready for school.

It was lunchtime; I was walking the halls with my friend Michael. I heard my name being shouted by another pal, David, down the corridor. I made my way over to him and he told me I had to go get my coat and bag and go to the office. David asked me, 'Why are you going home?' I remember my words: 'Because the Provos have come for my dad.' Somehow I knew even before I was told. When I got to the school office the headmaster was waiting and I asked him why I was going home, he replied: 'Your father has had an accident.' The headmaster and

John Olphert. (Mark Olphert)

I drove over to another part of the school to pick up my big brother, Peter. I was in the back of the car and I overheard the teacher and my brother talking. Peter was asking questions, but the headmaster couldn't answer them. I was worried and, like I said, deep down I knew.

We turned into Nelson Drive, heading to our house; we passed the shop and it was cordoned off, with soldiers and police outside the shop, where a crowd had gathered. It was obvious now what had happened as I'd seen things like this on TV. My young heart just crumbled as everything became crystal clear. My dad had been attacked and killed in his shop. My brother and I got home, where we were met by my grandfather, who lived with us. He didn't know what had happened, so Peter and I decided to walk down to the shop. On our way there, a car stopped beside us and in it were my mother and the vicar. My mum looked completely broken and devastated. I got into the car and went home with them. My brother went on up to the shop and when he got there he got a mop and bucket to clean our father's blood off the shop floor. Later on, we found out that my mum was holding dad in her arms and she pleaded for mercy. One of them said to her: 'Shut up, you Orange bitch or we'll shoot you too.' Then they shot my father through the head. As they ran out, they fired a shot into the roof to celebrate, shouting: '*Tiocfaidh ár lá.*'*

Our house suddenly filled up with uncles, aunts and some police. My mum just sat there, looking at the door repeating over and over again: 'John will be home soon; John will be home soon.' I didn't know what to do; I was just a child and my world had just fallen apart. I just couldn't understand why anyone would want to kill my father; he was such a good man. My father's body was brought home, and for two days I sat underneath his coffin, telling the scores and scores of people who called to pay respects, 'that was my daddy.'

The funeral happened, attended by over a thousand people, but after it the house went silent; people stopped calling. It was me, mum, Pete and Granda. Mum was a wreck, heavily sedated most of the time, crying in despair. Peter did his best and stepped up to try and hold things together, but he had only turned 15 the day after Dad's funeral. I didn't want to go back to school, but after a week off, my uncle made sure the headmaster came and picked me up every morning and took me to school. My mum's brother took over running the shop for a while, which caused bad feeling between my father's brothers and him. They felt they should have gotten the shop, but in her despair my mum made a promise to keep the shop doors open for as long as possible and her brother stepped up. The post office was run by a family friend for some months, until Mum felt strong enough to go back. I remember the police visiting the house regularly after the murder, making sure we were OK, asking if we needed anything, and keeping Mum informed of the investigation. I also remember friends and neighbours coming and asking my mum for money, which I thought strange, but as I've grown up I realise there were vultures out there trying to take advantage of my mum's situation. Sickening when I think about that now.

One memory I have is of the phone ringing over the next few days, but each time I answered, I could hear adult voices, in a sort of sing-song way shouting: 'We got him, we got him, we got him.' One day, we got off

---

* Tiocfaidh ár lá is Gaelic for 'our day will come'.

the school bus and someone had scrawled on the wall: 'John Olphert, ha, ha, ha.' The next time we passed there, it had gone, but I still remember. After the graffiti and the torturous phone calls, I went into myself. I was just a boy and my hero had been removed from my life. I do remember my anger; there was lots of anger. I only really dealt with that a few years ago in my 40s. At home, after Dad died, I tried my best to take care of my mum; she was in a sedated daze for a long time. I remember many days I would come home from school and Mum would be curled up in her bed crying. To this day I still rest my head on my father's pillow every night. I still have a few of his things, which I cherish. I've his watch and the jacket he wore. That was the only item of the clothing which he wore that day, which was returned to us.

As a family we were well looked after by RUC Welfare. Pete and I were taken away on trips to Fermanagh, England and France. We had a lot of support that way. There was a dedicated welfare officer who visited often and provided Mum with all the help and assistance possible. I do know my mum got a small five-figure sum in compensation, which she used as a deposit on a house in another more private estate. We moved out of Nelson Drive but a part of me has never left; I still pop into the shop from time to time.

My dad had been in the RUC over ten years and was highly liked and respected by his RUC colleagues. The murder was the third time that PIRA had tried to kill him. I have been told my father was a real pain to Gobnascale PIRA players, and he really must have annoyed a top player for them to come at him three times. Sadly, I think it was an article in the local paper about the new Mace Shop in Nelson Drive which alerted PIRA to my dad's new career; they were determined to murder him.

PIRA terrorists were very good when it came to killing people and not leaving much evidence behind. So, despite rigorous efforts, nobody was ever charged with my father's killing. House-to-house inquiries were conducted in the estate. Appeals for information were made and some Catholics from the area the getaway car was hijacked from even came forward and gave statements. I commend them for doing that as it could have brought deadly repercussions unto themselves. Lots of people gave statements to police and six terrorists were arrested and interrogated at Castlereagh but didn't give any information away.

It was the Provisional IRA who murdered my father, yet some local UVF members still decided to twice rob my mum. I have no time for paramilitaries/terrorists on either side. Growing up the son of a murdered former RUC man, I am firmly on the side of those who held the line. In October 1988 I had a motorcycle accident in which I broke my back, injuring my spine, so recovering from that became the main focus of my life for a while. I believe had it not been for that accident I'd have joined the RUC as well.

Mum had a visit from a senior police officer after the Gransha incident in which two PIRA men were killed, to tell her the gun used to kill my dad had been recovered. However, she already had an idea as she recognised it from the picture in the newspaper. The driver and the PIRA QM who supplied the guns used in my dad's killing are still alive but I hear life hasn't been kind to them. I believe that all the misfortunes they have since had to face were a direct result of their own actions earlier in life. I'm a firm believer in karma now. I won't name the other killers but I have let PIRA know that I know.

I'm 50 now, and it is almost forty years since my dad died. I've had intensive therapy and I've come to terms with what happened, as much as that's humanly possible. My father was a brave man and he loved Northern Ireland but I feel he gave up his life for nothing. Yes, we have had the GFA and yes, the killing rate has dropped, but there is no peace in Northern Ireland. The shooting war has turned into a narrative war. PIRA terrorists and their supporters are desperately trying to rewrite history so they can make their military defeat somehow look like a victory, and the likes of the late Martin McGuinness are lauded as 'peacemakers'.

'Set the truth free' was the cry; I just have.

✦

On 13 March 1984, the Provisionals struck again in the rural area of Co. Fermanagh, intensifying their border genocide campaign. Their target was Ronnie Funston, who had served in the UDR for a three-year period between 1973 and 1976. The Republican paramilitary group killed many times solely on the basis of guilt through past associations;

this was another murder on that most tenuous of grounds. Early that morning, a group of armed men crossed the Irish border at Pettigo, Co. Donegal, with their objective the killing of a former part-time soldier. The village of Pettigo is a small place, divided by the Irish border; the demarcation line crossing through Main Street. Close by is the townland of Lowery, where the Funston family farm was located.

Living on the farm was Ronald 'Ronnie' Funston, who had left the UDR to live and work on the farm with his parents and sisters. If the Provisionals were acting on intelligence gleaned from their army of dickers, it was, not for the first time, flawed. Their reason for killing the 28-year-old was very much in line with their tactics of stripping the Protestants from the border region, with the overall intention of creating a buffer zone, a no-go area in the border land. This tactic was designed to make the territory untenable for the security forces to operate inside.

At least two gunmen lay in wait in a hedge, close to the shed where Mr Funston fed some of his cattle at the same time every morning. With the British winter not quite over, the weather would have been cold, with warm clothing likely to have been the order of the day. As their victim started to use the tractor to move fodder to his animals, the gunmen opened fire with automatic weapons. They hit the vehicle eighteen times as the former soldier sat defencelessly – he was unarmed – in the cab. Alerted by the gunfire, his mother dashed over to the scene, finding her son slumped against the tractor's steering wheel. She witnessed the two terrorists running across fields, cheering loudly as they ran; with the sanctuary of the border so close, escape was by no means problematical for them. Ronnie Funston was buried at Muckcross Cemetery in Co. Fermanagh.

The RUC immediately issued a statement warning that they believed the Provisionals were planning a major campaign of murder designed to provoke Protestants into a sectarian war with Catholics. A spokesman said:

> They hope for a backlash of retaliatory killings, this in turn creates fear within the Catholic community. That is the intended scenario. The only sane course is for all decent, law-abiding people, regardless of religion or politics, to refuse to become involved in conflict and to refuse to be used and manipulated by paramilitary organisations.

Ken Maginnis, the Unionist MP for Fermanagh and South Tyrone, angrily demanded of Prime Minister Margaret Thatcher at Prime Minister's question time the following Wednesday: 'What message have you got for people who are likely to be victims, like Ronnie Funston, of the IRA's genocide along the frontier?' The 'Iron Lady' had few words of comfort for the dead man's family.

Joy Graham is the sister of the murdered man; her words come courtesy of SEFF.

Joy's Story

At times, it seems a lifetime away, and other times it seems just like last year. My brother was outside, as usual, feeding the animals before he went to work. He'd been out on his tractor, in the lane; he was giving silage to his cattle when a gunman came in from across the border at Pettigo and shot him on his tractor. My mother was a very short distance away milking a cow and she heard the gunfire, and she ran to where Ronnie was and found him slumped ... and saw the gunman running across the field. I was at school in Enniskillen and I was brought home by the police to a scene of something you couldn't describe. Army and police were everywhere that morning. We just couldn't believe what had happened.

Former UDR soldier Ronnie Funston, murdered by the IRA. (Ken Funston)

Obviously at the time it ruined my mother. It destroyed her completely. She couldn't stay on the farm; we had to leave because she was so distraught. Every day she got up, she was distraught – she could still see the gunman. I suppose a lot of people saw that as giving in to what the IRA and their supporters wanted, but we couldn't go on as a family living there … Until we moved away from the farm, our life couldn't start again.

Ken Funston is the brother of the murdered man.

Ken's Story

My family were from Co. Donegal; they moved into Fermanagh in 1959, mainly, my father said for a better-quality farm, and better standard of education for the children. I was the first one born in Northern Ireland, having six older siblings and one younger. The family were very well-known and respected in the area. We lived in Pettigo/Tullyhommon, a place divided by the border; it was a place subject to a lot of terrorism, especially in the early 1970s. My oldest sibling died at a young age from complications, but most of us eventually all joined the security forces. The only one not to have done so was my youngest sister. I had joined the Royal Marines as a 17-year-old and had been away six years at the time of Ronnie's murder.

As I said, our farm went right up to the border, so it was a dangerous area. In the early hours of 13 March 1984, two PIRA gunmen crossed the border river and hid in the overgrowth near an outlying shed. They obviously knew that my brother Ronnie fed the cattle at 0745 every morning. They were well informed but would have needed a guide to show them the route, which would otherwise have been impossible in the darkness of a winter morning. When Ronnie was at the shed sitting on his tractor, they opened up with two automatic weapons; he died almost immediately. Ronnie had left the UDR seven years previously to concentrate on farming. My mother was out in the nearby farmyard and heard the shooting and ran down the lane way to see her dead son. She saw the two gunmen running off up the field, cheering. As you can understand, the family were devastated and although we have managed to live with it, it destroyed my mother. She never recovered from the trauma, with cancer killing her within a few years. The family had to sell the farm and move inland near to the village of Kesh.

We believe the information was provided by a local man, who also acted as a guide; he was a man who had known the family all our lives. He helped out on the farm and would have crossed from the southern side using the same route the gunmen used. Through my own research, I believe one of the gunmen was Maze escapee Kieran Fleming,* who died later in 1984, drowning in the River Bannagh following a shootout with the Regiment.

As a family we felt badly let down, especially believing that a so-called family friend was the one who 'set up' my brother. After that it was difficult to trust anyone in the local area. We could come to only one conclusion: Ronnie's murder was part of PIRA's overall strategy of cleansing the area of local Protestant pro-Union people, and that was something that was condoned by the Nationalist majority. However, what made us different from them was we could never contemplate taking revenge or setting out to kill our neighbours in the name of some twisted nationalistic idealism.

The following words are those of the dead man's mother, reproduced by the kind permission of SEFF. Ronnie's mother discovered the body; she told the 1984 inquest:

> I was walking towards the silo pits, the next thing I heard was automatic gunfire. I was about 75–100 yards away. After the shooting, the

---

* A PIRA unit targeted the Drumrush Lodge Restaurant, stealing a van in Pettigo, Co. Donegal. It was loaded with devices containing 900lb (409kg) of explosives. Shortly after arriving, two of the ASU planted the device in a lane leading to the restaurant and wired up a further device that was connected to an observation point; the three other members set up a firing position. From there a hoax call was made in order to lure the Army to the restaurant. On the approach of the RUC, the device was detonated, but it failed to explode; one of the PIRA ASU, Antoin Mac Giolla Bhride (also referred to by Republicans as Antoine Mac Giolla Bhrighde), approached a car that he thought contained civilians, but in fact was a unit of undercover soldiers. He turned to run but was shot dead, sparking a fire fight that resulted in the death of Private Alistair 'Al' Slater (28). In the confusion, two of the ASU gunmen stopped firing and ran across fields and ditches into the safety of the Irish Republic. Fleming (25), however, ran straight for the River Bannagh and though a non-swimmer, attempted to cross; he made little headway and was drowned. He was wanted for the murder of several members of the security forces.

tractor stopped. On hearing this, I walked immediately towards where Ronnie had been working, calling out his name. When I arrived, I saw Ronnie slumped over the wheel of the tractor in the cab.

In all, eighteen shots were fired into the tractor cab.

✦

During The Troubles, almost thirty prison staff from HMP Northern Ireland were killed in terrorist attacks; their counterparts in the Irish Republic were fortunate to only lose one of their number to the same causes. That officer was Chief Prison Officer Brian Stack, who worked at the Irish Republic's highest-security jail, Portlaoise Prison. It was the place of detention for most of those convicted under the Offences against the State Act; these included, in the main, Republican paramilitaries.

Brian Stack's principal role was the reviewing and planning of security; in other words, the prevention of escape attempts; in this role, he was both successful and highly efficient. It is believed that while the planning for the attack was carried out at a local level, the IRA's Army Council approved the plan to shoot Chief Prison Officer Stack. Although the IRA's own set of rules – the Green Book – expressly forbids operations inside the Irish Republic, it is thought that they were aware, through inside sources, that he was getting close to uncovering an escape plan.

On 25 March 1983, the officer had attended an Irish Amateur Boxing Association tournament in Dublin's National Stadium. He returned to where he had parked his car, but as he reached it he was ambushed by waiting gunmen; he was hit once in the back of the neck, collapsing to the ground gravely wounded. The gunmen raced away on a stolen motorcycle, which was later found abandoned at a site in Dublin, where they were collected by other accomplices in a waiting stolen car. Mr Stack was taken to hospital, where he remained in a coma for six months. When he came around, it was discovered that he had suffered paraplegia and irreversible brain damage. He was allowed home to be with his family, but he was subsequently returned to hospital, where he died on 29 September 1984.

Both the Provisional IRA and the INLA refused to admit that they had carried out the killing, claiming that it was the unauthorised work of a Republican splinter group. It was only after courageous work by the dead officer's son – Austin Stack – that they finally admitted the killing in September 2013, some thirty years after the attack. In a statement, a spokesman told Austin: 'In Portlaoise a brutal prison regime saw prisoners and their families suffer greatly. This is the context in which IRA *volunteers* shot your father.' The attack that led to Mr Stack's death was consistently denied by the IRA and specifically Gerry Adams, the then President of Sinn Fein. It took the prompt-

Portlaoise prison officer Brian Stack, killed by the IRA. (Austin Stack)

ing and the insistence of Austin Stack to persuade the Provisionals to finally admit to the killing.

Two years later, the Gardaí unit NBCI (National Bureau of Criminal Investigation) revealed that they had interviewed a suspect living in Spain and had submitted a file to the Irish Director of Public Prosecutions. The author's understanding is that that the Irish police were interested in this man as it was thought that he was involved in the supply of at least two stolen vehicles used in the attack, and that he may have actually been inside the National Stadium while the shooting was taking place. There was also a suggestion that this same man was involved in the shooting of Garda Jerry McCabe, who was killed by the IRA during a post office van robbery at Adare, Co. Limerick, on 7 June 1996. The suspect was extradited back to the Irish Republic, but was inexplicably allowed bail. While on bail, he escaped out of the country and has never been tried for any of the alleged crimes.

Two years earlier, the Provisional IRA – presumably because of the pressure that Austin Stack had placed on Adams – announced that their Army Council (still in existence some fifteen years after the Good Friday Agreement) had conducted an internal enquiry. They admitted that some of its members had carried out an unauthorised shooting, but had been disciplined for acting without permission from their commanding officers.

Subsequently, Adams accused Austin of naming two of the perpetrators to the Irish Parliament, the Oireachtas, whom Austin had been advised that the Gardaí Síochána suspected of involvement in the attack. The former president claimed to have interviewed them and that they had denied responsibility. In late 2016, Adams made a personal statement to the Dáil Éireann (lower House of the Oireachtas) about the incident. In a response, Fine Gael TD Alan Farrell used parliamentary privilege to name Sinn Fein members; acting on the advice of his contact, the author declines to name these two men. It is the author's understanding that one of the men was not involved in the attack on Mr Stack and that the other named person was only involved by his attendance at a meeting to discuss the attempt on the prison officer's life. In any case, both men denied responsibility. To date, no one has been convicted of the murder of Prison Officer Stack.

Austin Stack's Story

I was 14 at the time, living in Portlaoise with mum and my two younger brothers. We knew that Dad was going to the boxing that night, but we were unable to go with him as there wasn't enough room in the car; we were all quite annoyed. I recall that I was in my bedroom – which faced the front of the house – and I remember that I was unable to sleep. It was dark and I felt uneasy; I just knew that something was going to happen; something was wrong. Then I saw some headlights sweep down the drive, illuminating my bedroom, so I went downstairs. Mum was there, along with other members of the family; she told me that there had been an accident and that Dad had been hit by a motorbike and was in hospital.

I went back to bed and listened to RTE radio until it went off the air at midnight. I stayed up all night long, unable to sleep. At six o'clock, the radio burst back into life, where there was an announcement, reporting the attack on Dad. I fetched my two brothers, bringing them into bed with me as I tried to explain what had happened to Dad. At six-thirty, the radio repeated the announcement, causing my brothers to finally accept what I had been trying to tell them. At that moment, Grandma came in; she hadn't wanted us to hear the news that way. I remember the announcer telling us that a prison officer had been shot at the National Stadium and was critically ill. They also said that the IRA had issued a statement denying responsibility.

Dad was taken to the Mead Hospital, where he was in a coma and had kidney failure. We knew that he would probably be paralysed as the bullet had severed the spine. He was in a coma for six months, being looked after at Dunleary Hospital, where we visited every weekend. I had been to a football match the day before one visit, and brought the match programme with me. We sat down with one of the doctors, who told us that although Dad's eyes were open, he wasn't really awake. He told me to hold the programme at Dad's eye level and read to him from it. I remember doing that, reading the teams out loud; when I came to one of the surprise selections that day, a name which Dad knew, his eyes opened wider as he reacted to the player's name. Almost a year after the shooting, Dad was allowed home, although he was paralysed from the neck down and only had the mental capacity of a 4- or 5-year-old.

We had an extension added to the house which served as both his bedroom and a sort of hospital room. I do remember that the Gardaí were often around, as it was thought that the IRA would try to come and 'finish the job' by shooting him again. Dad would try, but whilst his long-term memory was good, he couldn't remember what had happened five minutes earlier. When he died, me and my brothers were away at boarding school. One night in September 1984, the headmaster came to speak with me. He told me that Dad had been taken back to the Mead Hospital, where he had died; my aunt would pick us up in the morning. I requested that the two younger ones be allowed a final night's restful sleep, and we told them the following day in the company of a priest.

I saw dad's body at the coroner's funeral home; he was in an open casket, but as I went over to kiss his head, my aunt, who was a nurse, stopped me doing it because of all the post-mortem scarring. It shook me that all I was allowed to do was to touch his hand. The actual funeral was a State occasion, with leading politicians and my dad's colleagues from the prison service. I do remember being given a folded flag which had been draped over his coffin, but the rest was just a blur.

Brian Stack. (Austin Stack)

Over the years afterwards, we as a family felt that we were in a state of limbo as the IRA always denied that it was them, with the press speculating that it was the work of a 'non-aligned Republican group' or, 'off-shoot paramilitaries'. As I was only 16 by this stage, I wasn't told an awful lot – the Gardaí never once knocked at Mum's door – and wasn't in control of anything. Then, there was a startling development in November 1985. A group of IRA prisoners under control of their OC, Tommy McMahon[*] attempted to break out of Portlaoise Gaol, but the attempt failed when a bomb, which had been assembled within the prison itself, failed to detonate at the prison gates. I felt very uneasy as I was convinced that a particular gun which Dad had tried to locate before he was shot was used in the escape.

In December 1990, I was accepted in the Prison Service and at the same time Mum wrote to the Gardaí for an update on Dad's case. She received a curt one-line reply stating that the case was still 'open'. Six years later, I was based at Mountjoy Gaol, at Phibsborough in the centre

---

[*] Thomas McMahon was a volunteer in the South Armagh Brigade of the Provisional IRA and was one of the IRA's most experienced bomb-makers. In November 1979, he was jailed for life for his part in the murder of Lord Louis Mountbatten at Mullaghmore, Co. Sligo, and three others on 27 August the same year.

of Dublin, where I met a senior officer who had worked with Dad at Portlaoise. He sat me down and explained that Dad was on the trail of a gun which had been smuggled in by the IRA and that he suspected one of his fellow officers of being an IRA sympathiser. He did tell me his name, but as he is now deceased, I choose not to name him. It transpired that gun which Dad was searching for was used in the escape, but the man using the gun was a bit of a hothead and that the IRA's OC, McMahon, didn't want anyone killed, so he had 'doctored' the weapon. Sure enough, the man pointed the gun at an officer's head and pulled the trigger. Anyway, a bomb which they tried to use to blow open the gates failed to detonate and so they surrendered, handing the gun over.

In 2006, I agreed – with my family's blessings – to be interviewed by the writer Barry Cummins,* who was writing a book on unsolved killings. He was looking for information on Dad's murder. He spoke to a Gardaí contact, who allowed him fifteen minutes with Dad's files.

Barry was told that there was an eyewitness who could potentially identify the killers. The witness – a woman – had seen the gunman waiting outside the stadium, leaning against a car, reading a newspaper. As soon as Dad walked past him, he threw the paper down and shot Dad in the back of the neck. He then ran off to an identically dressed man and they raced off on a motorbike. Another witness – a soldier at the nearby barracks – had also seen the man and witnessed the shooting. So, the paper was found with fingerprints, the stolen motorbike, again with fingerprints and DNA, was also found and, he had touched the car; again there was potential forensic evidence. The killers were taken into Dublin in another car and were spotted by a Gardaí mobile patrol, who gave chase. The car crashed at some lights but the men raced off and were never caught; there must have been further fingerprint evidence in the crashed vehicle. What Barry found led us to conclude that all of this vital evidence has been buried by the Gardaí, but why, we don't know.

I believe that the OC of the IRA's Southern Brigade discussed the attack on my dad with a man who was run out of Belfast in the 1970s by the Provisionals after he had carried out paedophile acts against a 4-year-old child. I must decline to name this man, but I do know that he

---

* *The Cold Case Files* (Gill Books, 2012).

was brought back into the Provo fold to help reorganise the IRA in Co. Munster. I must tell you this, that I am very confident about the veracity of my information and I will tell you why. I spent some time with Sean O'Callaghan, the writer and former Provisional who turned informer against the IRA. I spoke with a senior Gardaí detective and I spoke with a very well-acclaimed writer who has very high-ranking IRA connections. This is why I am so certain about the allegations which I have made.

Brian Stack. (Austin Stack)

Do I forgive the killers, you ask? I have a funny way of dealing with this, following a long emotional journey which I went on for years after dad died. It is a process which I call 'giving them their monkey back'. For twenty-two years, I was consumed with bitterness and had a chip on both shoulders. For that period of time, I never once had a good night's sleep. Then, one day in 2011, whilst Martin McGuinness was running for president of Ireland, he was interviewed on television. The interviewer asked him, in light of all the allegations and rumours about him, how he managed to sleep at night. McGuinness[**] turned to the camera with a smirk and replied that he had no difficulty at all in sleeping.

The very next day, I wrote a very angry article for the *Irish Independent* newspaper and I poured out my venom. The next day, I rewrote it having toned it down a little. The paper printed it without any editing and a friend read it and contacted me. She told me that I had to learn to

[**] In March 2018, Senator Máire Devine of Sinn Fein re-tweeted a malicious tweet about Brian Stack that had described him as a 'sadist'. She was suspended from the Republican party for three months. She lost her seat at the 2020 Seanad election, but was later co-opted on to join Dublin City Council.

forgive them. A day or so afterwards, I was out for a drive and suddenly a light went on in my head: I could forgive them, but not for their sakes, for mine instead. I gave them the monkey which had been on my back; I gave it back to them and said: 'Now YOU deal with it.'

✦

At 0802 on Monday, 4 June 1984, a part-time UDR man, 34-year-old David Chambers, a father of two, was ambushed by gunmen as he arrived on his motorcycle to begin work at a factory in Co. Armagh. No one initially claimed responsibility for the killing, the second of a UDR man in two days; although the North Armagh Provisional IRA subsequently admitted their role in the murder. The soldier was a private from the Regiment's 11th Battalion. He worked as a foreman for Boxmore Eggs Containers at Dollingstown, close to Lurgan. Unfortunately, as in the case of many of his comrades, he had been dicked by PIRA members. He had been observed on patrols, vehicle checkpoints (VCPs) and clearly at his place of work. In instances such as these, PIRA personnel would follow an intended victim to and from work as they built up an attack strategy; as an organisation, they very rarely left anything to chance, having rehearsed their moves well in advance. The dickers would observe a local UDR several times before deciding if that individual would become a target. Republican terrorism became a patient waiting game, a quality of which the paramilitary group had in abundance. They could afford to take their time, make their plans, recce their routes as well as formulate escape plans before they struck. Consequently, 4 June was selected for the attack on what they termed 'a member of the Crown Forces'.

On that fateful morning, two PIRA gunmen, Patrick Steven O'Dowd and Kieran Murray,[*] arrived early at the factory, before donning balaclavas and hiding in bushes close to the car park. Private Chambers rode up on his motorcycle, but as he turned right from Belfast Road into Inn Road, the gunmen jumped from cover and one of them fired a blast from a shotgun that knocked the soldier off his vehicle. He was hit in the face, neck

---

[*] Both men were convicted of the murder in 1985. The RUC arrested ten men from the area, including the aforementioned O'Dowd and Murray.

and chest. As he fell, the second gunman opened fire with an automatic weapon, hitting him again as he lay prostrate. Sadly, he died before an ambulance could be summoned; the news was quickly relayed to his shocked wife, who worked for the same company. The killers had also planted a large explosive device weighing 200lb (91kg) in a nearby derelict building, knowing that the Army operated to a strict follow-up pattern. During the follow-up check, the device exploded, causing several minor injuries among the security forces, including a police

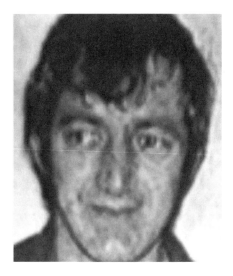

UDR soldier David Chambers, killed by the IRA. (Julie Tipping and Lynn Anderson)

officer and another member of the UDR; they were taken to a local hospital for treatment. Private Chambers' funeral was held at Lurgan Cemetery.

Julie Tipping and Lynn Anderson are the daughters of the murdered UDR soldier.

Julie's Story

I was 10 years old; my sister Lynn was 5 years old, and our mum was 33 years old when dad was murdered on 4 June 1984. My mum and dad worked together at the same factory, which is where Dad was going on the morning he was murdered.

I was at swimming lessons with my school class and my headmaster came in and asked me to leave with him. I was brought to my granny's house, where there were lots of people that I didn't know. My mum and auntie came into the house crying and screaming. My auntie took me into the hall and told me that my dad had been shot and murdered, and that he wasn't coming home.

After a while we went to my sister Lynn's school to collect her and explain to her what had happened. Later that evening, when we were back at our own house, I remember lots of UDR and police officers, and family and friends coming to see us. Mum was in a terrible way, and in complete shock, she had to be cared for by a local GP. Dad was murdered on 4 June 1984, 5 June was Mum and Dad's wedding anniversary, and Dad was buried on my sister Lynn's 6th birthday on 6 June.

Lynn's Story

I was only 5 years old when my dad was murdered. I remember on the day Dad was killed I was at school as normal. A teacher came and got me from class. I was brought to my auntie and my sister Julie. I don't think I understood what was happening, but I remember Julie taking me aside and telling me that our dad had been shot and killed and that we wouldn't be able to see him again.

We went back to the house and I remember lots of people being there, but as I was so young, I don't think I completely understood at that time what was going on.

Julie and Lynn

Mum's life and ours were completely torn apart on that awful day, which we will never get over. We have missed out on so much over the years. Mum lost her beloved husband and was left to bring up us two girls alone, and we have had to go through life without our dad. We will never ever forget or forgive the people who did this. We went through every milestone in our lives without our beloved dad.

Patrick O'Dowd is out of prison living his life, however on 4 June 1984 he ruined our three lives. One thing that still hurts and angers us is the fact that we could be face to face with this man at any time without realising who he is. We did at one stage with the help of local politicians try to set up a meeting with him, but this was declined.

Author's Note: The following quotation could be said to summarise the lack of remorse felt by one of the IRA gunmen Patrick O'Dowd; it is taken from *The Irish Times*:

> At first Paddy O'Dowd, a dark, quiet, guarded man, is reluctant to name the man he killed, but eventually he does. As recounted in the book *Lost Lives*, David Chambers (34) was a Lurgan man who served in the UDR. He was gunned down by O'Dowd and another IRA man

David and Carol Chambers. (Julie Tipping and Lynn Anderson)

as he arrived for work near Lurgan in June 1984. The IRA was hoping for multiple casualties that day as a 200 lb bomb exploded in a nearby derelict building injuring two policemen as they arrived at the scene. O'Dowd, like Chambers, is from the Lurgan area. Now 41, he was 22 at the time. He feels no guilt, he says. 'I can understand the family's point of view, but I am not here to make individual apologies for this, that and the other. I wanted a normal life. What I would say to people who are judgmental is, "wait until circumstances shape your life".'[*]

Soldier 'A', Ulster Defence Regiment

On the day that [Ronald] Reagan made his speech about not interfering in British politics, which to my mind was tantamount to a non-critical

---

[*] Source: www.irishtimes.com/news/outside-chance-1.348285

endorsement of the Irish Republic, and their agents, the Provisional IRA, a lad from another UDR battalion was killed. I have read much about the president's love for the Irish – his great grandfather was an Irish Catholic immigrant from Co. Tipperary – and his roots and all, and all about the jolly image that the Irish enjoyed in the world, but not one fucking word about Dave Chambers! Dave was gunned down by masked cowards who hid until he arrived for work and then blasted him to death; these 'brave patriots' shot him again as he lay bleeding on the ground, unable to defend himself.

His missus worked at the same place; they were due to celebrate their wedding anniversary, but instead she had to arrange to bury the shattered body of the man she had shared a bed with for years. I'll bet they were gloating all over Boston and places like that at the death of a soldier and crowing about 'stiffing' another Brit. What did that c*** Reagan say about it? Nothing, that's what; not a bloody dicky bird because he was scared of losing votes and being criticised by the Paddies in America. When he died about nine years ago, I bought a bottle of Bushmills and drank to the memory of David Chambers and my toast was 'Fuck Reagan!'. A few years back, they had September 11 and the terror attacks on the World Trade Center in New York. Talk about karma; I am sorry for the loss of so many innocent lives, but they encouraged and supported and financed Irish terror and they got a terror attack right back at them. When that race in Boston was attacked by their home-grown terrorists a few years back, they were there with their hearts bleeding, but if I remember correctly, Boston was one of the main collecting grounds for NORAID.

✦

By the onset of the 1980s, routine mobile patrolling by the security forces, particularly in the remote border areas of Co. Tyrone, Co. Fermanagh and Co. Armagh, was out of the question. The Provisional IRA's bombing teams controlled the border roads, with fifteen years of experience and expertise in the use of explosives and timers behind them; they were a ruthless and formidable foe. Many soldiers, policemen and even innocent civilians had died at their hands. By this stage of The Troubles it was far safer and certainly more expedient for soldiers and police officers to be airlifted in and out of trouble spots. However, it was still vital that the security forces commanded these strategic areas and regular shows of strength were necessary.

On Saturday, 14 July 1984, a patrol from 6 UDR was airlifted into the Corgary Road area of Castlederg, very close to the border with the Irish Republic. Indeed, it was the most westerly patrol point in Northern Ireland, situated a mere 100m from a tiny stream that divided the border with the Republic. A Lynx helicopter carrying eight members of the section was dropped in to patrol the immediate area, and set up a vehicle checkpoint (VCP). Shortly after the VCP was set up, a civilian car was stopped and the driver questioned; shortly afterwards, he was allowed to move on. Unknown to the soldiers, they were under observation from an IRA bombing ASU, some 100m across the stream in Co. Donegal. A device weighing 200lb (91kg) had been planted some time before, precisely where the checkpoint had been positioned; at this moment, the bombers detonated the device.

The explosion tore the section apart, killing Private Norman McKinley (32) from Castlederg instantly; his body was hurled over 300m, towards the high ground where the patrol had just been dropped off. Corporal Heather Catherine Jean Kerrigan (20) was mortally injured in the blast. Her brother, David, who was the commander of the section in the same patrol, was himself seriously injured in the contact. His radio operator sent through the contact report to base and it was also heard by the pilot of the Lynx helicopter that had only minutes previously dropped them. The pilot immediately returned to the location. The young 'Greenfinch' was too badly injured to save and sadly died in the aircraft en route to hospital in Omagh. Heather Kerrigan was the eleventh woman member of the UDR to die during The Troubles and the fourth and last female[*] to be killed by Republican terror groups.

Ms Kerrigan and Norman McKinley – who had just celebrated his birthday – were both buried in Castlederg Cemetery; today, they lay just a few feet from each other. There is a most poignant postscript to this

---

[*] A total of eleven female UDR soldiers were killed, including three RTA fatalities and two cases of cause of death 'unknown'. See the author's notes at the end of this chapter.

double killing. Both soldiers had earlier attended the wedding of Lance Corporal Tom Loughlin, who was himself killed just a few months after the Corgary explosion. Corporal Kerrigan was single, coming from a family of eight, living about a mile from the border with Co. Donegal; she was a also a part-time barmaid.

David Kerrigan, who called in the contact, is Heather's brother. Irene is his wife. This is their joint story.

David and Irene's Story

David: On 14 July, myself and my brother and my other sister, Heather, were in the same patrol being flown out to Castlederg. We were about 300 or 400 yards from the border, checking cars. We were flown up to the Corgaries, and we would have actually flown over where the bomb was, so the IRA would have known we were going to come back down that way. It was good weather – mid-July – and there would have been other patrols going on the same route, and it is possible that the bomb and the terrorists could have lain there for two or three days. They were about two fields from us and would have had a good view.

We were doing a foot patrol; I was on one side of the road, another man was opposite me, with Heather and Norman behind me. We stopped a car; the other man went across to speak to the driver. I went over to Heather to chat about the grid reference to check that we were in the right position. The car drove off as I stood up, and then 'Bang!', the bomb went off. I shouted at the radio operator to call the contact in. We thought that we saw movement in the area where we thought the 'plantin' was, so we fired about forty rounds in that direction.

Just then, I heard my brother Robbie shouting: 'She's still alive,' as he had found Heather lying in the crater; I collapsed then when I saw her. The helicopter which had brought us in was over in Clady and it came straight back. When it landed, the loadmaster jumped out and carried Heather in; he was cradling her; I could see that her clothes were blown off and her foot was hanging off. I was lying on the floor of the chopper and Heather's blood was running out of her, and running under my

UDR soldier Heather Kerrigan, killed in an IRA blast. (David and Irene Kerrigan)

belly. I was just lying there and looking up at her; I could see her lips moving but I didn't know what she was saying; she was dying. We were flown to the hospital in Omagh to intensive care. Shortly afterwards, they told me that Heather was dead, although they didn't tell me that Norman was dead, too. They actually couldn't find Norman until they went up in the helicopter, as he was blown way up the field; he was sitting directly on the bomb, and was killed instantly. Heather was only 20 years old when she was killed.

The next morning, I was taken to the military wing Musgrave Park Hospital. I had a collapsed lung and back injuries. I was lucky; I don't know how I escaped it, having been so close. The fourth member of our 'brick' was an English fellow who was all right. He must have been somewhere up further but I don't know how he survived.

Irene: I was 58 in November and Heather would have been 59 in May coming. I was born in November 1963 and she was born in May 1964. One time the two of us went up to a garden party at Hillsborough. The Greenfinches were there, and Heather and me were up to meet whatever dignitary was coming. She had only served a year and nine months at that stage, and she was already a corporal, so she was shooting up the ranks. She'd just been made a corporal; she was telling me that she had to get the stripes sewn on before she went out on patrol, the night before she was killed; I don't know if she managed to get that done.

David: I never got grieving or anything like, and I never even saw Heather in the coffin; I only learned years later that she was buried in her uniform. There were things I didn't know and it was never talked about in our house. Robbie did a full twenty-two years in the UDR/RIR and he is probably suffering from PTSD, but he never bothered looking out for himself. Heather was the youngest girl but there were two younger boys in the family.

When we went out that day, none of us went out to shoot anybody. Heather wasn't armed, as her job was to log any information we might gather that day. Even today, after time in the UDR and the RUC, I still feel as bad as I did the day of the bombing.

I had to look about counselling myself when I was in Newtownstewart. We had a call-out one night to where a UDR fellow had a bomb under his car and his two legs were blown off. I was first on the scene and I lifted him out of the car and put him into the helicopter. I folded up his trousers and put him onto the stretcher. That was a late turn on a Saturday night and we were back in the next morning at eight o'clock; nobody ever said anything about counselling; there was no such thing in the 1980s or anything like that.

It was about six months until I was back out on duty, because back then you didn't get any counselling. I went in to see the colonel and he said: 'Get back to work; there's nothing wrong with you.' To tell you the truth, I really wanted to get back to work again; you never give it a thought; it was a job, at the end of the day. We started back full-time; our status was still part-time, but we were working full-time hours.

Irene: The attitude was 'take a couple of drinks and sort yourself out', that was the way of it. We were engaged then and I remember the day of the bomb well. To tell you the truth, when I heard it on the news, I never even thought of anything happening to Heather and Norman. I was going for a driving lesson with my sister Joan, who lived in Trillick. The hospital phoned her and she took me down. On the way in, the nurse said: 'You know his sister's dead?' Well, if she had given me a kick in the stomach, it wouldn't have been worse. I had to go in and see him then tell him the bad news about Heather. I arrived at the hospital with my sister to the unit David was in and Reverend Fletcher was there, the Free Presbyterian minister, and David's cousin and they were telling David how lucky he was. The first thing David said to me was: 'I can move my feet.' Obviously they had told me he had injured his back, so he was just making sure he could move his feet.

I remember going into the room with David's mother, and looking at Heather and you wouldn't imagine that she was dead; the mortuary staff had sewed her foot back on. She was in full uniform: number two dress, her shoes and everything.

Then we went to the funeral, me and my brother and his wife. That was on the Monday, but we didn't get near the church because, really, I wasn't part of the family then. Then we left and went straight to the hospital to see David. Whilst we were there, the story of the bombing and the funerals was on the news that evening. It was just another story, but that was the thing at the time: shooting and bombing and killing coming from all directions.

Heather's inquest said that if she had got help, things might have been different; you know she bled to death. After that they started training team medics to go out on the patrols, but I don't think a team medic could have saved her ... because it was more internal bleeding.

David: Her spleen, wasn't it? It all hasn't gone away. Time doesn't heal; they say it does but it hasn't for me; it's no better for me at all.

Irene: In August 2014, there was a Republican parade in Castlederg; it was horrific. David didn't go to bed on the Friday night until three o'clock. On the Saturday night, he wasn't in his bed at all before it. He said that he wasn't going, but on the Sunday, he and the boys came with us. We brought the photographs of Heather with us, and the whole thing just erupted then. We got up to the barrier where David saw his mother; she was sitting, the tears dripping off her.

David: It was so insensitive; I was standing there and I don't know what came over me, but I just said: 'I'm going through this police barrier,' and through I went, because I had nothing to lose; I didn't care what happened to me. I just walked through it and that was it. Would you believe this? I got phone calls from all over after that congratulating me and praising me for what I'd done. I didn't think I'd done a good job but that's what people got out of it, but that made it worse again. I have an awful pain in my head, a heaviness in my head. I just know that I'm not well. Yet then there's times I'm not so bad but if I see photographs, it just hits right away and I have to go to bed. I take a couple of painkillers and a sleeping tablet and away I go and hopefully I get to sleep.

In 2009, the twenty-five years anniversary service was held in Castlederg. It brought it home to a lot of people, because a lot of young people went up to that anniversary service. It was unreal the amount of young people who were crying; they couldn't believe what we went though. My mother was only 49 when Heather was killed. How did she cope; there were people who lost their husbands in their 20s; how did they cope, these young women? Or even losing their son or their daughter; how did they cope knowing they were never going to come back?

Irene: How do you know when you get closure; that's the problem. You could think you have closure and then somebody says or does something, and that stirs it up again. Sometimes you can get your hopes raised as well. Some people say that we will get justice. I honestly don't think so. What is justice now? It's going to be two years at most in jail. And what are the chances of anybody being caught thirty years later? Why would anyone come forward and tell their story thirty years later, if they haven't been caught prior? And how do you know if somebody is telling the truth? The late Martin McGuinness never came forward; there was no way he would ever have admitted to any of this. And the British government didn't want him to admit to anything either, for fear the peace process would come crumbling down. I strongly believe he was a paid informer for the British forces.

The Irish Government and Garda gave the IRA a safe haven in the Irish Republic and there was collusion with Garda and IRA. There were items found at the firing point of the bomb that killed Heather, Norman and injured David but it all disappeared and why did the Garda not catch anyone that day as it would have taken them a while getting out of the forest onto the road?

David and I will never forgive those that made our family suffer so much. People say I know what you are suffering and been through but unless you have lived what we as a family have, you'll never know.

Trevor Loughlin, a Friend and Comrade of Heather Kerrigan

I was in the same unit as Heather and Norman and ordinarily would have been out on patrol with them at Corgary Road. However, prior to this, I had volunteered to take part in a radio cadre at our battalion's signals wing, which was scheduled to run for four weekends. As a result, three other soldiers were drafted in to take mine and the other volunteers' places. I remember that it was about the time of the anniversary of the worst atrocity in the history of the Ulster Defence Regiment to date; on the Ballygawley Road, we had lost four soldiers in a PIRA landmine on 13 July 1983.

We had been out on patrol the day before, which was Friday the 13th, and we were worried that the IRA might use the anniversary of the bomb to launch another attack on us. Just before we went out that day, I saw Heather, who told me she had just been promoted to full corporal, but she didn't have time to sew on her new chevrons. I told her I had a black pen in my pocket and I would draw one on for her. I joked with her that I could even make her a sergeant, if she wanted, but she said no just in case some big brass came out to visit us on the ground, which they quite often did. She said she would get the new one sewn that night before going out the next day; I never did find out if she got it done.

On the Saturday morning, 14 July 1984, a member of the unit – Charlie – drove us over to the course. When we arrived, the classroom was full, so I sat at the back. Across the hallway from me was the signals wing office, which had a radio on the battalion net. The door was open into the office so that the RSO could keep an ear to the comms and monitor what was going on around our TAOR – tactical area of responsibility. I suddenly heard a contact report come through, but I didn't catch the call signs which we used to identify casualties. About ten or fifteen minutes later the phone rang over in the RSO's office, which he immediately answered. He was on the phone for about five minutes before leaving us to go the ops room. When he came back, he asked if any of us was from the Rockwood unit, and of course, four of us were.

He told us that our call sign 25 had been attacked, but as he didn't have any further information, we should go to the cook house to await further instructions. As we did so, we could see the Quick Reaction Force all kitted up, ready for action. We could tell from the radio chatter that it was bad. Captain McFarland came back, singling me out, advising me on what was happening, so that I in turn would let the rest know the situation. He told me that the patrol had been blown up by a land-mine, with two dead and one seriously injured. He could tell instantly by our emotions that this had deeply affected us, so he decided to cancel the rest of the cadre and told me to take the remainder of us home. As Charlie was so upset and unable to drive his car back to Rockwood, I had to drive.

When we got into camp our PSI was waiting for us, and he told us what had happened, that Heather and Norman had been killed. The Lynx had returned, and the co-pilot had helped David Kerrigan on board, before lifting the badly injured Heather in beside him. As they were flying to the Tyrone County Hospital, David could feel the blood running underneath him, and at the same time he was shouting at the co-pilot that the female casualty was his sister, and to look after her. David himself sustained back and head injuries and was hospitalised for a week after, but Heather died en route to the hospital. David was unable to attend the funeral of both his sister and comrade Norman; he still suffers both mentally and physically from the injuries to this day.

The Corgary Road in the Castlederg TAOR; it was the most westerly road in the whole of Northern Ireland and a very dangerous road as it was just about 100 yards from the Donegal border, which was divided by a small stream. As the patrol started to move off they came under fire from just across the border from IRA gunmen. One of the patrol – Tommy – returned fire with the LMG (light machine gun), as did David, but on the follow-up by both the police, army and Irish forces there were no sign of any hits from the returning fire.

David was still in hospital when the funeral of his sister Heather took place in Castlederg; it was one of the biggest funerals ever to be held in the town. The following day the funeral of Norman McKinley took place; it was also a very large funeral. Heather and Norman had been at the wedding of her sister some time before; Heather was bridesmaid and

Norman was the best man. Heather's sister married Thomas Loughlin, himself a lance corporal in the UDR, and my cousin. Sadly, Thomas* was killed by the IRA on 2 March that same year, four months before the Corgary Road bomb. As the year 1984 ended 6 UDR Regiment CGC had lost five serving members and an ex-member; five of them were from 'B' Company.

On the Sunday, both my twin sister and I went to Heather's wake at her family home; there was such a large crowd, and with the house being so small, there were many people outside. Her coffin was in her bedroom; she was dressed in her number two uniform. She looked so lovely and smart, but I couldn't stay in the room as it was so upsetting; we left shortly afterwards.

My girlfriend and I went to Heather's funeral. One thing I can remember of that day which hurt me so much was when I went to one of Heather's brothers to shake hands, he just looked at me and as I held out my hand he turned and walked away. I think that he blamed me as I had been away when Heather was killed, but she had had the same opportunity to go with me to Omagh for the course. I also went to Norman's funeral – this time in the company of my brother, a fellow UDR soldier – but there was no trouble with his family.

---

* Thomas Alexander Loughlin worked for the Department of the Environment as well as being a part-time soldier in the UDR. The Provisional IRA planted a bomb under his vehicle outside his home in Drumnabay, Castlederg, on 2 March 1984. It exploded shortly after he drove off, having just waved goodbye to his wife and tiny baby daughter. She immediately ran to the wreckage to comfort him; he died a few hours later in hospital. Local PIRA man Declan 'Beano' Casey was linked in newspaper reports to the murder. He was arrested by the RUC on 14 June 1993. There was much controversy about this man, who is alleged to have been a police informer. He claimed that his RUC handlers allowed him to continue killing while he worked for them. It is further alleged that he was smuggled out of Northern Ireland in 1992 as it is believed that the Provisional IRA was close to unmasking him as an informer.

He claimed in the *Daily Mirror* that he was involved in fourteen IRA murders, six of which were carried out while he worked for the RUC. He also claimed that in two specific cases killings were carried out even though he had warned his handlers that the individuals concerned were being targeted. The then Chief Constable of Northern Ireland, Sir Hugh Annesley, was reported to have said that there was absolutely no truth in Casey's allegations. The IRA informant was said to have fled to the British mainland in order to start a new life.

Heather's grave. (Trevor Loughlin and Ken Wharton)

It's now been over thirty-five years since Heather and Norman were murdered, but there are many nights when I lie in bed and think about my feelings when the news of the bomb came over the radio. I have been told – unofficially, of course – that one of the IRA bombing team was killed in a motorbike accident in the Irish Republic. It may seem uncharitable, but I just think, thank fuck that he got what was coming to him; I hope that he suffered and I will lose no sleep over him. Do I forgive? Well, you have your answer there. He wasn't too worried about what he did to my friends.

When I think of my lost friends and comrades, I get such an awful feeling of what I am told is survivor's guilt and sometimes I think: it probably should have been me.

✦

On 3 May 1985, a young boy was orphaned as a result of PIRA's flawed intelligence. William Heenan (51), a widower, was shot dead by the IRA on his farm at Ballyward, near Castlewellan, Co. Down. The man was a former 'B' Special, but had left the force in 1970 when it was disbanded shortly after the onset of The Troubles. He was a digger driver who worked for the Department of the Environment Roads Division. The Provisional IRA's South Down Command claimed that he was a current member of the RUCR and that he had been seen at numerous VCPs in the area. The intelligence they had received was wrong; it was an allegation without substance. Mr Heenan had had no connection with the security forces for the best part of two decades, but he presented an easy target to the Provisionals, knowing as they did where he lived and worked.

At around 7 a.m. on the 3rd, at his remote cottage in Legananny as William was feeding his hens, a lone IRA gunman who had lain in wait in an outside toilet shot him in the head at point-blank range, killing him instantly. In a macabre twist, the dead man's body was dragged to the side of the barn in an attempt to hide his body. His 12-year-old son, Samuel, heard the shot that killed his father; he also saw the gunman's face as he stole the family car. He dashed outside to discover that his father was dead, but bravely ran over half a mile, clad in slippers and a dressing gown, to a neighbouring house to raise the alarm. In his shock, the young boy forgot that there was a phone in his house, instinctively running for help. He had already lost his mother and grandmother in the previous two years; one can only imagine the grief-stricken state in which he found himself, at the murder of his surviving parent. The killer abandoned the car a few miles away.

Sammy Heenan is the son of the murdered man.

Sammy's Story

I was 12 at the time of my daddy's murder. What I remember is that on the morning of 3 May 1985, around 7 a.m., he came into our bedroom, telling me to lie in as he was going outside to do the morning chores. I drifted back to sleep only to be awakened by a painful piercing yell, followed by a loud gunshot; I just assumed that he was out shooting crows, but then I saw his legally held firearm in the corner of the bedroom. I crawled across the bed to look out of the window; it was covered in the morning condensation, so I had to clear it first. As I looked out, I heard my dad's car start up, it reversed past my window where I could see a strange man in the car who I didn't know. He was looking over his shoulder while reversing, in his haste to make his getaway it would appear he didn't see me looking out at him, even though I was very close. He then drove away at speed, down the road which I lived on, then across

William Heenan, murdered at his farm by the IRA. (Sammy Heenan)

another road until out of sight. I suddenly felt sick with fear and unease that this situation didn't seem right.

I made my way outside, shouting for my dad over and over again; I just wanted the reassurance of an explanation. It was then that I witnessed a pool of blood and a smashed jug. I followed the trail of blood to the side of the barn. There I found my father's lifeless body. The image of his bloodstained face and him lying on the ground will haunt me forever. Here I was standing alone in the middle of the countryside in pure isolation, shocked and numb at what I was encountering. I kept my Grifter bicycle in the barn, which I frantically tried to get but couldn't find the keys. We had only installed a phone earlier that week but in the panic I forgot all about it. I then set off running to the nearest house, which was about half a mile away. As I ran along the country road crying and sobbing I hoped I would meet a car to secure help. The roads were very quiet as you would expect in such a rural area. At this stage I was experiencing shortness of breath due to my asthma. However, I knew that I needed to keep going to get help. I eventually arrived at my neighbour's house in a very distressed state shouting, 'Daddy's shot, Daddy's been shot.' The neighbours comforted me while they called the police. We then ran back to my house together. When we arrived back, the cold realisation dawned on me that my daddy was dead.

Three years earlier when I was 9 years old my grandmother died of a heart attack as she sat on the chair beside me. This tragedy happened one Friday afternoon at 4 p.m. on 11 December 1981. She died in the middle of a heavy snowfall, which prevented me from getting help. I was eventually found on the roadside in a distressed and shivering state by a neighbour. I also have vivid memories of my mummy dying four months after my grandmother. We shared the same bedroom and I found her in an unconscious state around 11 p.m. one night. I could see her across the room and knew she wasn't well. I called for my daddy, telling him to wake up as there was something wrong with Mummy. He wanted me to stay with her whilst he went for help, but I was too frightened to be alone, so I cycled to the same neighbours to summon help. She was only 43 years old and died of a brain haemorrhage. After that happened, it was just me and my dad; he was my rock and my inspiration in life. I was, naturally, a nervous and anxious child, so his death which left me completely alone just devastated me.

The emergency services arrived that morning with the forensics teams to seal off the scene while meticulously searching the area for clues. I was shown photo montages of known Republicans in the area and also took part in a photofit reconstruction of the suspect. The RUC later told me that the murderer had been dropped off about 6:30 a.m., where he hid in an outside toilet until my dad came out. The gunman then walked up behind my daddy, forced him to his knees before shooting him twice in the top of the head at point-blank range. The killer dragged him by his feet around to the side of the barn. One week later the South Down PIRA claimed the murder, claiming that he was in the RUCR, which was totally untrue; he'd been a 'B' Special until they were disbanded in 1970.

I was even more distressed when the undertakers came to take my daddy's body away in a coffin. I was sobbing and couldn't believe what was actually happening to me. I then went to live with cousins of my father who lived in Castlewellan. No one was ever arrested and no one was ever convicted of my father's murder. There were many anomalies in the case. This particular murder didn't quite fit the normal PIRA MO. The terrorists in Northern Ireland never leave anything to chance when they plan out their murders. For example, how could they have been so sure that my Dad's car would start, or even where he might have put the keys that morning. The gun which killed him had never been used before nor was it ever used again in The Troubles. Home-made ammunition improvised to suit the weapon was also used. This was rare as it could have necessitated the gun jamming, which would have resulted in the gunman being stranded.

The PIRA didn't admit to my father's murder for over a week, which makes me think that it was a more localised killing. Some believed it was a case of mistaken identity, but it wasn't; they selected our house quite deliberately. One theory was that they might have thought he was passing on information to the security forces. They might also have known that he was friendly with the RUC as he served with some of them in the 'B' Specials. The police would have sometimes called at our house for a chat and this might have been observed. That is only me speculating, because no one but them really know.

As a young child I can remember the outpouring of grief coupled with anger and revulsion at my father's murder.

I can vividly remember the funeral, which was on the following Sunday and it was a cold, wet, miserable day which reflected the sombre mood of everyone. People were so kind and generous towards me. My church and minister provided me with immense pastoral support at that particular time and for many years after. At this time I had to make a decision of where I was going to live as I had now lost my home. I opted for my father's cousins' home in Castlewellan, where I resided until I was 20 years old. I had started school in Castlewellan High School, where I had made many friends in my first year and wanted that continuity and familiarity.

Life was difficult as I missed my parents immensely and the after-effects of such trauma never leave you. I met Julie when I was 20 years old and married her when I was 25. She has been my rock and friend throughout my life and I especially appreciate the importance of my family unit. I have been blessed with two daughters who I am very proud of; Ellie is 20 and Katie is 16.

All my life I have battled for truth, justice and latterly against the incessant campaign to revise the narrative of the past. After all these years no one has been made culpable for my father's murder. One suspect was arrested in 1987 but he was subsequently released without any charge. He has now passed away.

At the time of speaking to the author, I circulated a letter to the South Down newspapers, to remind local Republicans of their thuggery across the South Down community over thirty years. The narrative of the approximately seventy South Down PIRA murders must never be allowed to rest, and Republican attempts to normalise terrorism in naming offices after terrorists will be bitterly opposed. I also attempted to appeal to moderate Nationalists to understand our grievance on this matter. In essence, the letter said:

I, like so many people, am rightly appalled at the continued naming of the South Down constituency office of Chris Hazzard MP after two PIRA terrorists. This office like every other should be impartial and free from the glorification of those who committed heinous and depraved acts of terrorism. The irony is that those named were an affront to democracy and what they represented only further compounds the traumatism and disregard to the sensitivities of South Down PIRA victims.

These names were a precursor of others who were later rampant across the entire constituency, predominantly murdering husbands and leaving widows, murdering fathers and leaving orphans with the legacy of anguish that has never healed or the pain that has never subsided. The depraved reign of PIRA terror in our constituency targeted ordinary working families, from a garage owner in Rathfriland, a carpenter in Kilkeel to a coalman in Downpatrick, with another seventy approximate murders (including that of my father), attempted murders, bombings and the manifestation of raw sectarianism through the targeting of Protestant businesses in many Nationalist towns. The uniform was used as a cover to assuage the sectarian bloodlust of the PIRA and their methods of murder were indicative of the psychopathic nature of their 'volunteers'. How can we as a progressive society in 2020 continue to countenance the naming of this constituency office, which is subliminally designed to condition youthful mindsets and reinforce the evil of PIRA legitimacy? It's even more intolerable that it continues to be subsidised by the UK taxpayer. It's imperative the regulating bodies of IPSA and Parliamentary Standard investigate and pursue this flagrant breach of ethics and good standards expected of our elected representatives and be cognisant of the impact it is having on the South Down victims' constituency.

I would personally ask Mr Hazzard, would he find it appropriate if his parliamentary colleague Gregory Campbell MP worked from an office named after the Greysteel killers in East Londonderry? I appeal to moderate Nationalism to please understand our grievances and hurt on the basis of this analogy. The innocent blood that was shed in your community was no different to that which was shed in mine and this naming inadvertently legitimises all brands of terrorism. It's the personification of hypocrisy to eulogise one group of terrorists and yet have the audacity to condemn the other. As a society we must stand together on these matters. In order for our country to prosper and heal, the ambition for everyone must be true 'integrity and respect', words which are often championed by Sinn Fein. This slogan is obviously a meaningless vanity mantra which this party adapts and exploits for political capital. This office naming dispels any resemblance of 'integrity and respect' for PIRA victims which exposes the fake sincerity of the Sinn Fein movement.

As victims we cannot rest on our laurels as we are up against a well-resourced and well-oiled propaganda machine, akin to the Mafia. They do not relent in their pursuit of denigrating the British, which is intended to question the integrity of every member of the security forces who served here. The recent exploits in relation to Finucane exposes their determination and they won't cease until they secure their public enquiry and they will succeed. All we can do as victims is hammer them with the truth and highlight their hypocrisy. I have repeatedly challenged Hazzard through every forum possible and he remains silent because I genuinely believe he can't reconcile his conflicting views. How do you condemn the murders of Catholics, yet defend the murders of security forces, Protestant civilians and Catholics who were deemed collaborators? I really want now to confront him in a public discussion and see how he handles the scrutiny of a victim's questions.

I have resigned myself to the reality I will not secure justice for my dad on this side of eternity, ultimately God will be their judge and justice will then prevail. I will strive to confront the lies and deception of the Republican movement and ensure the memory and integrity of our loved ones is not sullied or destroyed by the Republican revisionism which is now commonplace in Northern Ireland.

Trevor Loughlin

I joined the UDR two days after my 18th birthday in 1982; my dad was also serving with us in the UDR; he was a corporal. I was most friendly with one man in particular, Private Greg Elliott, as he was like a big brother to me; Greg was an electrician by trade. I was also very close to Privates William Pollock and Olven Kilpatrick; I was at school with William's brother and Olven was a neighbour of ours, living two doors from our house. My cousin, Thomas Loughlin, was a lance corporal and Private Norman McKinley lived about 500 yards from us. Then there was Lance Corporal Michael Darcy who, although not in our company, I had known since we were in the Castlederg Flute band.

My dad had asked these men to keep an eye on me, as I then had my training done and was attached to 'B' Company. I was even closer to them all as I was now working with them. One of the Greenfinches – Lance Corporal Heather Kerrigan – and I were both at primary school and high school; she was soon to be promoted to corporal. I was introduced to a girl by Lance Corporal Michael Darcy, who I hung out with in our local pubs. I am still married to the same girl, more than thirty-five years later. I have one other great memory of travelling back on the Stranraer–Larne ferry with Private William Pollock, standing out on the deck feeding seagulls with bread.

Sadly, as The Troubles continued, the men and women who I served with, and socialised with, are now all gone; I am the only one left. All of the others that I have mentioned were all murdered by the IRA; they are all now laid to rest in Castlederg New Cemetery. Some twenty-five years later, I still go to the cemetery and have a yarn with them. One of them in particular – Michael Darcy – was responsible for my marriage; I will never forget them. *Quis Separabit.*

The following UDR men and women – all from Castlederg, Co. Tyrone or the surrounding area, are the ones mentioned above by Trevor Loughlin:

Robert 'Greg' Elliott (25) was killed by IRA gunmen outside his home in Lislaird Road, Castlederg on 2 January 1984. The killers had lain in wait for him to leave the house, before firing fourteen shots into his car. They escaped on foot, running to a waiting car that was later found abandoned over the border with the Republic, only 2 miles (3.2km) away.

Thomas Loughlin (44) was killed by a PIRA booby trap that was placed underneath his car in Drumnabay, Castlederg, on 2 March 1984. He had just started to drive away when the device exploded, in full view of his wife and baby daughter. She comforted him until the ambulance arrived; he died a few hours later during emergency surgery to save his life.

Heather Kerrigan (20) and Norman McKinley (32) were both killed by a massive landmine planted by the Provisional IRA at Corgary Road, near Castlederg, on 14 July 1984. [Their story is told in more detail in this chapter.]

William Pollock (27) was killed by a PIRA explosive device attached to a stationary trailer outside his farm in Creeduff, some 4 miles (6.4km) from Castlederg. As the part-time soldier attached the trailer to his car, it exploded, killing him instantly. His shocked parents were parked next to the trailer, but escaped with only minor injuries.

Michael Darcy (28) had just returned to his home on Killeter Road, Castlederg, in the early hours of 4 June 1988, following a Loyalist parade. PIRA gunmen had lain in wait in a darkened hedge, running out to shoot the lance corporal as he parked his car; he was hit six times in the back and died very shortly afterwards.

Olven Kilpatrick (32) was a part-time soldier who ran a shoe shop in Main Street, Castlederg. He was serving in the shop on 9 January 1990 when two PIRA gunmen walked up to him, shooting him several times; he died at the scene. The gunmen then hid an explosive device with a timer inside a shoe box; the bomb exploded approximately an hour later, injuring two police officers and gutting the building in the subsequent fire. [His story is told in more detail in the following chapter.]

[Author's Note 1: Castlederg is only a short seven-minute car ride from the border with the Irish Republic, some 3.1 miles (5km) away. It was only a very short journey to the sanctuary of Ireland for the gunmen and bombers. Thirteen other members of the security forces, including a former UDR man, were killed in or around Castlederg during The Troubles.

Having visited the town on several occasions, I can attest to the sectarian tensions – experienced at first hand – which still exist in this divided town. The number of killings of part-time UDR soldiers in this small place gives weight to the Protestant assertion that the gunmen were aided, in their targeting and execution of attacks, by assistance and information from the local community, some of whom were neighbours of the dead UDR personnel.]

[Author's Note 2: As stated previously, a total of eleven female UDR soldiers (Greenfinches) were killed during the years of The Troubles, including three RTA fatalities and two cases where the cause of death was 'unknown' during the course of The Troubles.

Private Eva Martin was killed in a PIRA rocket and gun attack at Clogher on 3 May 1974; Lance Corporal Jean Leggett was ambushed and killed by PIRA while on patrol in Co. Armagh on 6 April 1976; Private Ann Gaynor died in an RTA on 9 August 1976; Private Margaret Ann Hearst was shot dead by the IRA at her caravan home near Middlestown, Co. Armagh, on 8 October 1977; Private Hilary Graham died of injuries after being knocked down at a VCP by a car that failed to stop on 15 November 1979. Three of her brothers were killed by PIRA; Private Mary Cochrane died in an RTA on 28 February 1980; Private Constance Beattie died on duty on 25 September 1980; Corporal Heather Kerrigan was one of two UDR soldiers killed in a PIRA landmine explosion near Castlederg on 14 July 1984; Corporal Diane Ousby died on duty on 20 July 1986; Captain Betty McCurdy died on duty 2 August 1991 and Private Heather Sloan died in an RTA on 13 April 1992.]

6

1986–90

On 18 May 1984, the Provisional IRA exploded a bomb underneath a Sherpa van belonging to four off-duty soldiers in a car park at the Forum in Enniskillen. The off-duty personnel were taking part in the town's annual fishing competition. The bombers had used a mercury tilt* mechanism, planted directly underneath the engine. Two of the soldiers were killed more or less instantly, with a third dying from complications arising from his injuries five months later. The men, dressed in civvies, arrived at the Forum car park close to the town centre to participate in the annual Sealink Ferries Classic on the River Erne. Unknown to the soldiers, their presence was noted and passed on to local PIRA commanders. It is thought that the attack had been planned several days in advance following leaked information, possibly from a member of the Forum staff. A large device had already been prepared before being transported across the border with the Irish Republic.

A PIRA bombing unit drove into the car park – in broad daylight – to place the device underneath the parked car. The mercury tilt device, similar in nature to the one that had killed Airey Neave, MP in the House of Commons car park in 1979, was designed to detonate once the vehicle moved. Once the device was secured, the team retired to a high point overlooking the Forum. While it has never been proven that the Provisionals

---

* A mercury switch is an electrical switch that opens and closes a circuit when a small amount of the liquid metal mercury connects metal electrodes to close a circuit, thus triggering an explosive device.

Forum soldiers Robert Huggins, Thomas Henry Agar, Pete Gallimore and Clive Aldridge.
(SEFF)

were certain that the four off-duty soldiers would be taking part in the event, spontaneous attacks were not their usual MO. They rarely left anything to chance, so it is extremely probable that later suggestions that one of their sympathisers, employed as a member of the Forum, passed on the information when the military party either booked in advance for the tournament or made initial enquiries were not without foundation.

At approximately 1730 hours, the soldiers were observed to return to their vehicle; as they set off, the device was triggered. The explosion was massive, tearing the car apart; Corporal Thomas Agar (31), a father of one, was killed instantly; Lance Corporal Robert Huggins

(29), a father of three, was mortally wounded. Lance Corporal Peter Gallimore was terribly injured, losing both legs; he died in October of a heart attack brought on by his blast injuries. A fourth soldier was injured, although he later made a tentative recovery. The blast also injured eight civilians, causing the *Ottawa Citizen* to note: 'The soldiers who had been given time off to take part in the contest, were killed when the device blew up as they started the engine. Parts of their car slashed into the crowd.' The *Sun* newspaper had dispatched a reporter to cover the contest for the newspaper's army of angling fans; he reported: 'When I reached the car park, I could only stand there stunned. One man was sprawled on the ground with his clothes on fire and another was lying motionless in a pool of blood. People were screaming and running in all directions.'

Craig Agar is the son of Corporal Agar.

Craig's Story

I was 8 at the time that my dad was killed, and we were living in Jarrow whilst he was away serving in Northern Ireland. He had just signed on for another three years, but Mum wanted to be away from Army camp life for a while. On that fateful day, Mum was having a drink with her friend, Maureen, watching the six o'clock news. I heard the announcer say that there had been a bomb explosion in Enniskillen and Mum remarked: 'That is where Tom is.' I don't think that it was very long afterwards there was a knock at the door. Mum answered it to find two officers and a policeman standing there. She knew straight away, dropping to her knees and calling: 'Tommy, Tommy …' Even at 8, I knew straight away that my dad was dead.

I was bundled upstairs out of the way. I just remember that there seemed to be lots of policemen in the house. Anyway, I was taken to Nan's for a while. When I returned home, Mum was on the settee in tears. I didn't really know what to say. They kept me away from the worst of it all. I didn't go to the funeral and was excluded from all conversations about Dad. Nothing was discussed while I was in the room; Ma really tried to protect me. Funny thing is that I talk to my kids about these things, but back in them days it was a taboo subject.

I do recall that the funeral of one of the other soldiers – Robert Huggins – was on the TV, and that made me realise that I should have gone to Dad's. It was not long afterwards that the police or Army advised us about letter bombs; I was told be wary of strange packages with our names on and that if it was partially transparent, to get help straight away. It was a very odd conversation for an 8-year-old boy to be having. Poor Peter; he went through the blast before suffering in agony for five months from the burns. I also recall that when he died, the Ministry of Defence gave his widow and family just five days to vacate their married quarters.

Afterwards, we were told many things by the Army and the RUC; some of it was lies and some of it was them covering things up. For example, we were told that they turned up in Enniskillen, in a hire car before checking into a hotel. They also told us that Dad and the others had been flashing their side arms around the town; I don't believe this and nor does the author of this book. We were also told that one of the bombers was known to them and that one of them had been killed in an SAS border ambush. I can't remember the name, but I am told that he was definitely involved; I know now that all the stuff we were told was just utter bullshit.

I know that Dad and the others were 'dicked' by the IRA and that a Forum employee, whose name I cannot disclose, was arrested and questioned before being released. There was a strong suspicion that this man, who registered the group for a fishing competition, had known that they were soldiers; it is alleged that he informed the local PIRA commander, who then had several days to plan a bomb attack. I understand that an employee at the Forum recalled that when the bomb exploded there was chaos as well as panic and confusion. This employee recalls that a fellow employee didn't react, just staying calm with a huge smirk on his face. Although I cannot legally name that man, I know that he was the dicker who started the chain of events which led to the murders. Incidentally, one of the bombers managed to get to Boston in the USA, where he laid low for many years until the Good Friday Agreement.

The investigation, both back then by the RUC and later by the HET of the PSNI was bollocks! We were told that there was a proper investigation and that everything was done properly; the fuck it was! In 2013, the HET announced that there was no interest in the case and that the evidence, statements, photographs etc. were either 'missing' or had been destroyed in an IRA bomb blast at an RUC station. Fair enough, we know that sort of thing happened, but then we were informed that three boxes full of paperwork and evidence had been found! More lies; it was a fucking disgrace and in the last seven years since we have been told nothing! Apparently, they don't even know what vehicle dad and the others were in; it is all a mess. We have been lied to consistently, and I think that they are scared of actually doing the investigation, frightened of upsetting senior politicians. If it was an Irish Republican wishing to have a soldier investigated, I am sure that they would leave no stone unturned! The terrorists get their cases opened but the soldiers are not being given the same level of thoroughness. All that the police and government are doing is covering their own arses and making up the rules as they go along.

Biggest thing apart from my night terrors is the image of my dad's charred face as he was laying in the car park; that particular photo of him covered in blood appeared in almost every paper up here. It is in my head constantly and I would like to 'thank' the reporters for my trauma.

I would like a small note to those brave people including two off-duty police officers who ran to help my dad and the other lads. I salute them all for being there and holding them in their arms to comfort them; I am in tears as I speak, but I salute them all. I also want to thank the fire service who got through the cordon and, despite the risk of a secondary device, tried to help, taking off their own tunics to lay the dead and injured on them. I cannot thank them enough, but I will never forgive the MoD for the way they treated us all; they kicked us when we were down.

How do I feel today? What reopening the case did do was to signal the onset of PTSD resulting from my childhood trauma. I keep questioning myself, doubting myself as I see no justice at all. It keeps producing question after question and I am only half the man I once was. As a child, I simply got on with it, but now I feel that I have been robbed of my dad, robbed of a good man and my poor ma was just abandoned; she had to get on with things on her own. The Army helped but an ungrateful

Government even taxed her tiny widow's pension; it was heartless the way that they took money from her.

The Government and the PSNI have left me in fucking limbo, in a no-man's-land. A lifetime of lies has left me in bits.

✦

On 26 March 1986, the Provisionals targeted and killed an off-duty UDR man at his place of work in Co. Tyrone; the murder left four children fatherless. Thomas James Irwin (52) was a part-time soldier who was employed by the Department of the Environment. He was working in a service manhole at a sewage treatment works in Mountfield, between Omagh and Cookstown. It is thought that he was selected for death after information was passed to the local Provisional IRA. The information could only have come from neighbours or even fellow workers. This is thought highly likely, as the gunman deliberately ignored other men on the site, striding directly up to the part-time soldier before shooting him dead. Private Irwin was acutely aware of the dangers he faced on and off duty, as his brother, also a part-time soldier in the regiment, was shot and killed by the Provisional IRA on 30 October 1979 while driving to work at Dungannon. Thomas left a widow, Anne, with whom he had five children, tragically one of whom died in 1983. The gun used to kill Thomas Irwin was taken from the dead body of RUCR Constable William Clements, killed on 7 December the previous year, 1985.

Alan Irwin wrote the following for SEFF and I have chosen to add it to his more detailed testimony below:

Alan's Story about Thomas

My father worked alongside two Roman Catholic colleagues who were with him when the IRA shot him. They seemed to think that it was more important to drive 7 miles to Omagh to raise the alarm, rather than going to a neighbouring house. We as a family weren't informed of his murder until at least six o'clock that day. The entire countryside around us seemed to know that he had been shot. The police were supposed to have come and informed us, but they didn't.

I would just like to start with the days leading up to the incident. Like all part-time UDR soldiers, my father worked full-time through the day and then patrolled at night on mobiles, stop and search and vehicle checkpoints etc. He always knew that he was a potential target, as the PIRA had killed scores of his colleagues at work or home and

UDR soldier Thomas Irwin, murdered by the IRA. (Alan Irwin)

his own brother was killed by terrorists in October 1979. We were at home having breakfast – I was 20 at the time – and we were discussing some intelligence which they had picked up the night before that there was a PIRA threat to part-time soldiers in the area. My father thought that it might be specific to him and told us that he suspected that it might be him who was being targeted by the terrorists. He thought that if it happened, it might well be at Carrickmore as he generally spent at least an hour there every day. Talk even got round to what would happen to his new car if anything happened to him. I was never sure if he was serious when he discussed this.

On the morning of the 26th, Dad went off to work and I went off to Omagh, where I worked. In the early afternoon, I heard the sounds of sirens from nearby and it crossed my mind that if anything had happened to him, the police would be calling. However, when no one came, I started to relax a little. I got home at around five-ish and I saw that Ivan Anderson, a part-time captain with the UDR was driving past looking very serious; Dad wasn't home and something appeared to be wrong. Mum said the phone had been ringing most of the afternoon asking if Dad was home. I entered the house and answered one of those calls myself; the caller was asking the same question: was my dad home. That week he was on standby at work, so we assumed he might be on a call-out. Ivan returned twenty minutes later at 1800 to inform us that Dad had been murdered between 1430 and 1440 that day. I should point out that Ivan, who was the principal of Sixmilecross Primary School, was murdered in a PIRA ambush on 21 May the following year.

The police eventually turned up to inform us, but Ivan angrily told them: 'I have done your job for you!' Their excuse was that they couldn't find our church minister to accompany them. They left at that stage, but I am still very angry and disappointed with them and what is hard to fathom is that there has never been an apology from them. The funeral was held in the same cemetery at Sixmilecross Parish Church where we had buried Uncle Fred. It was another military funeral with two pipers; it was very emotional. Afterwards, local Republicans daubed taunts and slogans along the roadside not far from the graveyard to intimidate us. We had been reliably informed, albeit off the record, that we would be watched in case we would retaliate. Months later, it appeared as if the PIRA were following Mum and I in a car, though we could not be certain.

I was very close to Dad and it was horrific losing him as well as my brother, but at least we had the comfort of an open coffin with him, whereas Fred's coffin was closed due to his dreadful injuries. It was difficult for all of us, especially my mum who never remarried. Nothing can be done to heal wounds, so you just stop talking about it. Families are torn apart and that plays into the hands of the cynical PIRA. The UDR welfare supported my mother but for those of us over 16 there was not the guidance and help, which we so desperately needed from any quarter. It has remained difficult over the years and it was our faith in God and support for law and order which kept us going over the years. At no point then or even now, did we ever feel that what we had experienced through terrorism, we should do the same to another. There are those who seek to defend the indefensible. They might feel that because this happened to me then I had no other alternative but to do the same, take up a gun or plant a bomb and murder someone in retaliation. What saddens me more is those who appear to have swallowed that feeble argument and lent their support in justifying the same. It is pitiful to say the least.

We were given lots of promises by politicians and the RUC but nothing happened, and when they told us that they would leave 'no stone unturned' it was mere words. However, there was one exception: a one young constable who attended after my brother's death and the murder of my father; he was supportive, compassionate, and a lovely lad. No one was ever arrested or charged, but I believe that the men responsible were later killed by the Army. Mum is still alive, now aged 78 as we speak, but her whole world was destroyed, taken in the blink of an eye. Time passes quickly but the memories never do.

My father's death was the third funeral the family had in just over three months at the same church and graveyard. Dad's brother-in-law, my uncle, had died on Christmas day 1985; his sister-in-law, my aunt, had died of cancer on 16 January 1986. My father was the one who assisted with the funeral arrangements for both.

✦

On the second Sunday of every November throughout the British Commonwealth countries, services are held to remember their fallen of both world wars, and also of hundreds of Britain's 'smaller wars'. At the eleventh hour of the eleventh day of the eleventh month, the nation falls silent to honour past generations. At Enniskillen, Co. Fermanagh on Sunday, 8 November 1987, that same silence was punctured by a huge explosion that rocked the town centre, leaving ten people dead at the scene. Two of the many injured would die later. The crowds had started to gather a little after 1000 hours; many of the watchers were standing with their backs to a wall, behind which the instrument of their imminent deaths – a bomb – had been planted by the Provisional IRA. The device had been left the previous evening, primed and ready to issue its death-dealing power. Poignantly, a survivor would later lament: 'At 11 a.m., we should have been remembering the dead … instead we were digging them out.'

At 1043, the bomb exploded with a blast that eyewitnesses recalled went on for at least ten seconds. After that millisecond of whiteness, and those ten seconds, nothing could ever be the same again, anywhere. For those eleven people and for their children and grandchildren, and other loved ones, their worlds were changed forever by that flash of whiteness. An eyewitness who described the bang told of the sobbing and crying that followed. Some people were already dead, others were badly injured and would soon be dead.

Of the dozens of injured, there were some who could be saved. In the aftermath of the blast, the triage determined that those with a chance of life must have priority. A survivor – David Grimsley – described the explosion as 'a big black cloud', speaking of 'an awful noise with alarms going off'.

The scene was utterly chaotic; the stench of explosives, the clouds of swirling masonry dust, pulverised by the explosion, lent the scene a nightmarish haze, a red fog through which it was difficult to penetrate. As people came out of the immediate shock, they struggled to their feet, those who could stand. There was a sudden realisation that a child was missing, or a husband or a wife. The dazed survivors were scrambling around in the bricks, the rubble and the dust, desperately seeking their loved ones; hoping against hope that they were alive. Many experienced the ecstasy of finding them wandering around, dazed like themselves. Then there were those who felt that icy dagger to the base of the stomach when a pile of smoking and bloodied rags on the ground proved to be the man or woman that they had shared a bed with for thirty or forty years. Within minutes soldiers and police had taken off their raincoats to cover the dead; limbs protruded out from underneath the rubble, marking their temporary graves like makeshift crucifixes.

Those killed instantly or at the scene of the blast were: Wesley Armstrong (62) and his wife Bertha (55); Kitchener Johnston (71) and his wife Jessie (62); William Mullan (74) and his wife Nessie (73); John Megaw (67); Alberta Quinton (72) a retired nursing sister; Samuel Gault (49); and RUCR officer Edward Armstrong (52).

Marie Wilson (20) – who was a student nurse – was still alive and trapped under the rubble along with her father, Gordon; she died later in hospital. Underneath the masonry, bricks and wood, they had held hands and prayed. One man, Ronnie Hill (55), was so badly injured that he never recovered, dying some thirteen years later.

Aileen Quinton is the daughter of Alberta Quinton.

Aileen's Story

At the time of the Poppy Day Massacre, I was 29 and living in London. On the day itself, I was watching TV as I crocheted my mother's Christmas present. It was a lace tablecloth and was going to be a surprise. I wanted to give her something that she would know I had spent a lot of time over. It was putting a wee bit back of all the time she had spent on me. I didn't go to any Remembrance Sunday ceremonies as it was just too emotional for me. This was a mixture of homesickness and thoughts of my father who used to parade with

Alberta Quinton, killed in the Poppy Day massacre. (Aileen Quinton)

the other ex-servicemen and who had died only a few years before. The programme *The Waltons* was interrupted with a newsflash that there had been a bomb at Enniskillen war memorial and there were seven dead. I was so shocked and wondered for a moment if I had imagined it. When I collected myself I rang home, but the number was continuously engaged. I just thought that that was our phone, but I later found out that the Enniskillen exchange was overloaded.

I rang my Uncle Dick in Belfast but he knew nothing. In desperation, I called the operator, asking her if she could interrupt whatever call was tying up my family's phone. She said that it could only be done in an emergency. So I explained what had happened and that they might be trying to ring me as I was trying to ring them. She said that she would try and get through and ring me back, so I could keep the phone free. I nearly said to her: 'Pray you don't hear the name "Quinton" on the news tonight', but I told myself off for being dramatic. It was so hard to sit and wait for the call back and not ring round other people who might know something. I tried to keep calm and rationalised that it was unlikely to be any of my family. The newsflash had said seven dead and I thought that it was probably those who were laying wreaths. Statistically it was unlikely to be my mother or any of my brothers but she was going to be so upset as the day meant so much to her, remembering those she served with in the RAF in World War Two. I was looking forward to the guilty relief at knowing for sure that the dead were other people's loved ones but not mine.

The phone rang and it was the operator, who had got through to one of my brothers, Christopher. He told me: 'Aileen we can't find her.' That was actually reassuring as I thought it meant she was not one of the dead and, having been a nurse, was probably focused on helping any wounded. I found out later that Christopher had been driving around the various places he thought she might be, and at one stage he went to the Territorial Army (TA) centre as he had heard that some of the injured were being taken there. When he arrived he just asked: 'Any injured here?' He left when he was told that it was only the dead. He was not ready to consider that she might be dead. She probably was there at the time. He bumped into a friend of his who had been trying to dig out those buried in the rubble. Their exchange was: 'Andy, you know what I am going to ask?' with, 'I haven't seen her,' in reply. So many people had trouble recognising those they dug out, not just because of the injuries but everyone was covered by a layer of dust. He drove to the Erne Hospital, seeing all the wounded being carried in, all covered with dust; it was like actually being in the operating theatre, he told me. He saw Jim Dixon on a stretcher, but his face was so damaged that he was only recognisable as a male by his clothing.

Shortly after talking to Christopher, a cousin got through to me and said that she had heard where the bomb was and that it was well away from where my mother normally stood, which added to my belief that she would be shocked but otherwise unhurt. I called some of my friends, who came around to collect me so that I wouldn't be alone as I waited for news to come through. When we got to their house I tried to ring home again, but again got the engaged tone and then I tried my Uncle Dick. I said: 'It's Aileen, I was wondering if you had heard anything.' His answer started with: 'Awk, Aileen,' and I thought he was irked at me calling him again, but then he broke down and said: 'I am so sorry …'

Alberta with her daughter, Aileen. (Aileen Quinton)

I knew that she was gone; it was a voice of no hope. I gave a cry and dropped the phone. My friend picked it up and spoke to him, offering her condolences, and I heard her adding: 'Yes, we'll look after her.' My friend's husband said to me: 'You must be very bitter.' I said that I was sorry for them as they didn't have the example that I had.

Shortly after I managed to get through to my brother Derek, who had identified her. He was with Bishop Hannon at the hospital when someone said that a lady hadn't been identified and they had her hand-bag. Derek recognised the photos of us as children that she carried round with her. The bishop went with him to identify her and indeed he related this in future sermons. I wanted to know what the bomb had done to her apart from killing her. The first form of words that entered my head was: 'How many bits was she in?' but I managed to amend this to a less stark: 'Was she all in one piece?' Derek assured me that she was.

The next day, Monday, I flew with a cousin to Belfast, where we were met by my uncle, who drove me to Enniskillen to the family home. As soon as the door opened, I could see that the house was packed. I hugged my brothers and the next wave of the family circle, lined up to greet me. It was so strange not to have my mother there as she always was when I came home, if she wasn't actually in the car that was collecting me. In Northern Ireland, that is how we do death. People flock to the house when someone dies and there were lots of hugs and lots of tears.

Just as an aside, one of my parents' closest friends, Angel, was at the war memorial for the parade. When the bomb went off she came across Julian Armstrong (16), who was standing with his parents dead at his feet. He was brought to hospital and Angel went to let his sister (her husband's niece-in-law) know. She then went to church, the one my family also attended, where she was told that my mother couldn't be found. After church, she popped home to see her husband, who wasn't well and said to him: 'I am just going to Quintons to see if Alberta has been found.' She was at our house when Christopher took the call from Derek, who had just identified my mother's body. Angel's nephew, another Derek who was an RUC detective, had been murdered by the IRA the year before.

[Author's note: Detective Derek Breen (29) was murdered while off duty on the evening of 11 February 1986 as he drank in the Talk of the Town pub in Maguiresbridge. IRA gunmen burst into the pub, opening fire indiscriminately, also killing barman John McCabe (22).]

Afterwards? I am not sure if the RUC were allowed to make arrests and the PSNI didn't even seem to want to; the investigations seemed half-hearted, as the person whom the author of this book feels was responsible – Martin McGuinness – was clearly a protected man. We have been told the HET investigator was prevented from questioning him. I have asked for a public enquiry into the protection of senior terrorist leaders from prosecution and even interview and investigation. I recall some years ago BBC's *Question Time* programme was aired from Belfast with McGuinness on the panel. Had I been there, my question would have been: 'When did you hear about the Poppy Day massacre, and was it before or after the bomb exploded?'

Do I forgive the IRA? To me, it is totally and absolutely immoral to forgive people who are not sorry. Forgiveness to me is an acceptance of the person in the present despite what they did in the past and that included their current moral stance regarding what they did. Their moral stance can only be acceptable if there is remorse. If I forgive them and they are not sorry then I am saying that it is OK for them not to be remorseful. Some people seem to think that the only two options are forgive or hate. This is simply not true. I was not forgiven as a child by my parents if I was not sorry for any wrong I did. I was still loved though, they expected more of me. That is another reason I don't approve of unconditional forgiveness. It is dismissive of the potential of the other person to reach the moral position with regard to what they have done.

Gordon Wilson, the father of Marie who was killed in the blast, did not mention forgiveness in the interview he gave after the bomb, despite the media and so many commentators since 'talking about the interview where he forgave the killers'. He simply said that he prayed for them and asked that there should be no retaliation. This forgiveness thing placed a huge burden on all of us as pressure was put on to forgive the bombers. The IRA have never apologised for the murders; there is no forgiveness from me and I will always maintain that the more heinous the crime, the more wrong it is to forgive them in the absence of remorse. It was bad enough that this world was where a horrible thing like my mother being murdered happened but on top of that to have so many other people promoting forgiving unrepentant bombers made it so much harder to want to stay in that world. Even worse that some people thought that we did forgive them. It wasn't that I couldn't live up to it, I couldn't live it down. My father told me once: 'You should never hate people, just the things that they do.' I have held to that and I know he meant that there should be no exceptions and I shouldn't hate the people who took her from me. I consider it the far more realistic and far more moral stance.

The Provisionals later claimed that the outrage was the work of a maverick Republican group. They also claimed that adequate warning had been given, but ignored. Ed Carty of the Press Association disputed these explanations, writing that: 'it may have been a carefully planned, premeditated attack on Remembrance Day, aimed at provoking a loyalist backlash'. There was to be a deadly reaction from the Loyalists, although provocation was never an essential motive for them.

The *Daily Express* wrote the day afterwards: 'The IRA knew the casualties would be civilians. At 11 o'clock, when Enniskillen wanted to pay tribute to its war dead, the air was heavy with the cries of the injured and the dying.'

✦

The day after the terrible explosion at Enniskillen, with the air still thick with smoke and the acrid smell of burning, the UFF killed a young, innocent man in Belfast. It has always been claimed that the murder was in retaliation for the events of the previous day. Adam Lambert (20) was shot by a Loyalist gang, alleged to contain William 'Billie' Stobie[*] and Stephen Harbinson; Adam is known as the 'thirteenth victim of the Enniskillen bomb'. Often overlooked in the aftermath of the bomb, he could so easily have become a forgotten victim had it not been for the valiant efforts of his mum, Ivy Lambert.

The gang had intended to kill a Catholic male by the name of Sean. The young man they murdered was in fact a Protestant from Ballygawley, Co. Tyrone. Adam Lambert was working on a housing project just off the Springfield Road, in the Loyalist Highfield Estate. He was on work experience while studying for a degree in civil engineering. Several UFF men – including Stobie and Harbinson – had earlier been drinking heavily while they hatched a plot to carry out a sectarian murder. With violence in their hearts, it was clear that any Catholic would do. Their first port of call was near the Springfield

---

[*] Stobie was accused by the UFF of being an informer. On 21 May 1992, he was seized at a house on Snugville Street in the Shankill by a gang sent by the paramilitaries to shoot him. He was hit five times but survived. On 12 December 2001, the paramilitaries finally caught up with him again. He was shot dead by the Red Hand Commando outside his home at Forthriver Road, Glencairn, Belfast. The RHC was considered a flag of convenience for the UDA/UFF, although others felt that it was a stand-alone organisation.

Road in Belfast; they opened fire on a bus that was coming from the direction of the Catholic Ballymurphy/New Barnsley area. Fortunately for the passengers on the bus, which included children, their automatic weapon jammed, forcing them to seek other victims elsewhere. Their next attempt to kill involved opening fire on two children going into a Catholic-owned shop; again, they were thwarted. It was tragically third time lucky when they chanced upon a house on the Highfield Estate.

Adam was shot several times by the gunmen at very close range; he was mortally wounded, dying at the scene. The killers roared off in their stolen car, driven by Stobie.

The tit-for-tat killings in the wake of the Enniskillen outrage continued; on the 16th, nine days after the bombing, the UVF killed café owner Thomas McAuley (32) at his premises on the Crumlin Road in Belfast. They shot the father of two several times from close range, mortally wounding him. Despite the proximity of the Mater Hospital, the innocent Catholic died of his wounds.

Ivy Lambert is the mother of Adam Lambert.

Ivy's Story

Well, it was a shock to us when it happened, the day after the Enniskillen bomb. I never thought when I heard the news about Enniskillen on the Sunday, that I'd be hearing the same thing about my own child the next day. When the news came through, my husband Brian was out working. There was a knock at the door and it was a clergyman and an RUC officer; when they told me, it was such a shock. Brian was in 6 UDR based at Clogher, while I was a retired teacher. I was doing work with the UDR, helping with bereaved parents and widows. I had to be very discreet as you didn't know who was for you and who was against you in the country.

He used to come home from university every weekend to play rugby for Dungannon. I used to spend the weekends washing his filthy, muddy kit. He went back on the Sunday night, but sadly I can't remember his final words; it may just have been something as simple as: 'Bye; see you on Friday.'

We had just to get through the funeral as best we could. Adam was sort of the forgotten one. The Enniskillen bomb was such a big thing and he was just a single person, so people thought that he had become forgotten in the middle of it all. I don't want him to be forgotten, I want him to be kept alive in people's memory. We were never sectarian in any way, and both sides of the community gave us great support. In fact, Adam wouldn't have even known who was Catholic and who was Protestant. All faiths came to the house and the funeral to pay their tribute to him.

Adam wouldn't have wanted us to have been bitter or complaining. He wouldn't have wanted us to be constantly talking about him. Remember that we had three other children to look after and this is what Adam would have wanted. It's been thirty-three years now; it was very hard in the beginning but we had so much support. It has been such a very long time and sometimes I think, did we ever have Adam? At other times I feel he's very near. He was a handsome and popular man, studying building science, and well-liked by all who met him. He was an absolutely superb young man. He would have been a great member of society. He was meticulous about everything, particularly in his studies – he never missed a lecture. It's a long, long time ago now. People say time isn't a great healer, but I think it is. Thankfully, we never had vitriol or anger. I suppose we accepted it; we thought that's the way Adam was supposed to go. A lot of people will think that's a silly way of looking at it. But I think that Adam has done as much in twenty years as many people do in a lifetime. He shed a lot of love and light around and he was very well liked. We were lucky to have him for that long.

A man called Stobie was one of the ones who killed Adam. I remember the trial when one of the solicitors got out a file on him; all the things that he had got up. It was several inches thick as he had been in and out of court for years because of his paramilitary activities. We had no strong feelings about the men who were sentenced; we took it for granted and we took it in our stride. Sorry that is a bit vague, but I had a stroke a few years ago, and I have spent a lot of time recovering, learning how to walk and talk again. It has been a few years, but we were involved with the Stevens' Enquiry, which also looked at the killing of

Pat Finucane* as it was thought that some of the men who killed Adam were also involved in his murder.

We are glad that we lived in the rural area as there wasn't as much paramilitary influence there as there would have been had we lived in say, Belfast; it would have been harder to keep the kids out of their clutches. Although Adam wasn't that sort of boy.

How do I feel about the men who killed him; do I forgive them? That is difficult to answer as they have never actually asked us for forgiveness, but anyway forgiveness is for a higher authority than me. I don't bear a grudge, but as I said, no one has asked me for forgiveness.

On the anniversary of his death, SEFF put a photo of him up on their website, and I thought that a few people might remember him. However, 520 people remembered him and had lovely memories of him. He did as much in his twenty years for others as most people ever achieve in an entire lifetime. From the life that he led, there is still a fallout of goodness coming after him. He was meant to be an example to others by the way that he lived his life.

On 15 June 1988, several hundred people, including both military and civilians, had just completed a fun run in the centre of Lisburn. Several off-duty soldiers, having taken part in the charity race, returned to their vehicle, which they had parked in the town's Market Place. During the run, a PIRA bombing unit had placed a 7lb (3.2kg) device under their van. The vehicle set off around 2100 hours, but moments later, the device exploded, tearing the vehicle apart, hurling razor-sharp shards of metal into the departing spectators, participants, shoppers and shop workers alike. Four soldiers were killed instantly, with two more dying later. Those killed were: Corporal Ian 'Metty' Metcalfe (36), a father of two daughters, aged 10 and 8, from Bradford, West Yorkshire, a soldier in the Green Howards; and RAOC Lance Corporal Derek Walter Green

---

* Pat Finucane was killed by the UFF at his home in North Belfast on 12 February 1989. He was a Northern Irish civil rights' solicitor. UFF member Ken Barrett was convicted of his murder. William Stobie, Adam's killer, was charged – but not convicted – of supplying one of the weapons used to kill Mr Finucane.

(20), from the St Helens, Lancashire area. The other four soldiers were all from the Royal Corps of Signals: Sergeant Michael James Winkler (31), from Llanelli, Wales; Lance Corporal William Paterson (22), from Glasgow; Lance Corporal Graham Patrick Lambie (22), from Dinnington, Sheffield, killed just a fortnight before his 23rd birthday; and Signalman Mark Robert Clavey (24) from Trimley St Martin, near Ipswich.

Church leaders and politicians were quick to condemn the no-warning attack. British Secretary of State Tom King described it as: 'a horrific act of brutality ... a terrible loss of young men's lives. That terrorism is a vile and destructive thing was shown all too clearly by this latest horrific event.' The Mayor of Lisburn, William Bleakes, called the bombing: 'diabolical; an act of wanton savagery'. The Northern Ireland Office suggested that the soldiers had failed to follow proper security procedures as they had left their vehicle unguarded for over two hours and had then driven off without having checked under it beforehand. Margaret Thatcher, who described the attack as a 'terrible atrocity', at the same time rejected demands from Conservative back-benchers to bring back internment.

A spokesman for PIRA claimed responsibility for the murders, promising to: 'wage unceasing war' against the Army and RUC. Gerry Adams later stated, somewhat bizarrely, that the killings were: 'vastly preferable to killing members of the Ulster Defence Regiment or Royal Ulster Constabulary'.[*] As a further postscript, the PAF (a cover name for the UVF) threatened that Catholic members of the leisure centre's staff – whom they claimed had collaborated with the planting of the bomb – were now considered legitimate targets. Their words were roundly condemned by the Lisburn Lord Mayor, William Bleakes.

[Author's notes: the term 'legitimate target' was used by the UFF, at that time under the control of John McMichael. This unwarranted description was applied indiscriminately as the paramilitaries of both sides sought to justify their respectively barbaric campaigns. One can, with a dispassionate objectivity, understand the term when it is applied to the enemy of a cause – in this case, the Army and the police – but

---

[*] Sharrock, David; Devenport, Mark, *Man of War, Man of Peace?: the unauthorised biography of Gerry Adams* (Macmillan, 1997), p.263.

Scene of Lisburn fun run bombing. (Belfast Telegraph)

Memorial to those killed in the Lisburn fun run bombing. (Ken Wharton)

never when applied as inaccurately and outrageously to justify sectarian murder. It is also worthwhile noting that the late Martin McGuinness, PIRA commander in Londonderry's Creggan, later Northern Command and ultimately, the Army Council, used the term to describe the death of Catholic civilian Patsie Gillespie.

He was employed by the British Army at Fort George barracks in Londonderry. On 24 October 1990, a PIRA ASU abducted him from his home in the Shantallow district, holding his wife and children at gunpoint. He was strapped to the wheel of his own car, into which they had packed explosives. He was then forced to drive to the border Permanent Vehicle Checkpoint (PVCP) at Coshquin. He tried to shout out a warning to soldiers of the King's Regiment who were manning the PVCP. His warning came too late, as the watching PIRA unit remote-detonated the bomb, killing Mr Gillespie as well as five soldiers. This was one of the earliest uses of the proxy bomb. His widow Kathleen told me in a private meeting that McGuinness's use of the term 'legitimate target' caused her great and lasting offence.]

One of the injured civilians was Andrea Brown, whose father was murdered five years earlier, in 1983 at Rostrevor, Co. Down. On the day of the Lisburn blast, she was in a bridal shop at Market Place in the town centre. She was shopping for bridesmaids' dresses when the bomb detonated; she was among those badly hurt. Her mother, sisters, her fiancé's sisters and mother-in-law to be, who were also in the shop at the time, were lucky to escape with only minor injuries.

Andrea's Story: Part Two

On that day in the bridal store, there were no seats left, so I was sitting on the floor of the shop. Then there was a huge blast and the force of the bomb lifted me into the air; I landed on a mahogany writing bureau and then down onto the concrete floor. I was 18 at the time and about to get married. I suffered spine, neck and leg injuries, which changed my life dramatically; it had a devastating impact on my physical and mental health.

After undergoing weeks of treatment at Musgrave Park Hospital, I decided that I had to do my best to get on with life, despite my injuries, so I went ahead with my wedding in September. I remember having to remove my neck brace for the service and wedding photographs. I spent three years on and off in hospital; I basically had to learn how to walk again. Sadly, my physical health deteriorated in the years that followed and I eventually lost the use of my left leg. There were days I woke up and couldn't get out of bed because the pain was so bad. There were days I was able to be a mother and other days when my daughter had to be a 'carer'.

I was unable to work and felt guilty that I was a burden to my family. My mental health began to suffer, to the point that I even considered taking my own life; I needed psychiatric treatment. The events of the 'fun run bombing' as well as the murder of my policeman daddy in January 1983 left me with PTSD, although it would be years before the medical health authorities recognised that. I have to say that the mental effects of those horrific events have been far worse than the physical ones. It is an awful way to live; it dictates everything in your life. I'm not living life, I am just existing.

It is now thirty-two years since the attack, but I have no clear memory of the day of the blast. But I still have nightmares and flashbacks, often triggered by certain sounds and smells. My health problems are now so acute that I have to rely on a carer coming to my home four times a day, and for the past ten years I have needed a wheelchair to get around.

The IRA attack in 1988, and the murder of my daddy in 1983 by the same organisation, has ruined my life. I'm past the anger stage, but I can't forgive. But then again the way I look at it now forgiveness isn't mine to give. These people have never asked for forgiveness, and you can only forgive someone who is sorry for what they've done. To me the IRA and Sinn Fein are not sorry for what happened.

I don't think anyone will ever be prosecuted for the Market Place attack but I believe that the money being spent on legacy investigations could be better spent elsewhere. I think the money could be used to help victims rather than chasing dreams. The Republicans are calling for investigations into this, that and the other thing. That's fine and police and soldiers have to be held accountable. But when they did the historical inquiry investigation into my dad's murder they arrested a guy, brought him in and he didn't have to open his mouth. It's not fair. Even if someone is convicted at this stage they're only likely to serve two years anyway. I have lived over thirty years of pain and suffering – physical and mental. My whole family has been affected. There is just no justice.

One more thing that I can tell you is that had my daddy not been murdered, there is no way that I would have been involved in the Lisburn bombing. If he had been alive, he wouldn't have allowed me to get married at 18. I wouldn't have been looking for someone to love to try and replace him.

I often worried about the families of those poor soldiers who died. I met Billy Paterson's mum and dad, who later moved to Northern Ireland as that had been their son's dream after his Army career was over. I also met Sarah Carter, the daughter of Ian Metcalfe; once when she was due over, I had the sad news of informing her that Republicans had defaced the monument to her dad and the other soldiers in Lisburn town centre.

✦

We have spoken previously about the Provisional IRA's tactics of targeting off-duty members of the security forces. The strategy had a two-fold purpose: it was part of the terror process, designed to show the British Government that Northern Ireland was ungovernable. It had a second purpose, in that it was intended to demoralise the men and women of the UDR and RUC; forcing them to 'take their eyes off the ball' thus reducing their operational efficiency as well as actively discouraging recruitment into the services.

On Tuesday, 11 October 1988, the IRA murdered an off-duty RUC officer in the Lisburn Road area of South Belfast. Constable John Larmour (42), a father of a boy of 13, had agreed to look after his brother George's ice cream shop – Barnam's World of Ice Cream – as they were taking a family holiday in Spain.

The officer was a seasoned professional and would have been only too aware that if his stint of duty was picked up by PIRA intel he was extremely likely to become not only a target, but an easy one at that. His brother, George, had not discussed his brother's background to either staff or customers, and John himself had invented a cover story, stating that he was an electrician. Although occasionally flawed, PIRA intelligence was very good. The off-duty officer was recognised either by a dicker from the area or his details were passed on to local commanders by a customer with mischief in his heart.

The assassination was timed in line with the shop's closing time of 2200 hours, and just two minutes before John was about to shut down for the night, two men walked into the parlour. There were only two customers in the shop at the time: a young couple finishing off their ice creams. One of the men remained at the door, while his colleague walked across to the counter, requesting a 'slider', better known in the rest of the UK as a sandwich. John politely informed the man that he didn't stock them, prompting the man to ask instead for chocolate ice cream in a cone.

As the off-duty officer bent down to get a cornet wafer, the first man fired four shots at the policeman, causing him to slump, mortally wounded to the floor. The man at the door then turned off the shop's lights before firing a total of eight rounds at the young couple, sitting at a nearby table; both of them were wounded by the volley of shots.

The first gunman leaned over the counter, firing a further two rounds into John Larmour's prostrate body. They then ran outside to a waiting car, which sped off in to the night. The wounded officer was rushed to hospital for urgent medical treatment, but despite extensive attempts at resuscitation, he did not survive. The young couple both recovered following treatment in hospital.

Perhaps it was a casual remark from a customer that found its way to the ears of the IRA; perhaps it was a case of active dicking or, more disturbing, maybe John Larmour was acceptable collateral damage. Was he a pawn in the intelligence game of chess, being played out on the streets of Northern Ireland. Perhaps his murder was allowed to proceed in order to protect a double agent. The truth can often be stranger than fiction in the murky world of informers and their handlers.

Forensic evidence later showed that one of the weapons – a Browning 9mm pistol – had been taken from Corporal Derek Wood after he had been beaten by a mob before being shot alongside Corporal David Howes in March 1988. The two soldiers had wandered into an IRA funeral cortège at Andersonstown on 19 March, earlier the same year; they were abducted, beaten and tortured before being shot dead by local gunmen. The second weapon – a .357 Magnum Ruger – was used by the Provisionals to kill an off-duty UDR soldier, Lance Corporal Roy Butler, at the Park Shopping Centre on 2 August. The same weapon was also used by the IRA to murder Colin Abernethy on the Belfast–Dublin train at Finaghy Halt in South Belfast, also in 1988. The Provisionals made a spurious claim that Mr Abernethy – a man with no Loyalist paramilitary connections – had been involved in sectarian murders.

George Larmour is the brother of the murdered policeman, and author of *They Killed the Ice Cream Man*.

George's Story

I'm sure there are some who will be reading this and already formulating their own whataboutery words in response. That he was a policeman and even off duty he was a legitimate target during our casually referred to 'Troubles'. They will use words to justify his murder. I won't waste my time debating that narrative. It is pointless wasting words on those who will never listen.

To me he was simply my older brother John and I miss the lost opportunities and memories we would have made together. My mum and dad certainly weren't legitimate targets. The gunman might as well have killed them

John Larmour, off-duty RUC officer, murdered by the IRA. (George Larmour)

too that night back in 1988. He effectively killed them anyway. They died from broken hearts.

All murders are wrong. All our mothers' tears are the same. And all words stirring up hatred are wrong. History tends to get rewritten by some who wish to change the wording to sanitise the part they played in the mayhem they helped create and view their past through nostalgic rose- or green-tinted spectacles.

I accept our politicians have a difficult balancing act to perform at times but it would be refreshing if they could think before selecting some of the provocative words they use. It would also be good if they could stop predictably behaving like feet-stamping tantrum children throwing their toys out of their respective political prams every time they have to make decisions that affect us all.

Maybe they will finally learn to have the courage to stop looking over their shoulders to get approval from those pushing their prams. Instead they should use appropriate words to help heal us instead of rhetoric that has the potential to cause the wheels to fall off the fragile Pram of Peace or stir and reheat our simmering 'Troubles' cauldron of division.

I hope everyone in positions of power have learned something from the now infamous siege of Capitol Hill, Washington when Trump's reckless words lit the fuse and were interpreted by his followers as it being OK to resort to violence. Social media can be dangerous. For the sake of a new impressionable Twitter- and social media-savvy generation, I hope our local politicians learn to choose their words carefully when expressing their opinions on such platforms and in public. Their message should always be unambiguous: that violence is never the answer.

We have a tendency here to glorify individuals who played significant roles during our 'Troubles'. Particularly former participants who chose violence to achieve their goal. If you want to use words to eulogise those who died for a cause, eulogise the innocent victims. They are the people who died for a cause they played no part in. They are the real people deserving of such glorification, not perpetrators and their armchair social media supporters.

✦

The following testimony was written anonymously for this book, and while it names a man who died as a consequence of his own actions, the intended victim does not wish to be named. Two respected colleagues – Trevor Loughlin and James Henderson – testified as to the veracity of the account. On 5 February 1989, PIRA man James Joseph Connelly was fatally injured in the act of placing a bomb underneath a vehicle belonging to an RUCR man. It exploded prematurely, blowing off both of his hands. He underwent emergency surgery at Tyrone County Hospital in Omagh but died the following day. A gun he had been carrying was later found to have been involved in the murders of RUCR officer William Monteith and UDR soldier Michael Darcy. Darcy was shot outside his Castlederg home on 4 June 1988 by the IRA; Monteith was also killed in Castlederg, shot by IRA gunmen on 21 November 1988.

Helping a Hungry Workmate

I was a part-time member of the RUC, working at a Construction Yard at Drumquin near Castlederg. It was one lunchtime and I was feeling really hungry. As I sat down to tuck into my sandwiches, I noticed a workmate – a Catholic by the way – sitting there, with nothing to eat; I could tell that he was hungry. It was hours until home time and I knew that he would be starving by then. I knew that we didn't see eye to eye on politics, but out of kindness and compassion, I decided to share my food with him. He had expressed a hatred for the security forces to which I belonged. In other places, political differences mean nothing, but this was Northern Ireland in the 1980s and the differences meant everything; and I do mean everything.

As I mentioned, I had another job, but the other job was much different and far more dangerous: I was a part-time soldier. I didn't talk about my role and nor did I discuss politics with anyone at work, but this particular workmate did, and I know that he held Nationalist opinions. On this particular day, he was hungry and that was all that mattered. I couldn't talk to anyone about being a soldier, but because you are a member of the security forces, fighting terrorism, within the law, keeping the community safe, you put yourself in harm's way in an effort to inhibit the actions of dangerous people. I knew that around me were people who deliberately maimed and murdered those they disagreed with, or whoever got in their way.

Anyway, I finished work for the day and went home, as did that colleague. When I got home, I shared another meal, but this time it was with my family. Later that night, I checked around the house, I checked my car and then locked up. I drifted off to sleep, not knowing that the man with whom I had shared my food was now intending to kill me. As I slept, he was outside my home, preparing an explosive device which was designed to kill me, maybe even injure my family as well. He wasn't there to repay my kindness, he was messing around with my van. He was armed, as was his accomplice.

The plan was for the device to detonate in the morning, as I drove out of my lane on my way to work. On an ordinary day, I might have shared my food with him again. His plan was to blow me to pieces; that was the extent of his hatred.

But, as he set the detonator, it exploded prematurely, injuring him very badly. He was rushed to hospital, but he died the following day. That workmate – and neighbour – was an IRA member, but I take no pleasure from his death, even though it was a death intended for me. That incident was almost forty years ago, but I am eternally thankful that the terrorist failed in his efforts to murder the man who showed him nothing but kindness.

✦

A terrorist-related death occurred on 6 November 1989 in an attack by the Republican splinter group the IPLO. A man who had once been a Protestant was killed by the tiny but vicious terror group. They admitted responsibility, claiming that the dead man was a member of the security forces. It was a classic case of mistaken identity. The murder gang was from the Nationalist Twinbrook in south-west Belfast. Shortly before the murder, they hijacked a taxi and then drove the 2 miles to Derriaghy, across the southern part of the city. Robert Burns (49), a father of four children, including a grown-up daughter, lived in Milltown Avenue, close to Derriaghy Primary School.

Mr Burns was in the hallway of his house when the killers arrived; one was armed with an AK-47 and another with pistol. They saw a shape through the frosted glass of the front door. The men, despite being uncertain if that shape was their intended victim, or his wife or even his adult daughter, opened fire with their weapons. Mr Burns was shot five times and slumped to the floor, mortally wounded. His killers fled back to the Twinbrook, while two of his neighbours who were nurses rushed to help. He was taken the 3 miles to Lagan Valley Hospital, close to Lisburn, but was dead on arrival. The dead man had no connection with the security forces, nor was he connected to either a Loyalist or a Republican terror group. The murder was carried out by the IPLO, although it was claimed under their flag of convenience title of Catholic Reaction Force. The terror group maintained that he was an agent, although this was mere bluster to disguise that they had made a grave and fatal error of judgement. It was yet another terrible sectarian attack.

Laura Burns is the daughter of Robert Burns.

Laura's Story

Basically, I was driving towards my parents' house in Milltown Derriaghy with my two young children. As I approached, another car came scream-ing past me and although I wasn't to know at the time, it was the getaway car of the men who had just shot my daddy. My sister came running over to my car in a great state of distress, frantically pulling at the door handle, which for some reason wouldn't open. There was terror on her face and she screamed at me: 'Someone has shot Daddy!' I was shocked but it was so surreal as people just seemed to appear from nowhere. I could see that Daddy was lying in the hallway; there was blood eve-rywhere and he had been shot through the glass. I later found out that they had used an AK-47 and that he had been hit five times.

I remember trying to run to him but people were pulling me, but I could see his body. I felt anger towards them that they were stopping me reaching him but also relief that I wouldn't have to see the mess that his killers had left him in. I experienced anger, relief but also guilt. A policewoman was soon on the spot and she told that one of our neighbours – a nurse – had told her that he was still alive, although I knew that he wasn't. It was only some years later that the nurse revealed that she made up the story about detecting a pulse so that an ambulance would come out and he would be taken on a stretcher and not in a body bag.

Robert Burns, murdered by the IPLO.
(Laura Burns)

The ambulancemen came and he was taken straight away; he had no trousers on, clad only in his underpants; I remember that they were purple with holes in them and there wasn't even a blanket to cover him. Some years later a medic explained to me that it was a 'scoop and run', with time being of the essence to try and save his life.

I just remember at the time that it all wasn't real; things like this only happened in the movies. Even though this was the twenty-first year of The Troubles, I had been cocooned from the violence, spending time in the countryside with my grandparents; it was a million miles from Belfast and The Troubles. Nothing had seemed to affect us as my daddy wasn't in the security forces and he wasn't a paramilitary. I am aware that many people on the mainland, when they heard of a murder in Northern Ireland, they simply assumed that he or she must have done something to deserve it. Well, I will tell you this: my daddy was completely innocent.

The RUC arrested some suspects from Twinbrook but after interview they were released without charge. A few weeks afterwards, the chief inspector came to see me and I protested that my daddy wasn't involved with terrorism; what he said will stay with me forever:'I know, pet, I know that he was an innocent man; we know who they are and we arrested them. One of them was a big, greasy lump of lard and throughout the entire interview, he refused to sit on a chair, just sat on the floor. He had that look which said: "I know that you know that I did it: prove it!"'

As you know, my daddy was a Protestant who converted to Catholicism in order to marry my mum. I remember her saying on the day of the murder that she just didn't know where to bury him. He was a gentle giant; a big child in a man's body. He wasn't like other men, even in a pub with others, he just looked out of place. He was a member of the Ulster Grand Prix Association; he loved his motorbikes, which were his passion. At his funeral, his motorbike mates arranged for the hearse to be taken on one final circuit around Dunderod race track, stopping in front of the grandstand for a minute's silence.

From one of Laura's poems about the bullet that killed her father:

I can see you, you're dead inside, but still you won't look at me. Ignoring me won't change the facts that I took your dad away from you. There's more of me at the front door; I smashed the glass and took a life; I settled in your wall. You know I'm here. Don't look, don't look all you want, but I'm inside your head.

✦

On 17 November 1989, the IRA's campaign tactic of targeting off-duty soldiers resulted in the death of Lance Corporal Samuel David Halligan at Stockingman's Hill in Co. Armagh. The murder took place less than a day after Sinn Fein had launched a new statement under the grandiosely named 'Scenario for Peace'. The organisation purportedly offered conciliation with the UK Government; a step towards a permanent ceasefire.

The Armagh Provisionals targeted and killed the part-time UDR soldier after he finished work for the day at Drumadd barracks in Armagh City. He was employed as a civilian storeman with the MoD, as well as being a part-time soldier with 'C' Company of 2 UDR. Lance Corporal David 'Davy' Halligan (57), a father of three, left the base, intending to play in a darts match at Richhill, some 4½ miles away. He then intended as was his routine to drive back home to Loughgall. As he drove along the Hamiltonsbawn Road, he slowed in order to negotiate a bend at Stockingman's Hill, close to where the main road branches to the right. PIRA intel had done its job, with a three-man unit in position at the exact spot where they knew that the soldier would have to decelerate rapidly to negotiate a severe bend. At the point where they had placed the ambush, it would have been impossible for the victim to avoid. The unit, concealed in bushes at the roadside, opened fire with automatic weapons. They fired between thirty-five and forty rounds, the bulk of which hit the car, mortally wounding the lance corporal. The car ground to a halt, before slewing across the road. The desperately wounded man managed to stagger out of the wreckage, where he returned fire at his attackers. He fired several rounds before collapsing and dying. His killers raced away to a stolen car, waiting on Stockingman's Hill Road, before escaping towards Newry. His killers were never caught; he is buried at St Luke's Parish Church, Loughgall.

The PIRA unit was known to be from a very active gang in Armagh City; no one was ever convicted of the UDR soldier's murder. He was a married man with three daughters, and was one of a family of eleven.

Bryan Walker was a nephew of the murdered man.

Bryan's Story

I was 19 at the time and had also joined the Ulster Defence Regiment a year previously, when I turned 18, serving part-time in 'A' Company, also based in Drumadd, along with my brother Mervyn. My father had also served; he was with 'C' and another uncle, Davy's brother, also served in the same unit. The company in which I served had a small platoon of men who carried out full-time duties. I would have done twenty-five to thirty duties a month.

With 17 November being a Friday night, I decided to go out with my mates to a local bar in Armagh. We were enjoying a few beers and playing pool when someone came in and said that there had been a shooting close to Drumadd. No mobile phones back then, so I got on the payphone in the bar. At this stage a lot of thoughts were going through

David Halligan, UDR soldier murdered at work. (Bryan Walker)

my mind, with the main one being that something bad had happened. I phoned the int cell in Drumadd and, as I suspected, they were very busy; however, as I was told to ring home I realised something was indeed very wrong. I rang home and my father answered and said: 'You need to come home, son.' I remember saying: 'Who is it, Dad?' He told me that it was Uncle Davy. I immediately wanted to go to Drumadd but realised there was nothing I could do there, and I needed to go home to my mum, Davy's sister. My mate took me home to Orchard Park in Loughgall; Uncle Davy lived in number 14, we lived in 21. Total devastation had hit my family, and although I had grown up with this, now it was personal.

The next morning, I decided I was resigning from the regiment; there was no way I could risk this happening to me, putting my mother through what she was going through that day. Davy was buried with full military honours, in one of the biggest funeral gatherings ever seen in our tiny village of Loughgall.

After the funeral, my mind was all over the place. I was not dealing with things very well and alcohol was playing a big part. I did not speak to anyone about it, but I made the decision I wasn't leaving the UDR and got back to what I was good at. It was hard for a while, especially when patrol briefings mentioned Armagh city PIRA; I knew at some stage I was going to engage with them, because on patrol we would regularly stop and search them. Only two weeks later it happened on the Cathedral Road in Armagh.

We were on a foot patrol and one of them was stopped in a vehicle. The patrol commander immediately told me to search him, but I hesitated. I just looked at him, but he just winked and nodded his head. I will say this: I was nervous, but I had a duty to do and carried out the body search. There was no verbal interaction until he spoke the words: 'Where's Davy Halligan today? I stopped and looked him straight in the eyes and could see the evil; every emotion was going through me and I was standing in front of him with a loaded SA80 rifle. I turned and walked away.

I continued to serve another eighteen years and had many more good comrades murdered over the years. Today I remember them all with pride but I also feel sadness as the very terrorists who murdered them are walking around free men with letters of pardon. Our politicians thought it right to forgive them and elevate some of them to my country's government, so I also feel rage. I feel guilt that I survived, and so many good soldiers are in their graves for nothing.

No member of Armagh city PIRA ever faced justice for the murder of my Uncle Davy, but I have no doubt whatsoever which one of them pulled the trigger. I will never forgive and I will never forget. I think back to that day on the Cathedral Road; yes, I now wish to God I had emptied my magazine into him.

✦

The Ulster Defence Regiment (UDR) lost a total of 368 personnel between its formation in 1970 and its disbandment in 1992, although there are other sources that put this total much higher. The deaths were from a variety of sources, which included death at the hands of terrorists, road traffic accidents, accidental shootings and Troubles-related suicides. Many of these deaths took place in situations where off-duty personnel might reasonably have expected to be safe. Attacks were carried out in the soldiers' homes, while out socialising or shopping, at work, or travelling to and from their place of employment.

On 9 January 1990, the Provisionals killed a part-time UDR soldier in Castlederg, Co. Tyrone. Private Olven Kilpatrick (32), a father of two young girls, had served for fifteen years as a part-time member of 'B'

Olven Kilpatrick, murdered by the IRA, Castlederg. (Sylvia and Ronnie Porter)

Company, 6 UDR. He was a partner in a shoe shop in Main Street, Castlederg; he and his wife were in the process of saving up for a new house, away from what had become a most dangerous area for the security forces. Earlier that day, a PIRA murder gang had burst into a house close to the family shop, holding the family hostage at gunpoint. Two of the gang stole the family's Vauxhall car, before driving into Main Street.

Shortly before 1730 hours, as the main shops were beginning to close on a cold, dark and wintery night, two PIRA gunmen entered the premises. The part-time soldier was just finishing off with his final customers of the day when he was approached by masked men holding guns. Without a word, they shot him several times at point-blank range, hitting him in his chest and mortally wounding him. As he lay dying, one of the gang placed a bomb in a shoebox; he set the timing device to explode approximately an hour later. They knew that there would be a follow-up by the police, with the premises searched for forensic evidence. The gang escaped across the nearby border, where they abandoned the stolen vehicle. They were never caught.

The terrorists deliberately chose a shoebox as it would sit there, identical to hundreds of others. The bomb was intended to kill and maim. While RUC and ATO officers were investigating, the device exploded, injuring two of the police officers and setting the building ablaze. The dead man's body could not be retrieved until firemen had doused the heavy blaze. Mr Kilpatrick was described by the minister who conducted his funeral as: 'a dedicated Christian who helped others quietly and discreetly'.

During a personal chat with the family in 2021, they made it very clear that they were most disappointed with the lack of any meaningful action or support from the Government departments with regard to murders in Castlederg. One family member remarked: 'The Republicans seem to get public enquiries at the drop of a hat.'

Sylvia Porter is the sister of the murdered soldier.

Sylvia's Story

There were only five years between my brother Olven and me; he grew up to be a hardworking family man with a wife and two kids. He was innocent, and maybe a bit naïve but he loved his civvie job and being in the UDR. He was a regular at church and an officer in the Boys' Brigade. He was a member of the Orange Order, but didn't bear malice towards anybody. Eventually he bought the shoe shop S&K Shoes, which he had been working in. I'll never forget the day that I heard Olven had been killed; it was a neighbour who had heard. She landed at our house, and she knew when she saw me all cheerful that I didn't know a thing about it. She told me that the IRA had been involved, and I knew that meant he had to be dead. I went into the sitting room; I just went numb. We had just had a son two weeks before. I was in shock the whole time that he was growing up; I couldn't cry or talk about it, and I couldn't relax and enjoy being a mum.

Olven Kilpatrick. (Sylvia and Ronnie Porter)

I just remember it coming on the news. It was like an ordinary death; you just got up the next day after the burial and got on. I couldn't cry;

I couldn't cry for years, never cried. I took it that bad. After Olven was buried, my whole body just closed down. I was on top of an open fire and I didn't feel the heat. I was shivering. It must have been the shock. My whole body from top to toe came out in a rash; it was the trauma. I was in shock for years. Every morning I woke, he was in my head: every morning.

There was a legacy to what happened; within one and a half years Olven's wife just upped and left, and didn't want to know anything more about Castlederg. We lost contact with her to a large degree as a result of that. You try to move on with your life, but when you had to endure the likes of Republican parades, it makes it very hard when the people you live among can treat you so badly and show so little respect for your loss. How can you trust them? We know that the politicians just want this to go away, and that is a huge betrayal because we have done nothing wrong. They want victims and their families to disappear; we're not even allowed our traditions. People don't even know what the Orange Order is about, yet they blacken its name. Yes we have peace, but at what price?

Ronnie Porter is the brother-in-law of Olven.

Ronnie's Story

On the evening of 9 January 1990, at 5.20 p.m., I came in from work, and Sylvia was making the dinner, with a Walkman playing in her ears. Just then, there was a knock at the door; it was our neighbour who had heard on the news that something had happened to Olven in his shop. I was part-time in the RUC then and was able to find out that the IRA had shot him, and put a bomb in a shoebox in the counter beside the body. It had exploded forty minutes later. I could see the fire streaming out of the shoe shop as I came into the town with Olven's mum, who lived on her own in the village of Killen, 3 miles from Castlederg. Thankfully, whilst a couple of police were injured in the explosion, it was nothing serious; Olven was dead, but his body was unharmed.

I know it seems petty, but it's hard these days when we see people who support what happened in those days, like at the IRA march through Castlederg a few years back. I've stood at hunger strike protests and it didn't bother me, but when I heard the Republicans cheering, it made my blood boil. They were jeering the victims' families; did they really know the pain they were causing? I would say: don't judge people until you know how they feel. Even in the days after the parade, family members of the victims were blanked as they went about their daily business, and even taken off social networking sites. We accept that only a minority supported the violence during The Troubles.

We have Roman Catholic friends and we feel no bitterness towards them, but it is very hard to trust people in general when you know some of them were involved in violence. That is why we need people to understand why we are the way we are; it is because we just don't know how to trust. Also, there was collusion and the authorities let certain things happen, so the likes of informers could be saved; I think there is a lot more information to come out. We have opened our hearts to all the politicians but it didn't matter; they didn't stop the Republican parade in Castlederg, even though we asked repeatedly. This was not an orange versus green thing to us, but rather it was about right versus wrong! Victims really need to be brought to the fore in all this; nobody asked to be a victim, we didn't go out and murder. There needs to be a differentiation between the victim and the victim-maker. Of course, the society that young people are growing up in is a lot better now, but we still need more tolerance. I think that Sinn Fein still calls the shots on everything; how many more times can the Orange Order give in? There is no tolerance of Protestant culture, and we are dictated to about where we can march; we feel alienated no matter where we turn.

I am a member of the Orange Order and Royal Black Preceptory, but this is a religious thing to me; I don't go out throwing stones. Sure we have peace, but we didn't want peace at any price! It is just a case of giving in all the time to the demands of Sinn Fein. We have to grieve behind closed doors, but I often ask myself: who really cares what was achieved by others losing their lives? Because of the hours I worked, I lost out on seeing my family grow up, but why? I loved being in the RUC, and what happened to Olven made me determined not to back

Olven Kilpatrick's grave. (Ken Wharton)

out. But I didn't consider what Sylvia was going through as it was easier to be the person in uniform rather than the family member sitting waiting for the knock on the door.

While Sylvia understands that it is the next of kin who gets all the attention, and rightly so, no one from any support agencies ever got in touch with either her, or her late mother. It was only in later years that a local victim support group visited her mum; maybe twice a month or so.

As far as forgiveness goes, we are an upright Christian family, and we would not wish ill on anyone, never mind carry out a murder. However, when it comes to those who set Olven up and those who carried out the murder, forgiveness is not that easy.

✦

On the evening of Sunday, 10 June 1990, Noel Downey, then aged 27, stopped outside The Weavers pub in Lisnaskea, Co. Fermanagh; he was en route to meet his fiancée Helen in Newtownbutler. He was a part-time soldier in the Ulster Defence Regiment (UDR), having served eight years in the war on terror. Unknown to him, a PIRA bombing team had planted an explosive device containing Semtex underneath his car; he was horrifically injured in the subsequent blast. He was later taunted by Republicans, who also sought to delay his emergency flight to hospital in Belfast.

Noel's Story

I joined up in 1982, the same year as the Falklands War was raging on. I was one of three who joined up, living in Maguiresbridge at the time. I worked at Sir Arkwright Cotton factory through the day and was stationed at RUC Lisnaskea. I served alongside some of the Regular Army, including the Paras, the Light Infantry and the Queens; I got to know them all quite well.

It was a Sunday evening on 10 June; I was on my way to Newtownbutler to pick up my then fiancée – now my wife – and thought that I would stop at The Weavers pub for a game of cards.

UDR soldier Noel Downey. (Noel Downey)

I must tell you that I was always very security conscious religiously checking under my car for booby traps, but on this occasion, when I returned to the car, I omitted to do so; I can't explain why I didn't. The next thing, I was falling into my car; I was blinded and knew that something was wrong. It just hit me that there was a bomb underneath

Noel Downey's wrecked car.
(Noel Downey)

the car, but as I didn't feel any pain and was conscious throughout, I sort of dismissed it. I got out of the car and immediately fell over; I did this three times and fell over each time.

Then I looked and saw that my left leg had gone. I didn't know at the time but my severed leg had hit me in the mouth, knocking out several teeth, which were embedded in the shattered limb; it was found in the back of the car. I noticed bizarrely that my socks and new trainers were still on the leg. As I lay there in shock, a wee guy who I knew was a fireman ran out of the pub to help, as did a friend – Albert Ebbitt, followed by Eric Brown, who had heard the explosion from nearby. Soldiers were quickly on the scene, one of them holding onto my badly injured left hand, which was just hanging off. I was sitting there, blackened by smoke and petrol and oil, my clothes blown off; I looked like a zombie from Michael Jackson's 'Thriller' video.

There was a long snake-like trail of blood from the car to where I lay and I am conscious that Eric kept slapping me in the face to stop me from passing out, although we laugh about it today. I remember asking one of the RUC officers to see if my balls had been blown off; that really scared me, but he had a look and replied: 'Yes, they're fine.' I was rushed to Erne Hospital in Enniskillen, where they found that I had only four pints of blood left inside me. I was treated there for three days but they soon realised that I needed to be in the Royal Victoria in Belfast [RVH] and a helicopter flight was arranged. However, word was leaked and several Republicans drove their cars onto the helipad, thus preventing the helicopter from landing. In the end, I was rushed by ambulance with two RUC vehicles clearing the route for me.

I was in the RVH for three months and had several life-saving operations before being transferred to the military wing at the Musgrave Park Hospital in South Belfast. I had an artificial limb fitted and learned to walk again. I also had to learn to write again, as I was left-handed and my left hand was badly damaged in the blast. I am here to tell the tale, but there are plenty of young lads who never got the chance to live their lives.

In the end, I got justice and one of the bombers, called McHugh, was sentenced to twenty-five years at Crumlin Road Courthouse. I was there to see him in court, but he only served three years before being released early under the Good Friday Agreement.

Noel and Helen Downey. (Noel Downey)

I just need to go back to the Tuesday after the bomb; Republicans erected a huge placard in the centre of Lisnaskea on a telegraph pole with a picture of me on it. The sign read: 'If you want to get legless on a Sunday night head to the Weavers Bar.' Sinn Fein/IRA talk about respect and shared space, but it is just spin; they have no respect whatsoever. It is the biggest load of rubbish and if people believe them, they are just fools.

So, thirty years later, I am still bitter about the bomb attack which maimed me. I will never forgive them. What makes it worse is the way that they are in power today. I see the released bomber and other former IRA men in Lisnaskea as it is such a small place. McHugh actually laughed in my face and I am taunted by him and the others every time we pass in the street.

✦

In the very early hours of 22 September 1990, a young UDR soldier, Private Colin John McCullough (24), was murdered by the Provisional IRA. The soldier and his fiancée, Leslie, were chatting in their parked car, close to Lough Neagh in Co. Armagh. The recently engaged couple had been followed at least once previously by dickers, who had noted where they went, when they went and, more importantly, how long they spent on their trips. These undercover agents of an undercover terrorist group reported back to the local IRA command in Lurgan. It is thought that the local unit was based in the Republican estate of Kilwilkie. Colin and Leslie had been observed to stick to a regular pattern, thus presenting the terrorists with an easy target. Earlier that evening, the pair had been to the cinema in Lurgan with friends, before setting off on one of their regular late-night drives.

They duly arrived at the beautiful but isolated shores of Oxford Island Nature Reserve, on Lough Neagh. Shortly afterwards, at around 0130 hours, several PIRA gunmen who had lain in wait silently approached until they were at the driver's side. Without warning, they opened fire, pouring at least twenty rounds into the vehicle. The soldier was hit a total of thirteen times but somehow all the shots miraculously missed the terrified woman, who was sitting in the passenger side. The young soldier died more or less instantly. The gunmen escaped in their waiting car, driving the short distance back to Lurgan.

It is thought that the same gunmen also shot and killed a former UDR soldier from Lurgan, John Lyness (57), who was attacked outside his home on 24 June 1993. A local PIRA member, Colin Duffy, was jailed in 1995 for this murder – he was also allegedly involved in the shooting of Colin McCullough – but later acquitted after one of the key witnesses, UVF member Lindsay Robb, was arrested in Scotland for gun running, thus rendering his evidence as unsound. In 1997, Duffy was charged with the shooting of two RUC constables in Lurgan town centre, but these charges were also later dropped. The dead RUC men, Roland John Graham (34) and David Johnston (30), had been on foot patrol in Lurgan town centre, close to the RUC station, when they were attacked from behind. Duffy has been linked to the dissident Republican group Éirígí in an article in *The Irish Times*.[*]

Roberta McNally was a comrade and close friend of Colin McCullough.

Roberta's Story

I knew Colin well; we were friends and we served together in the UDR. My husband, George, was on duty the night that Colin was murdered, but I was at home, although I can't remember when I heard the news or where I heard about it.

Apparently, Colin and his girl-friend, Leslie, had taken one of their regular late-night trips out to the Nature Reserve at Oxford Island, which was only a few miles away from Lurgan. The problem was that they made regular trips, same time, same place, and if we knew, the IRA also knew. There was a very

Colin McCullough, murdered by the IRA at Lough Neagh. (Roberta McNally)

active unit on the Kilwilkee Estate in Lurgan. The night of the attack, they were lying in wait for him and Leslie to drive into the reserve and park up. They came and they shot him and it is a miracle that Leslie wasn't hit.

Can you imagine how terrified she must have been? Her boyfriend dead, she herself covered in blood and remember that the place was so remote and pitch black at the time. She must have been devastated by the horrendous incident, but ran and ran until she saw a light in one of

---

[*] Source: www.irishtimes.com/news/republican-colin-duffy-has-walked-free-from-five-murder-charges-since-1993-1.448756

the few houses around, where she was able to get some help. George's unit was among the first to arrive and he was on a cordon around the scene; he could see poor Colin's body lying there in the car.

As I said, we knew that he and Leslie went up every weekend and he was advised to avoid this pattern of behaviour, but like all young men he was young and invincible. He could be very quiet at times, but he was well loved and I liked him very much; he didn't deserve what he got. His mum asked me to go see her after the murder, which I did a few times. She had his UDR beret plus a photo of him in the centre of the room; poor woman was just devastated as she idolised him. I visited her for several years afterwards. I also used to see Leslie around the town on occasions, but she sadly died from cancer and I don't think that she ever recovered from the shock of the murder.

When we found out about Colin, I was very sad, but I was also very angry, because we knew the people who did it and we knew the main man but we couldn't touch him or them. I am sure that the *Lurgan Mail* named the man, but I can't be sure. The same gang was also involved in the murder of an ex-UDR man called Johnny Lyness; he had left the regiment about a year before. I actually spoke to him a few minutes before he was killed and several witnesses saw the faces of the men who killed him. There was an investigation into Colin's murder by the RUC, but it wasn't much of one and I don't think that any of us were actually questioned about it.

Afterwards? We were devastated and angry but we had to go back on duty; we had to be professional, even when we saw the men we knew were the killers. We got lots of abuse and taunting about Colin when we did VCPs, patrols etc., especially in places like the Kilwilkie.

Thirty years later, I am still devastated; I feel the same today as I did then; there is absolutely no difference in how I felt and still feel. Some people have moved on since The Troubles, but I can't, just can't move on from what happened on the night, but also on nights before that and nights afterwards. Even today, I don't feel safe in the 'other end' of the town. I should explain that in Lurgan, Catholics live in the north of the town and the Protestants live in the south. I am often seen in the newspapers at memorials and the like, proudly wearing my beret and my medals; 'they' know who I am, but I am proud to be me. I was UDR from being 18 until I was 34 and it is engrained in me. I spent my twenties in this state and I will never change.

George McNally was a friend of the murdered soldier.

George's Story

On the night Colin was murdered, I was part of a three-vehicle patrol which left Mahon Road, Portadown for Lurgan. At 0145, we got a radio message to report to the RUC station. On arrival, the patrol commander and myself went into the operations room, where we were told that there had been a shooting in the outskirts of Lurgan. As we were waiting for further information, we were told the car details; we immediately recognised it as Colin's.

We then proceeded to Oxford Island, a local beauty spot, where the shooting had taken place, to set up a cordon. I was located approximately 70m from Colin's car – a green Ford Orion – and I could see that the driver's side door was open; I could see Colin lying on the front seat. We waited all night until daylight to allow forensics to do their work at the scene. His body was removed later that day, and his vehicle was then taken away by a tow truck. As the vehicle was lifted, blood could be seen flowing out of it. We then left the scene and returned to our base for a debrief.

Having witnessed all of the above, it has had a profound effect on me; the images never leave your mind, and periodically come back to haunt me. Colin's murder was cold, cowardly and callous. My wife and I regularly get our army photos out and talk about all of our comrades who were murdered.

7

1991–97

On 17 August 1991, Simon Ware, of the Coldstream Guards, was on rural patrol in Carrickovaddy Woods in South Armagh. A unit from the regiment's 2nd Battalion had been tasked to search an area where documents and photographs of PIRA personnel were thought to have been lost. They were unsuccessful and were en route to rendezvous with an extraction helicopter from Bessbrook Mill. As previously mentioned, by that stage of The Troubles, even more so in the very heart of 'Bandit Country', it was far too dangerous to travel by road. Lance Corporal Ware (22) walked past a mound of earth by the side of the track that, unknown to him, contained 300lb (136kg) of explosives. The landmine, planted by PIRA operatives from the South Armagh Brigade, was remotely detonated, resulting in the young Londoner being killed instantaneously. He had married his wife, Carol, in March the same year, in the Guards' Chapel in Wellington Barracks, London. Sadly, his funeral was also held there.

Carol Ware, Simon's Widow

I lost my husband that day, he was my best friend too, and my soul mate. I lost my mum to cancer the previous year and without Simon's love and support I don't know how I would have coped. I didn't know then that only one year later I would lose him too. The worst two years of my life! And also the best if that makes sense (because I was with Simon).

Only a few months before our wedding, Simon got the news that the 1st Battalion were being posted to Germany, I had just started a new job so wasn't keen on the idea of being in Germany for two years, so Simon put in for a transfer to the 2nd Battalion, so that we could be together in England. Not long after the transfer, he was given the news that the 2nd Battalion was doing a six-month tour of Northern Ireland, leaving two days after our wedding. I was gutted! But also relieved as we then heard that the 1st Battalion were going into Iraq for the first Gulf War; far more dangerous, I thought. It didn't occur to me that Simon wouldn't came back.

The families officer Keith Robinson arranged a couple of trips for the wives; the first was an assault course and barbecue at Pirbright barracks. It was a great fun day and a big morale boost. The second trip was a day trip to France. That day was Saturday, 17 August 1991, forever engraved in my mind and heart. A day I shall never be able to forget.

We left very early, about 6 a.m., a great bunch of girls off for a day out. We were having a fantastic time, a really good laugh all the time, not knowing what had happened. During the ferry trip home the families officer disappeared for what seemed a long time. When he reappeared he gave some story about there being a problem with the coach driver. One of the wives later told me that she had sussed that something was badly wrong and tried to ask him about it; he more or less confirmed it without speaking out loud but told her she wasn't to say anything. He made the decision to keep quiet until we got back to Dover, which as I recall was another couple of hours away. The trip home was the first time that the army had been able to get word to the families officer about what had happened (no mobile phones in those days).

I've no idea how he must have felt, having to pretend to have a good time all the while knowing what awaited me at Dover, but understandably he felt it would not be right to tell me on the ferry.

When we got to Dover one of my friends was taken off the coach first. I didn't know why at the time, but Keith (FO) wanted to ask her how well she knew me as he was worried about how to tell me and who should be with me when I was told. Another of the wives on the coach was someone I had known during my nurse training, so she was called off the coach too. Then I was led off by Keith. Coming towards me were two WPCs and a man in a suit. I was completely bewildered, I thought I was about to be arrested for bringing back too many fags and too much booze but I hadn't bought any more than anyone else so I couldn't understand why I had been singled out.

I was taken into a sort of toilet block ante-room, and then this man in the suit who introduced himself as the regimental adjutant told me that Simon had been killed. I screamed. I've never screamed before, at least not in any kind of emotional way. Then I just cried and cried.

Simon Ware, Coldstream Guards, killed in an IRA blast in South Armagh. (Carol Richards & Darren Ware)

The adjutant sat on the floor with his head in his hands, not knowing what to say. He looked about the same age as Simon. The two WPCs were crying, and the friend who had come in with me was swearing. Ironically, she was a Protestant girl from Northern Ireland.

Myself and two friends were taken by car to my brother's in Hertfordshire. We stopped at services en route, and unbeknown to the driver we had stopped at the same services as the coach with the rest of the wives on. I remember walking into the restaurant area and seeing their faces. They were all completely devastated. They obviously felt for me while at the same time relieved it wasn't them.

I spent a sleepless night at my brother's, who then took me home to the home I should have been sharing with my husband. We had actually only spent one week together there when he was home for R&R.

I remember the morning he went back to Ireland, he stood in the bedroom doorway and told me he loved me. Little did I know I wouldn't see him again. I spoke to him the Wednesday before he died. He told me he was on operations and wouldn't be able to talk to me until Saturday. When he signed off he told me he loved me just as he always did, but then he added: 'Remember I'll always love you.' I will never forget it because it was almost as if he knew he wasn't coming back and that was the last time I heard his voice.

I went to Heathrow to meet his body being brought home. I was completely unprepared to see his coffin draped in the Union flag emerge from the hold, and it was taken to a waiting hearse. I went to the hearse and placed a red rose on the coffin. I said goodbye to him in my head. I wanted to say goodbye out loud but I couldn't speak. Everyone said I was really brave but I didn't feel very brave. I felt as though my heart had been ripped out.

The funeral was at the Guards' Chapel, the same place that we were married. How different an atmosphere walking behind his coffin to how it had been only months before. I was overwhelmed by the amount of people that were there, a fitting tribute to a truly wonderful person.

Although time has moved on and I have had happy times since, I still think about Simon a lot and every time another soldier dies and I see a Union flag-draped coffin my heart breaks for that soldier's family.

Darren Ware is Simon's brother.

Darren's Story

I am writing this on the thirtieth anniversary year of my brother's murder in South Armagh in August 1991. He was Lance Corporal Simon Ware, 2nd Battalion, Coldstream Guards. I have dealt with his death following an IRA bomb attack in my own way, helped by many things that I have done to deal with it. Many others directly or indirectly involved may not have dealt with it easily, and I respect that. These are my reflections on the past thirty years.

Not every day, but on many days, there is a reminder and there are many different themes: a picture, flag, Remembrance Day, a social media post and much more. I am lucky to say that I have not had any mental issues, merely manageable emotional ones with many tears over the years. I was once asked: 'If you had the opportunity to talk to a converted IRA terrorist, wanting to talk to you, would you?' 'No way!' was my immediate response; I have no reason to allow any gain from those people.

I had the advantage of being a soldier serving with Simon in Northern Ireland at the same time; on that day I was dealing with someone whose house had been targeted in a grenade attack. I was not to know that other soldiers were dealing with a bomb attack which had killed Simon only about 70 miles away. We were both soldiers, taking a high risk, and that helped me deal with it. Other parents, partners, siblings and close friends did not have that advantage of being in the armed forces to know how it worked. My company commander wanted me to transfer out of Northern Ireland to somewhere else less risky; that was not going to happen! I was staying in Northern Ireland, as that was my way of dealing with it. I was not letting the terrorists beat me! I was determined to get my own success against them and I did.

Many years of anger and hatred ensued, not towards Northern Ireland or the genuine people, but just to the IRA! Northern Ireland is a beautiful place and so are the good people. I encountered many of those people and those places in the two and a half years. I have strong resilience which I think has come of many difficult life-changing experiences which I have 'just picked myself up from'. I have had some difficult times, which have kept me strong. I have been a police officer for twenty-three years; twenty of those on the armed response unit; I have experienced many incidents of trauma, death and high risk.

I asked to visit the scene of Simon's murder only six months afterwards; I was not allowed very close and only managed to oversee the wooded area from about 50m away. Close enough to see the gap in the middle where the bomb had detonated, ripping up a few trees. But then I returned twelve years later. I walked the last few hundred metres of the patrol route and I stood in the crater where the bomb had exploded. These are two other examples of my resilience to face my fears and deal with the challenge. Nothing was going to get in my way.

In 2008 and 2009 I took part in three television interviews for Northern Ireland documentaries, with BBC, ITV and Sky wanting me to tell my story. It's what I wanted to do, having been asked. It was not a case of, 'Hey look at me, seeking attention.' I wanted to tell the world how hard things were in Northern Ireland, how people suffered and to tell the story of me, at a time when the Northern Ireland 'Troubles' were about to be forgotten.

On 14 August 2019 I was asked by the Royal British Legion to speak at the Op Banner 50th Anniversary event at the National Armed Forces Memorial … wow what an opportunity I could not turn down. I spoke in front of 1,700 guests in an outdoor event attended by dignitaries including the Defence Secretary and presided over by Alistair Stewart. I was immensely proud to have been asked, but it was the toughest thing I've had to do to tell my story. I was praised by many people that day, including Alistair Stewart (who became a good friend that day) and the head of the Royal British Legion, Lieutenant General James Bashall, who took time to come and speak to me. In 2010 I became a published author with my book *A Rendezvous with the Enemy* (Helion Books). This was a very good way of dealing with it too. I researched for two to three years in many ways and got my story out in a book.

The year 2021 is the thirty-year anniversary when historically 'all the evidence comes out'. I spoke to a senior Member of Parliament last year of my intention to find out all those unanswered questions. His reply was: 'They won't tell you,' but my thoughts were: 'They will have a good job not to, because I am not giving up!'

On 3 January 1992, there was yet another sectarian attack by the UVF, this time in Moy, Co. Tyrone. The small village had been the scene just thirteen days before of the murder of a young student, Robin Farmer, killed by gunmen from the Irish National Liberation Army (INLA). Their original target was Robin's father, who was a former member of the RUC Reserve (RUCR). On this occasion the gunmen from the UVF were acting on flawed intelligence that had linked the McKearney Butchers' shop with Republican paramilitaries.

Just before closing time on a cold dark winter's night, gunmen in a stolen car dashed into the shop, brushing by a cardboard Santa left over from Christmas. The gunmen opened fire, hitting Kevin McKearney (32) in the head and killing him instantly. Also hit was the man's uncle, Jack (69); he was fatally wounded, dying on 4 April. A spokesman for the Loyalist paramilitaries claimed that the attack was carried out against Republicans, when in fact both victims were innocent Catholic civilians.[*] The gunmen, part of the UVF's mid-Ulster Brigade, escaped in a waiting car, later found abandoned in a nearby Protestant area.

Allegedly, the order was given by Billy 'King Rat' Wright, leader of the UVF in mid-Ulster, in succession to Robin 'The Jackal' Jackson. There is also informed speculation that Alan Oliver was involved. Oliver was also the suspect in the triple murder of three Catholics at a mobile shop in Craigavon in 1991. He was named in court documents as being involved in the murders of Eileen Duffy (19), Katrina Rennie (16) and Brian Frizzell (29) in Drumbeg, and also the 1994 murders of Gavin McShane and Shane McArdle, two 17-year-olds who were killed in Keady, Co. Armagh in 1994.

As the gunmen ran out of the butchers to the getaway car, one of them, as later described, took up a military-style stance before firing quite deliberately at two people in a nearby parked car. It has been suggested that this man is likely to have received weapons training previously from a military unit. A little girl in the car was hit as her mother bravely tried to pull her across to her side of the car in order to protect her. That little girl, who was 10 at the time, is Ruth Patterson.

---

[*] A later report by HET concluded: 'Kevin and Jack were not members of any paramilitary groups; they were both completely innocent victims.' The murders were investigated by the police Historical Enquiries Team, amid relatives' claims that a death threat received by the family days before the shooting was not properly investigated by the RUC. In 2012 the HET concluded that police had not done enough to prevent the killings, but found no evidence of collusion with the killers.

Ruth's Story

I was Ruth Emerson at that time, aged 10. We lived about 2 miles away from Moy, and we went there a lot, for school, for shopping etc. You mentioned the killing of Robin Farmer; I was aware of The Troubles and the shootings going on as I was growing up. One night, weeks before the attack in which I was injured, I recall coming downstairs one night, terribly afraid of something. Daddy was there, which was quite unusual as he was often out late, working away. I told him that I was going to be shot; I wasn't sure how I knew, but I was crying, absolutely convinced that it was going to happen. Naturally, Daddy kept trying to reassure me, telling me that I would be all right.

On the day concerned, Mummy drove us into Moy to have a haircut before we went back to school. I was in the front – because I had won the argument about who sat where – and my brother and cousin were in the back. A car was right outside the butcher, blocking the road so that we couldn't get around it. All of a sudden, we heard loud bangs, and someone came running out of the shop; it looked as though they were trying to get into the passenger side of the car in front of us. Then, one of them dropped to one knee before opening fire straight at our windscreen. I remember seeing the sparks fly from the barrel of the gun as I was hit. Mummy grabbed me to pull me over to her side, but the seatbelt prevented her from pulling me very far, as four shots were fired at the car. One of the shots went through the windscreen, leaving a bullet hole in the glass and then hit me, making four separate holes, because of the way my arm was curled; it went in and out and then in and out again!

I am not sure if I passed out, but I remember that Mummy, who was a retired ward sister, went in the doorway to the shop to see if she could help any

Ruth Patterson. (Ruth Patterson)

Scene of the shooting of Ruth Patterson in Moy. (Ruth Patterson)

of the wounded; she hadn't realised that I had been shot or how badly I was hurt. All I really could feel at the time was a stinging sensation and it wasn't until she hugged me that she could feel how much blood there was. I remember the Presbyterian minister, the Reverend Boggs, coming over to us, taking all four of us to his house, where his wife began to bandage me up. Then he put Mummy and I into his car to drive us to the hospital, as he didn't want me travelling in the ambulance to upset me anymore. I was in there for two days, but had to return daily for my wounds to be dressed. It wasn't particularly sore on the day it happened, but it was stinging; and the pain then came, and even today, nearly thirty years later, I still have a funny sensation and pain in my arm. Daddy came to see me when I was in A&E, and I made sure that I said to him: 'See, Daddy; I told you so!'

Over the years, I tried to put it to the back of my mind as best as I could as I was determined not to let it prey on my mind too much. It was never talked about in school, in fact, Kenny Donaldson was in the same class as me for five years and he never knew that I had been shot until we met at SEFF, years later. I believe that two men were arrested for the murders, so Mummy had to appear at the Crumlin Road courthouse in Belfast. Although I went along, I wasn't called to give evidence as I was too young.

You have asked me why that gunman fired at us, and to be honest, I still don't know why they did; maybe they panicked, maybe they thought that we could identify them; I don't know. I don't understand why people just can't get on with each other. I try not to let it get me down and I use my sense of humour to find release from the memories, but it is a difficult event to forget.

I'd also like to add that Daddy and Mummy took me to see Jack McKearney in hospital and he said: 'Isn't it great to be alive,' even though he was lying there paralysed. Unfortunately he passed away a short time after. I always remembered him saying those words and, even as a child, I was amazed that someone so ill was so grateful for life.

How do I feel today; can I find forgiveness? I am still cross, because they never apologised to me for catching me in the gunfire. They have no idea of what they have done to me. Even today, I don't like the dark as I worry that they will come back to finish me off. When it gets dark, I can't see what is going on. After the shooting, I never wanted to go in to Moy again, but Daddy made me go, made me brave and made me face it. Even today when I go there, I feel uneasy and get a sinking feeling in my stomach.

[Author's notes: McKearney's white-coloured butcher shop is still there, sandwiched between an empty building that is for sale, and an off licence, Daly's World of Wine. The white building is a grim reminder of the day on which a Loyalist paramilitary gang carried out two murders, and came close to killing an innocent child.]

From very early on in The Troubles, the Provisional IRA's Army Council decided on a profound but unsurprising change in tactics; their avowed strategy was to kill members of the security forces, whether they were on duty or not. To this end, they allied their long-term intention of destroying the Northern Ireland economy with bombs. They would continue to cause damage to business premises as well as intimidating shoppers. This, not unexpected, change would include the elimination of businessmen and the companies they represented, as well as their ordinary employees. This new target category were overwhelmingly Protestants. Their crimes: building, repairing or refurbishing security bases, for this made them 'agents of the Crown Forces'. These men were tarred with the epithet 'collaborators'.

One such company was Karl Construction, which in 1992 was contracted to repair the bomb-damaged St Lucia barracks in Omagh. Their workers were ferried daily to and from their homes in the Cookstown area. The route was never varied, giving the Provisional IRA a wealth of time in which to plan and execute an attack. At some point on 17 January 1992, two massive landmines were planted close to Teebane Crossroads on the Omagh–Cookstown road. The devices – packed into two plastic bins weighing 1,500lb (680kg) – were linked by a command wire next to a local quarry. The bomb was the brainchild of James Kelly of PIRA's South Londonderry unit, although the attack was claimed by the East Tyrone Brigade, commanded at various times by Kevin Mallon and Jim Lynagh. At the end of the working day, the company-owned minibus set out from Omagh to take their workers home to the Cookstown area.

During the drive home, on a cold, dark winter's evening, a stolen car, driven by a female PIRA operative, pulled ahead of the minibus in order to 'shepherd' it towards the location of the bombs. As the car reached the crossroads, the PIRA member flashed her lights to the bombing team, to give the signal to detonate. She then accelerated away from the slower-moving works bus to avoid being caught in the blast. The bomb was detonated; the massive explosion ripping into the target vehicle, before hurling it into the air. It came down on its side as it continued sliding for another 100ft along the road.

Author and former police officer Colin Breen wrote in the *Belfast Telegraph*: 'No one had ever paid any great attention to them because no one ever thought that they would become a target. We were immediately diverted from where we were. Ambulances were arriving as we got out of the helicopter. The ambulance people were making their way through what was left of the van to see if they could help people.'

Those killed at the scene were William Gary Bleeks (25); Cecil James Caldwell (37), a father of one; Robert Dunseath (25); John Richard McConnell (38), a father of three; Nigel McKee (22); and Robert Irons (61), the father of a grown-up child. The driver, Oswald Gilchrist (44), was rushed to the RVH in Belfast, where medical teams fought for almost four days to save him; he died on the 21st. Part-time soldier Robert Dunseath was a ranger (private) in the Royal Irish Rangers and is listed in the Military ROH as a member of the Territorial Army (TA). Another of the dead was David Harkness (24).

Ruth Forrest is the sister of one of the murdered men, David Harkness.

Ruth's Story

Friday, 17 January 1992, was a dark, dreary day with a constant drizzle and six days after the 24th birthday of my darling only brother, David Harkness. David, who was a Joiner, was the youngest of six, having five older sisters, Heather; Doreen; Dorothea; Louise; and Ruth (me). He had returned from Australia after a two-and-a-half-year period and only came home because Mum was very ill. She had suffered a perforated bowel and pneumonia.

Dave Harkness, killed in the Teebane massacre. (Luke and Ruth Forrest)

There was a scarcity of work for Joiners and reluctantly he took a job with a firm called Karl Construction to make ends meet until he would return to Australia. This firm mainly worked for the security forces. David had been home approximately eight months. Mum, who had made a remarkable recovery, had travelled along with Dad to London to visit her brother and family. David had come to visit me on the Wednesday, 15 January and I had cut his hair and trimmed his beard. We had a great night together, but I wasn't to know that it would be our last together. I had been speaking to him on the phone on the following night, and he said that he was considering not going into work on Friday, 17 January. He told me that if I was passing by the house and the blinds were up, I would know that he went to work. I was passing by the house on my way to style a neighbour's hair and when I went past, the blinds were up.

Just after 5 p.m. that evening, I could hear sirens in the distance and I opened the front door. We were living in temporary accommodation as my husband and I and our children had lost our home and entire contents in another bomb eight months earlier, which the IRA had been responsible for. When I opened the door, a neighbour was also outside and I asked him if he had heard anything. He said that he thought there was a large explosion somewhere outside Cookstown. I knew it was in the direction of my home place, near the Omagh road, Cookstown. I had a gut instinct immediately that something terrible was wrong.

A newsflash came on UVT around 5.45 p.m. and it was saying that three workmen were feared dead. I fell to my knees to the ground, crying to my husband that it was David. He told me to 'not jump to conclusions' but I just knew within myself that it was. I can't explain it, I just knew and I had the most sickening feeling. Immediately, I contacted my three other sisters, who also had the exact same 'gut instinct'. None of us knew exactly who David worked for because it had never been discussed in our house. Meanwhile, Mum and Dad, being in London, also heard the newsflash just as we had. Mum said: 'Cyril, phone home, that's David!' Daddy phoned Cookstown Police Station, but there was so much confusion that they were not sure who owned the van. East Tyrone Brigade of the IRA had made a coded telephone call claiming responsibility but stated that it was 'Henry Brother's van', who were another construction firm who also worked for the security forces. Mum insisted that they get a flight home, but just before they boarded the flight, Cookstown Police confirmed to Dad that 'David Samuel Harkness is on this van', but they didn't know if he was dead or alive. Mum and Dad flew home, not knowing, until they landed in Belfast International Airport, what had happened to their darling only son.

Back home, my sisters and I were ringing frantically trying to get in touch with David at home. There was no response; there were no mobile phones at that time. At approximately 8.30 p.m., my sister Louise phoned me; she said: 'Ruth, I want you to prepare yourself for the worst; my husband has checked every hospital in Northern Ireland and no one has David.' I naïvely thought he could be helping someone at the roadside. She then stated: 'The hospitals don't accept the dead.' I was praying that David would be alive, no matter how serious his injuries were. How selfish of me. At exactly 9 p.m., my sister Heather phoned; her exact words were: 'Ruth, it's all over, David is dead.'

Life changed dramatically for us all after the death of David. He was a quiet, inoffensive, beautiful soul who didn't deserve to be taken in such a selfish and needless manner. He never got the opportunity to enjoy married life; have a family of his own; and has missed out on our children and grandchildren. Mum and Dad did not get enough time with their beloved son. Dad passed away on 22 March 2006, aged 72 years. Mum passed away on 28 February 2012, aged 79 years. They never got justice for the murder of their son. Twenty-five years later, we are no further forward, even though we were assured by the highest authorities that 'there would be no stone left unturned'.

It has been an extremely difficult journey for so many people, but for me, God has been my guide and refuge along with the support of my husband, Adrian, my children, Aaron, Clarke, Luke and Stuart, my sisters, my father-in-law, Ted, my grandchildren and extended family and friends.

✦

On 3 December 1992, the IRA's England team struck at the capital of the North-West: Manchester, detonating two bombs. Their objective was to wreck the city's economy by intimidating northern folk, making them too nervous to spend their money. The British economy traditionally has a much-needed boost at Christmas time; this meant that the Provisionals had a double-edged sword: terror and economic ruin. The bombs were timed to explode at the height of rush hour. When they did, it caused traffic chaos and spread pandemonium among city centre workers and shoppers alike. The first bomb exploded in the city's Parsonage commercial district, near a tax office. Sixty-five people were injured by flying glass as they sought refuge near the Anglican Cathedral and Renaissance Hotel following the first blast. The second bomb was cynically designed to catch those who were escaping from the first.

It was the IRA at its most cynical. Amongst sixty-five people injured in the second blast was Neil Tattershall. He had been moved to what was thought to be a safer point after the initial blast. The location and timing of the two bombs was deliberately chosen by the IRA to maximise casualties.

Manchester bomb, 3 December 1992. (Neil Tattershall)

Neil's Words

It was coming up to Christmas and I had recently been made redundant, so I had found part-time work with Argos in the Arndale Centre. My girlfriend was pregnant with my daughter, so I very much needed to bring some money in. On that particular day, I had gone into Manchester on the bus, oblivious to the fact that there was an IRA bomb warning right where I was working. In fact, just before I got there, a bomb had exploded behind Kendals at about 8.30. As I arrived, people were just going about their normal daily routines, so unperturbed, I went into the canteen for a quick cuppa. We were then told to immediately evacuate the store and assemble in St Anne's Square. As we did so, several police officers came rushing over and informed us that the IRA had telephoned with a warning that there was a second bomb in a bin. Apparently, the only safe place was in front of the Renaissance Hotel, so off we went, but once there we were told that that the hotel had also been targeted. We were then moved into Cateaton Street, where several found a wall to sit on in order to make ourselves as comfortable as possible.

The atmosphere was fairly jocular and people were joking that the pubs would be open soon. I jumped down from the wall, intending to walk towards the grass verge, when there was an enormous bang! The bomb had been placed behind the wall and it suddenly went off. I instinctively covered my head, and then felt a huge thump in my back, but there was no pain; it was strange, it felt as though I was in a vacuum and I was aware that the building had blown out. Everyone was running; I felt that I should too, but I couldn't move; I was rooted to the spot.

It was only seconds, but then two people – I now know to have been a man and a woman – grabbed me and dragged me to safety. As they did so, a policeman took me and told them to go, and I remember him getting me down a ramp next to Lloyds Bank. I was aware of four or five people in forensic boiler suits, milling around me to help. I could see that I was losing a lot of blood, and one of the officers removed some huge shards of glass and wood out of my back, presumably from one of the windows which had hit me in the blast. As they did so, the blood just began to flow out of me as I drifted in and out of consciousness, forcing one of the officers to keep slapping me in the face to keep me awake as I just wanted to sleep. I experienced what I call a series of 'white outs' as people would suddenly be in front of me but the next second were dozens of yards away.

At that moment, a bomb disposal officer came over and told the police to get away as there was another bomb in the area. The officers refused and to my horror, the bomb disposal guy said: 'Leave him alone; he is fucking dying anyway!' I remember looking at my legs, which were drenched in blood, thinking that I was going to die. I thought about my fiancée and my unborn child and how she would manage without a dad and I thought about my mum and my dad. It was due to the courage of the police officer with me that I got to the ambulance, which had bravely driven into the danger zone. As I was put on board, the adrenaline kicked in and I was shaking like a leaf. From there, I was taken to Manchester Royal Infirmary (MRI) and I could see lots of the 'walking wounded', including several of my workmates; a girl I knew just screamed out: 'Oh, my God, it's Neil' and tried to come to me, but the medical staff kept them away. Mum and Dad and my sister arrived not long afterwards, having been alerted by the police.

Neil Tattershall (centre). (SEFF)

Things just seemed to go so fast as there were many concerns about my survival. Indeed at one stage, a Catholic priest asked my parents if he could have a word with them in private away from me, presumably to get their consent to give me the last rites? I remember that Mum was crying and it was all a blur. I would like to point out that there were dozens of reporters besieging the hospital to get to speak to me and several tried to get in by disguising themselves as doctors!

The whole thing damaged me emotionally as well as physically and the psychiatrist I saw didn't help when he asked me if I was a member of the IRA. The follow-up by the police was no better as they investigated if myself or my family had any links with the very bombing group who had done their best to kill me! Because of the interest from dozens of reporters, we were all becoming fed up and when the *Manchester Evening News* asked to run an exclusive interview with me in order to get the rest of them off my back, I jumped at the chance. However, when it happened, it was just too much for me and I had to go hide in a park for around seven hours.

I had a long period of therapy, back treatment etc., but in the end I was just thrown back into society without any acknowledgement that I was suffering from flashbacks and PTSD. Not long after, my dad died and I went through hell, attending a PTSD course at Withington Hospital, which I later learned was about suicide prevention. It screwed me up and I couldn't handle any sort of relationship. I lost my home and I was living rough under a stairwell at Manchester Airport for a while. The *Daily Express* came to see me and took some photos of where I was sleeping. From that, Kenny Donaldson of SEFF got in touch but I couldn't believe that anyone wanted to help me, so I kept hanging up on him, especially when I heard his Northern Irish accent. Thankfully, he persisted and he promised me that he was going to help me and he did.

I get asked a lot if I forgive the IRA, but to be honest I say no; I cannot forgive them. My daughter has never known me as the man I was before the bomb; 3 December 1992 was the day that I died.

✦

Thomas Begley was a PIRA gunman from the Nationalist Ardoyne area; he was to later achieve infamy when he killed himself and nine others in a bomb blast. The outrage took place at Frizzell's Fishmongers' shop on Shankill Road, Belfast, on 23 October 1993. Some ten months earlier, on the evening of 30 December 1992, Begley and two other gunmen, in a stolen red Ford Sierra, left a safe house in the Republican Ardoyne area. Around dinner time, they made the 1-mile journey to Westland Road, Belfast. They parked very close to the house of Private Steven Archibald Waller (23), a young full-time soldier from the Royal Irish, home on leave from Episkopi in Cyprus. He was relaxing at his home between Cavehill Road and Cliftonville Golf Club. As he watched *Neighbours* on TV with his family and wife, Tracey – they had been married just eight months – there was a knock at the door.

Mrs Waller recalled hearing someone ask for her sister-in-law, Pamela, who had house-sat for her while they were in Cyprus. Mrs Waller had become suspicious of the two men on the doorstep and tried to slam the door shut, but they managed to force it open. A 'smirking' man pushed his weapon through the partially open door, firing either side of her. She would later recognise and identify one of them as Thomas Begley. Although she was unable to identify the second gunman, this author understands from a former RUC source that it was probably Sean Kelly, who was one of the bombing team at Frizzell's with Begley the following year. They fired fourteen rounds from an AK-47 at her unarmed husband, hitting him six times. He was mortally wounded and collapsed on the lounge floor. Begley and the other man ran back to the car, which then raced away, later being abandoned in the Nationalist Ardoyne. It is thought that one of the murder gang was a woman.

The young soldier died within hours despite medical treatment at the Mater Hospital on Crumlin Road. His funeral was held at Roselawn Cemetery in Castlereagh, Belfast. His killers were described by an SDLP leader as 'gangsters' and local councillor Nelson McCausland said: 'How many more deaths will there have to be and how much more destruction before the Government effectively cracks down on terrorism?' Another local politician told UTV: 'People are going around at this time of year wishing each other a merry Christmas and a happy new year, but for this family and this estate, there's not too much that is merry or happy about it. It is a tragic situation.' Private Waller's father had been shot dead in an internal Loyalist paramilitary feud in the Shankill Road area on 29 November 1975.

The same weapon was also used in March the following year when PIRA gunmen shot UFF member Norman Truesdale. The father of four was shot dead by the Provisionals in his shop at the junction of the Oldpark Road and Century Street, Belfast, close to the local public library. It is thought that IRA commander Eddie Copeland dispatched a three-man unit alleged to include Begley to the sectarian interface to kill Truesdale.

Tracey Magill is the widow of Steven Waller.

Tracey's Story

On the day of the murder of my husband, my brother came to our house at 79 Westland Road to take us to get some food shopping. Later on in the day I went into Belfast with him and my mum. Steven went to the local pub and we met up again there after 4 p.m. It wasn't until after Steven was killed that my brother told me that both himself and Steven had seen two men parked facing the house[*] but that the odd manner in which they were

Steven Waller, Royal Irish, murdered by the IRA. (Tracey Magill)

changing a wheel seemed quite suspicious. It is probable that Begley and another man were doing a 'dummy run' before the attack at the house later on that evening, a fact later confirmed by the RUC.

We got home and I made a proper Ulster fry-up for dinner; around 1835 there was a knock at the door. Before I opened the door a bit I asked who was there. A voice said: 'Is Pamela there?'[**] I was about to say that he should try her mum's house, which was close by, but before I could speak, my eyes were drawn to a large gun which he was cradling. There was one man – whom I know to be Thomas Begley – and to his side was another man who looked familiar. As I was trying to take in what I was seeing, I looked at his face again and I saw that he was smirking. At that moment I pushed my back against the door to try to keep it closed whilst shouting to Steven to get out.

---

[*] A Belfast woman – Jacqueline Donnelley – was interviewed by the RUC but released without charge due to insufficient evidence, following allegations that she was scouting the area close to the scene of the attack. It is alleged that she approached a retired policeman and his family asking where 79 Westland Road was. She appeared in court alongside another person who was charged with hijacking the car used in the murder.

[**] The police did say that Pamela definitely was a link but didn't have any concrete evidence to charge her.

Then Steven appeared in the hallway and the gunmen began firing. As my hands were at the same level as the gun, I received gunpowder burns to both hands. I also remember that one of the men reached around the door and grabbed my head in both hands. The first shot hit him in the arm, causing him to cry out: 'Tracey: I've been shot; get out!' Another shot him in the thigh, after which he was hit three times in the stomach; finally he was hit again in the left side and he went down. I was in a state of shock but still trying with all my might to keep the door closed. I felt the tension in the door relax and realised that they had left. What I didn't realise at the time was that he had been hit in an artery and he was bleeding to death.

I must have gone into survival mode, as I remember jumping over Steven before running outside and meeting a neighbour, who then went in the house to Steven. I was terrified! I then went and telephoned for an ambulance from Steven's mum's house; the dispatcher told me it had already been telephoned through multiple times. I did try to go back into the house when the police and paramedics arrived, but they wouldn't let me as they were working on Steven. I also remember that I had lost a slipper in my flight and that my gold chains had been ripped off in the struggle at the front door. My brother arrived and I asked him to ride in the ambulance with Steven. The last words Steven ever spoke was to my brother in the ambulance, and it was to ask if I was OK. After everything his only concern was me. That was just him all over the world, making sure I was OK.

We got to the Mater Hospital, where we were put into a family room and waited and waited. All the while I was praying: 'Please let him live, let him live.' I just kept thinking that all this wasn't happening. At about 2145, one of the surgeons walked into the room. At this, my sister tried to leave as she knew that it wasn't going to be good news. He just told us that Steven had severe internal bleeding and was dead. I just screamed and carried on screaming. We were taken up to see him on another floor. There is one thing which I will never forget: he was normally of a naturally ruddy complexion, but with the sheet pulled up to his throat, his face was very pale.

We went back to Mum's. Although I had to go home first to check on our cat, as she was upstairs when the shooting began. As I entered,

I could see a massive patch of blood on the carpet, with bullet holes up the stairs, in the kitchen and in the lounge. There were also loads of blood-stained bandages lying around where they had been discarded by the medics as they frantically fought to save Steven. It just hit me that all of my plans with Steven, children, everything, now would never happen. I didn't sleep much that night as I felt that my heart had been wrenched out of my body. It was especially bad when the TV news showed photos of our

Steven Waller. (Tracey Magill)

house as they discussed the murder. The next day, we went down to Antrim Road RUC station, where I helped make up an identikit photo of the killers. In the days following, we went to Donegall Pass RUC station to take part in an identity parade, but they definitely didn't have any of the men concerned.

Steven had a funeral with full military honours; some of his comrades from the regiment fired a volley of shots over his coffin, but the gunfire scared the life out of me. Ian Paisley and Nigel Dodds, MP, came to the house as well as the funeral; the latter gave me a cheque to help me out financially. I remember staying in the lounge where Steven's coffin was the night before the funeral with my brother and my dad and laughing out loud as though he was in on the conversation with us. We had been due back to Cyprus on 4 January, but were delayed until the 6th. When we arrived at the married quarters, the painters, who were Cypriot, had painted the outside of the quarters. However, they had also managed to get inside and all of our family jewellery, including Steven's dad's ring, had been stolen, and the thieves – who were never caught – had stolen a carriage clock, which was the first thing I'd noticed missing. I just kept wondering, 'What else can go wrong?' I had to explain the theft of Steven's ring, a ring which belonged to his dad, to Steven's mum, which wasn't easy.

Back in Northern Ireland, I had this feeling that I knew one of the killers. I had seen him before, but I couldn't remember when. Then it hit me. On a number of occasions, my sister-in-law Pamela would go off for days and no one knew where she was, much to her mum's dismay. She either just turned up again out of the blue usually, or her mum would go looking for her. On one such occasion a friend of hers knocked on my door and told me she was down in the Waterworks in North Belfast. I went down to get her back home again and I saw two men brazenly lying on the grass, on their sides. One of them, I distinctly remember, smirked at me; it was Thomas Begley. This took place back in May/early June 1992. The guy lying beside him was the other person I seen at the door the night of the murder. I did report this to the RUC, but heard no more about it. Then, after the Shankill bombing in October of that year, I saw Begley's face staring back at me from the pages of the *Belfast Newsletter*. It was the same man in my photofit; the same man who killed my husband. I felt sick at what I was seeing.

I did give a statement to the police. They told me that the likeness of the photofit to the picture in the newspaper was: 'A better likeness I couldn't have given.' They came out a few weeks later to tell me, just in case I'd heard, that Thomas Begley wasn't an informer, as there had been talk of it. Yes, I had heard it and had wondered why he wasn't in any of the line-ups I'd attended straight after the murder. Interestingly enough, there was a newspaper report that Begley had been stopped and questioned a week before the Frizzell's bombing. In his car was a bag of whelks, which he had purchased from the same shop he would bomb a week later. It had clearly been a dummy run, but if it was Mr Frizzell himself who served him, how could he have even imagined that his 'customer' would wreck his shop and so many lives a short while later?

Incidentally, I had to give evidence at the later court case. On the second day, and as we were leaving the court, all their supporters in the gallery were jeering down at me and the police took me out the back door.

Do I forgive them? No never; I will never forgive them as long as I live. People say you have to forgive to be able to move on, but I can't and won't forgive them for the impact which it has had on my life. I have suffered every day since. Due to my vulnerability after Steven's murder I've had several abusive relationships, which almost destroyed me, but with true Northern Irish spirit I've got up, brushed myself down and started all over again, numerously. I don't even have to close my eyes to see a rerun of that day. I often think what might have happened in my life had Steven not been murdered; what if? You never get over it, you just learn to live with it. I was diagnosed with PTSD last year and although I know that I can talk about it, sometimes I have to shut my mind down and remember I'm in 2020 not 30 December 1992 where all my nightmares and trauma are. I even had to mentally prepare to speak to you.

✦

On Saturday, 23 October 1993 – as referred to in the above account – a three-man team from the Provisional IRA in the Ardoyne drove a stolen car to Berlin Street just off the Shankill Road. While the driver remained in the parked car, two men – Thomas 'Bootsey' Begley (23) and Sean Kelly, who was 21 at the time – set out to walk the short distance to Frizzell's Fisheries, which was expected to be packed with Saturday shoppers. Begley was carrying a haversack, inside which was a 5lb (2.3kg) bomb and a detonator. The bomb had been assembled by a PIRA unit in the Short Strand district of Belfast, before being transported to a sister unit across the city in the Ardoyne. The haversack was carried in a stolen taxi, driven by an unknown man, plus the bombing team. The Provisionals, in seeking to provide justification for the attack, claimed that the real targets were not Saturday afternoon shoppers. Apologists for the bombing maintained that the leading lights of the UFF's 'C' company met on Saturdays in a room above the shop. They alleged that these meetings included the likes of Johnny 'Mad Dog' Adair and Steven 'Top Gun' McKeag. The IRA's plan was to wipe out the senior members of a sectarian murder gang, with any civilian casualties being 'collateral damage'.

Just before 1300 hours the car containing the bombing team parked up on Berlin Street, roughly halfway between Riga Street and Pernau Street, just off the Shankill Road. Begley and Kelly – dressed in white coats – began to walk the short distance to Frizzell's, mingling in with the crowds. As expected, the shop was packed with Saturday shoppers; in

Aftermath of the Frizzell's bomb. (Belfast Telegraph)

Memorial outside the former Frizzell's. (Ken Wharton)

fact it would have been more of a surprise had it not been so. Kelly positioned himself in the doorway as Begley pushed his way through the throng of shoppers, all patiently waiting their turn to be served by either Desmond Frizzell or his daughter, Sharon McBride.

One can only speculate if those about to die reluctantly moved to one side as Begley roughly pushed past them; did they grumble at a possible queue jumper or did they shrug their shoulders at the sight of another fish man dropping off supplies? Only the dead can answer these questions. Again, it can only be mere conjecture, but did Begley hesitate for a split second before he triggered the device; did he think that he was striking a blow for Irish unity? Did he think that he was going to wipe out the leading lights of the UFF? Like the innocent dead, the guilty dead are equally unable to speak for themselves. He reached inside the haversack to set what he thought was a nine-second timer. However, it exploded instantly, killing him as well as nine other innocent shoppers.

The nine innocent civilians killed that day were: John Desmond Frizzell (63), a father of three, the eponymous fishmonger from Kilcoole Park; his daughter, Sharon McBride (29), who served in her dad's shop, mother of a small child; George Williamson (63) and his wife, Gillian (49), parents of two, from Drumard Park, Lisburn, who were in Belfast shopping for curtains for their new house; Michael 'Minnie' Morrison (27) and his partner, Evelyn Baird (27), parents of three, and their little girl, Michelle Baird (7), from the Forthriver area. They were on the Shankill for two specific reasons: to buy a wreath as Michael's father had died two days earlier, and to buy some crab sticks, their favourite delicacy. Leanne Murray (13) from the Shankill was in Frizzell's to buy whelks, her favourite snacks; her mother and stepfather were next door in the fruit and veg shop. All nine were living their lives as best they could under the awful and violent conditions visited upon Ulster by both sets of paramilitaries. In this particular incident, the fault lay squarely with the Republicans, with the ultimate tragedy that their dreams of a united Ireland were all but unachievable by this stage of the conflict. The final victim, Wilma McKee (38), was a mother of two, from Westway Gardens, just over a mile away from the shop. She died the following day from her terrible injuries.

Michelle Williamson is the daughter of George and Gillian Williamson, who were killed in the blast.

Michelle's Story

It was a sunny Saturday morning as my mother and father decided to go shopping in Belfast for some fabric to make curtains for their new home. They had only just moved in the previous day. Normally I would have gone along with them, as Mum and I shared an interest in sewing and crafts. She taught me to sew and knit and we loved to go around the fabric shops in Belfast looking for a bargain, but on this day, I was busy finishing curtains for my own home.

The television was switched on and I was half listening to it in the background, but then a newsflash interrupted the programme to announce that a bomb had gone off in Belfast. This was unfortunately a common occurrence and didn't concern me too much, but I remember thinking: 'I hope mum and dad don't get caught up in the chaos.' I carried on with what I was doing but as the afternoon wore on, I started to worry as they said they wouldn't be long. Then at about 5 p.m., there was a loud knock at the door. I knew it wasn't mum and dad as they wouldn't have knocked. As I came down the stairs I saw the unmistakable silhouette of a policeman. My heart pounded as I opened the door.

A policeman asked me: 'Are you Michelle Williamson?' I answered: 'Where's Mum and Dad?' but he kept asking me if I was Michelle Williamson? When I eventually said yes, he told me my mum and dad had been caught up in an explosion on the Shankill Road in Belfast. He told me that Dad had severe head injuries and that Mum was with him; he also told me to go to the Royal Victoria Hospital as soon as possible. I was anxious, but from the way that he phrased things, I presumed Mum was OK and was looking after Dad.

The next thing I remember is being in a small room at the hospital and a doctor was telling me that Dad had sustained severe head injuries and was already in a coma on arrival. Then he announced that he had died just before I got there; I asked where my mum was, as I had been told she was there.

Nobody seemed to know, so they started ringing around all the hospitals in Belfast to find her. I wanted to see Dad, so they led me to the corner of a corridor, where behind a screen lay my father. Until my dying day, I will not forget that image; seeing my daddy lying there on his own with his head bandaged and blood seeping onto the pillow. I held his hand, kissed him gently on the cheek and told him how much I loved him and said goodbye. Next thing I remember is being back home in Lisburn awaiting news of where Mum was, but eventually at about 10.30 p.m., word came through that Mum had been found and that she was in the mortuary in Foster Green hospital. She had died at the scene and had been lying on her own all day. I wanted to go and be with her, but my relatives wouldn't let me go as she was so badly injured. I will regret that for the rest of my days!

Since that awful day my life has changed in so many ways; I am no longer the carefree girl I used to be. My heart is full of pain at the loss of my parents, but I have so much anger and hatred of those that carried out this heinous atrocity and for all that they claim to stand for. Whenever I see Gerry Adams, my blood boils! Words cannot describe the hatred and contempt I feel towards him and his ilk. I cannot forgive, and I will never forget what they did to my family.

It is now approaching the twenty-fifth anniversary of that awful day. I still hurt, and I still miss my mum and dad and I still spit venom at Adams and his fellow killers. I no longer live in Lisburn, as I was hounded by the press after I tried to challenge the early release of Sean Kelly and all the injustices innocent victims have had to swallow, whilst the killers parade themselves like movie stars! But my life has changed too; I married and became a stepmum to my husband's son. I never had the chance to have my Dad walk me down the aisle and give me away, nor did my husband and my stepson get the opportunity to meet my mother and father. I think they would have approved that I married a proud Ulsterman, and both he and his parents have stood by me and supported me through some very tough times when nobody else seemed to care. Sometimes the only thing that keeps me going is knowing that my mum and dad are looking down on me and that we will meet again someday, and that Adams, Kelly and Begley will all be joining McGuinness in hell.

✦

Charlie Butler is the uncle of Evelyn Baird, who was killed on that terrible day with her partner and their 7-year-old daughter Michelle Baird.

Charlie's Story

I was born in the Shankill and have spent all of my life here, at one time living in Seventh Street just up from North Howard Street Mill where the soldiers were. The whole area was known as the 'Black Pad' with reference to when the Black Forge was working. The Army took over the old forge and turned it into a base.

When the bomb went off on that October day in 1993, I was 39 and ran a taxi company based on the Woodvale Road, whilst living in Glencairn. My wife was out shopping that Saturday afternoon, so I picked her up as requested near Berlin Street. Just as I was setting off up this street, the radio crackled into life warning us that a bomb had gone off on the Shankill Road. I don't think that I heard the blast, but as I stepped out of the car, all I could see were clouds of dust everywhere. I yelled to my wife: 'Sit there; don't move,' and began to run towards the main road. I didn't know this then, but around the time that I stopped in Berlin Street, the IRA getaway car driver was heading in the opposite direction.

As I said, there was nothing but smoke, but as I got close to Frizzell's, I saw a woman lying in the road with severe head injuries; someone was attending to her. I then looked at where the shop was, but all I could see through the smoke was a huge gaping hole, walls, floors, everything all collapsed. Now you must remember that this wasn't the first indiscriminate bomb on the Shankill – it was the fifth! I had seen the IRA blow up the Bayardo Bar, the Mountainview Tavern, the Four Step Inn and the Balmoral Furniture shop; and now Frizzell's.[*]

I ran over to a huge mound of rubble, where there were already people there: police, soldiers as well as ordinary civilians were tearing at the bricks and timber to find survivors. All that was in my head was to help, so I joined in. We had been digging for about twenty minutes when I spotted under the bricks a black, curly mop of hair. It was just so surreal. I screamed out for a medic to help me and we dug down

---

[*] The attacks to which Charlie refers are as follows and were all carried out by the Provisional IRA:

The bombing of the Four Step Inn took place on 29 September 1971; two Protestant civilians were killed.

The Balmoral Furniture Company bombing took place on 11 December 1971, killing four civilians – one of whom was a Catholic – and included two small children.

The bombing of the Mountainview Tavern happened on 5 April 1975; the blast killed four Protestant civilians and one Loyalist paramilitary.

The Bayardo Bar attack took place on 13 August 1975; it killed four Protestant civilians and one Loyalist paramilitary.

to find a very still body. Although I didn't know it at the time, it was Leanne Murray. Do you know, it took me twenty-five years before I could bring myself to tell her mum that it was me who found her, although she already knew. We put Leanne on a stretcher. God forgive me, it will be with me to my grave. The bones were shattered; it was just like jelly; the poor wee girl just rolled off the stretcher. We put her back, covering her with a blanket, before we carried her to one of the ambu-

Michael 'Minnie' Morrison, Evelyn Baird (27), and Michelle Baird. (Charlie Butler)

lances. I remember that there were four of them. Inside each one was a body, covered in a blood-stained white sheet. Everywhere you looked there were arms, legs, feet; it was just terrible.

We kept digging and digging and digging for several hours. Just then, someone called out 'Quiet' so we all went silent. They had found another body; I could see a pinky-coloured coat, but we were told to back off as there was a risk of trampling over people buried underneath us. I didn't realise at the time, but that pinky-coloured coat had enormous personal significance to me. Remember that the bomb went off at exactly 1303; we didn't have everything cleared until 1730.

We were told that the Mater Hospital had announced that there were eight[*] dead and 240 injured. I was exhausted and joined a few others in the pub, where I sank a few large ones before going home, still covered head to toe in dust. When I got there, there were several messages as friends had seen me on the television news carrying poor little Leanne. I want to say this, but Mr Frizzell was a good, Christian man. He loved kids and he would always have crab sticks in for them.

I was just sitting in the bath – I can't even remember what I was thinking – trying to get the dirt off me, when my wife came in to tell

---

[*] A ninth civilian, Wilma McKee, died in hospital the day after the blast.

me that my niece, Evelyn, her partner, Michael as well as her daughter, Michelle, hadn't returned home from their shopping trip. I wasn't too worried as I thought that they might just be up the town, enjoying themselves. Anyway, I popped next door to my sister, who was also called Evelyn – we called her 'big Evelyn' and my niece was 'wee Evelyn' – to see if they were OK. I reassured them that in all the time that I had been on the rescue work, I hadn't seen them. Shortly afterwards, an RUC detective came to the door, asking for photos, identifying marks, what type of clothing the three had been wearing that day. My sister told him that Michelle had been wearing a pink coat. It hit me like a ton of bricks. I turned to my nephew Joe and said: 'They're dead,' but he told me not to say that. I explained that I had seen the pink coat in the rubble and that it couldn't have been a coincidence.

The detective returned, explaining that there were three bodies in Foster Green mortuary; they needed someone to go and identify them. Joe and my brother-in-law, Jim, went off, where they were able to identify all three; they had perished in the blast. When they broke the news to us, it was terrible, it was devastating. I think that I had felt it more because I was at the scene and didn't even see that members of my own family were there. It turned out that the three of them were on the Shankill Road, and little Michelle ran into the shop as she loved crab sticks, so Michael and Evelyn followed her. As they did so, Begley pushed past them and then the bomb went off. We don't believe for a minute the IRA story that they wanted to kill the UDA leaders who were supposed to be meeting above the shop. Their idea was to rip out the hearts of the people on the Shankill, but they never managed it.

When the coffins were brought home, they were sealed because of the terrible injuries. As you know, it is a big thing in Northern Ireland to have open coffins so that we can say our proper goodbyes, so this was hard, hard to take in. I have nine sisters and four brothers; we are a big, strong family, but it was even harder for us. Some of us left the wake early on to see Gena Murray, mother of the other murdered little girl; she was alone with her son, Gary, so we tried to comfort them.

Do I forgive the bombers? No, I can never ever forgive them for what they did. To be honest, as time went on, I started to think about the bombers' families; what did the parents of Begley and Kelly feel about their sons being mass murderers of women and children? Not so long ago, I spoke to a journalist about a Sinn Fein plan to place a plaque to honour Begley. Through him, I sent a message to the parents of Begley and asked them not to attend the ceremony, and the message came back that they wouldn't go. Then they appeared on stage at the ceremony to 'honour' a murderer. It was a kick in the teeth for all the Shankill families who lost loved ones in the blast. We held a little protest at the ceremony and one of them threw a pipe bomb at us, which fortunately didn't explode. That speaks more about them than it does us.

The bombing of Frizzell's shocked the whole world; we like to think that it was the beginning of the end.

✦

Ian Millar was a detective constable in the RUC at the time.

Ian's Story

I was on early shift that day at Tennant Road police station, when, suddenly there was burst of radio transmission; there had just been a huge explosion on the Shankill Road. We immediately grabbed our flak jackets and weapons, boarded our vehicle and proceeded to the scene. As we exited left onto the Shankill Road, I could see immediately a massive scene of devastation just a few hundred yards away. As we neared, we could see tons of rubble spread all over the road; far too many people to count, either lying on the road or milling about totally dazed. I drove as close as I could, and I could see that there was a wide gap in the buildings where Frizzell's fish shop and the wallpaper shop next to it used to be. When I got out of my vehicle, I was immediately aware of many people shouting and screaming in pain, with injured people lying about, some bleeding, others obviously with other physical injuries but mostly a huge pile of rubble where the pavement area was.

There were quite a few other police and Army vehicles already arriving at the scene and I could hear sirens from other emergency vehicles on their way. I saw many of my colleagues attending to the injured on the road, including one man who was wearing a white coat; the sort that a fishmonger would wear. This, I found out later was Sean Kelly, one of the two bombers who had carried the bomb into the fish shop, but I took no more notice of him at that time. It took a few minutes for people to gather themselves, including myself. There was too much happening at once to immediately take it all in. Once we had gathered ourselves, we could hear many people saying that there were people trapped under the huge piles of rubble on the pavement and in the shop itself. Some members of the public were already clearing away some of the rubble to get to those buried, so we formed into an orderly clearing party.

I was at the shop front, next to a pile of rubble. Close to me was a colleague, a fireman and a paramedic. We lifted a pile of rubble and passed them in a chain to members of the public on the roadway. After a while – time had stopped for me – I uncovered what was obviously the foot of a female child who was wearing a white-coloured boot. Eventually, we uncovered her full body, but as we did, the fireman uncovered the head of a woman and detected a pulse. Because the poor little girl was clearly dead, we knew that we had to concentrate on the one who might survive. What happened next will haunt me to the day I die. To lift the rubble off the woman, I had to stand on the body of the child; I had no choice. This was not done out of callousness, but I had to get the rubble off the woman. Because of the crush injuries to the child, she had no bones left and it felt like I was standing on a bag of jelly; I will never forget that, and my heart is breaking even now whilst I am writing about it. Seconds later, the fireman announced that the woman was dead also and when I looked around, someone had removed the child's body. We continued to dig the woman out and she was gently removed. It got even worse, as under the rubble we found another young girl who was also dead and her body too was removed. Then we found the dead body of a man; the time just blurred, and I have no idea of how long we were there, and you must remember that there was 2 or 3ft of rubble; tons of it, lying on top of these poor people.

During the clearing, I found a handgun – obviously from the area of the explosion – so I passed this to a fellow officer. The Salvation Army had arrived and were passing out much-needed drinks of water. We were now into the ruined shop, where we found the body of a man, but couldn't move him as a large roof beam was trapping him; in fact, we had to get on 'all fours' to lift the beam enough to release him; it was hard taking that weight on my back. Time continued to fly by, but it was too hectic for us to even notice. Then we reached where the stairs had been, and obviously the seat of the explosion. There, in several lumps, were bloodied human remains. I helped a fireman to hold open a body bag whilst other firemen literally shovelled up the lumps. Later, I was to find that this was Begley the bomber, who was blown to pieces by his own bomb. You will recall Gerry Adams later carrying the coffin of this 'freedom fighter'.

At this point I was totally exhausted and could take no more, so I walked back to Tennent Street RUC station, some five hours after we had left to attend the explosion. I went to the canteen and found many of my colleagues there in a similar condition to what I was in. I had a cup of tea and got changed into my civilian clothes. Some of my equipment (gun belt, personal weapon etc.) and my uniform and boots were covered in dust and filth, so I put them in a bag to take home to clean.

It wasn't until 2001 when, because of many other incidents, I was diagnosed with PTSD. I still struggle with this today and it is only through my own efforts to gain expert psychological treatment that I manage to keep my feelings under control. I must point out that the actions of the members of the public and of the emergency services on that day were nothing short of magnificent. This was after a few years of gradually sliding into an abyss, doing things that I would not normally do such as having extra-marital affairs, racking up debts, etc. In the intervening years, my marriage broke down. I went through a period of ten years where I felt like I had been abducted by aliens. My life totally fell apart. But for the fact that I have an amazing circle of friends and family and a loving and understanding wife, I would not be here today.

At the end of June 2019, I left home with the intention of killing myself. It was only through excellent intervention of mental health workers and a two-week stay in a mental health ward at the Ulster Hospital in Belfast that I was able to come to terms with my thoughts. I have had years of counselling, including EMDR and CBT, but even today, the blanket of depression/PTSD can strike from nowhere. I do not forgive and I do not forget. I feel badly let down by politicians of all shades. The 'good guys' are now portrayed as the 'bad guys' and vice-versa.

✦

On the morning of 26 October 1993, just two days after the terrible blast at Frizzell's, the UFF struck at the council cleansing depot at Lower Kennedy Way in Andersonstown. The attack was the brainchild of Johnny Adair, head of the UFF's 'C' company. Adair had allegedly planned the attack some time before, so it was somewhat self-serving for the Loyalist terror group to label it a retaliation for the events on the Shankill Road the previous weekend. It is alleged that Adair dispatched Gary 'Smickers' Smyth and Robert 'Rab' Bradshaw along with Thomas Beggs* in a stolen taxi to the home of Wendy Davies in Moltke Street near Belfast's City Hospital. The following morning at 0745 hours, the gang arrived outside the depot to carry out the attack.

Adair, who was known to brazenly travel into Nationalist areas to carry out reconnaissance work, knew the optimum time to make the attack. He was aware that this particular time would be the moment that some workers would be reporting for work, while others would be in the canteen enjoying a hot drink before work commenced.

Armed with a pistol and an automatic weapon, clad in yellow high-visibility jackets, the two men ran through the gates and opened fire; James Cameron (54) from Lenadoon, a father of three, was hit and died almost immediately. Shouting sectarian slogans, they fired indiscriminately at the twenty or so workers in the yard. Seconds later, Mark Rodgers (28), a father of two, also from Lenadoon, was hit in the chest. He was mortally wounded, falling close to a tanker leaking diesel that had been hit several times. At this moment, the gunman with the automatic weapon experienced a stoppage, forcing him to stop firing. He was observed standing with his foot on the dying man's body as he attempted to clear a stoppage. It was a monumental display of callousness, demonstrating the psychotic nature of the paramilitary murder gangs.

That was the final moment of the attack, as the gunmen fled to the waiting getaway car, which was later found abandoned in the Lisburn Road. Mr Cameron had a 12-year-old son, who simply could not

---

* Lister, D. and Jordan, H., *Mad Dog* (Mainstream Publishing, 2004) pp.164–66.

understand the tragedy that had bludgeoned its way into his young life; tragically he was later observed in a distraught state outside the depot, crying for his lost father. With a tragic irony, it was later revealed that James Cameron's wife was a nurse at the Royal Victoria Hospital in Belfast; just days earlier she had worked very hard to treat the survivors of the PIRA bomb attack at Frizzell's.

Mark Rodgers is the son of one of the murdered men, Mark Rodgers Senior.

Mark's Story*

I was only 6 years old when my father was murdered; it had been my birthday two days before. Ever since that day, my birthday has been hard. On one hand, yes, it's your birthday and people want to celebrate, but I always know that just two days later, it'll be the anniversary of my father's murder. A lot of the media focus has been on the Shankill bomb and next we'll have Greysteel. But there were others who died, other families who suffered and we have to remember that. There was so much hatred on the streets. And while there are still walls between some, there's not between normal people. The people who did these things weren't normal. The people who did this to my family are absolutely evil – pure, pure evil. My dad had never judged anyone by religion. Mostly all I have is stories of him. My sister Leanne has even less. She was only 3.

Every five years we hold a memorial service; that's our own personal thing. Anyone is entitled to remember a loved one. What angers me is people who are supposed to represent political parties, getting involved in commemorating the sort of people who brought this trauma to people like me and my family. It's unsympathetic to the victims of the Shankill bomb and the families of the victims in the wake of that day. Representatives of political parties never seem to see the suffering of people like me, like my mother, my sister and families like ours.

---

* *Belfast Telegraph* www.belfasttelegraph.co.uk/news/northern-ireland/people-who-killed-my-father-were-pure-evil-says-son-of-depot-worker-killed-in-1993-uff-attack-37464014.html

None came to remember my father. Instead they seem more interested in remembering the so-called brave volunteers who put all these families through hell. And it was hell – just ask my mother. But in a way I like to think my dad's death paved the way for peace. The ceasefire started the next year and I like to think my father's murder helped politicians realise that the brutality we were all being forced to live through had to end.

My family has lived through a terrible, terrible thing. Our children need to read about months like October 1993, see the trauma it caused and never allow it to happen again. All people want is to live free from the hatred and brutality that robbed me of my father.

Just seven days after the terrible carnage at Frizzell's, some 70 miles north of the Shankill Road another bloody massacre took place. The repercussions of this atrocity, like the Shankill bomb, are still being felt today. On the evening of 30 October 1993, several drinkers were enjoying a night out at The Rising Sun pub in the small town of Greysteel, which sits at the side of the wind-lashed North Sea. It was a Catholic-frequented pub in a mainly Catholic community, although several members of the Protestant community also drank there regularly.

The evening began in good spirits – literally – with a Halloween party; many guests were wearing fancy dress, with the place, as the author was told on a visit in 2016, 'rocking on its foundations'. As the evening was in full swing, a stolen Opel Kadett pulled up in the pub car park; it contained three UFF members: Stephen Irwin, Geoffrey Deeney and Torrens Knight.** They took their weapons, donned balaclavas and entered the packed, noisy, pub. The men created quite a startling sight as they brandished weapons, their faces covered. However, as many people were wearing Halloween dress, they were not, for a second or two, taken seriously. That changed very soon afterwards, as Irwin levelled his weapon at the customers. He was armed with a Czech-manufactured VZ.58; it used the high-velocity 7.62mm round, combined with a

---

** A fourth gang member, Brian McNeill, had driven ahead of the Kadett to nearby Eglington. The plan was to torch the Opel and escape in his car.

terrifying rate of fire. He called out the words: 'Trick or treat,' to which at least two people – Karen Thompson and John Burns – responded angrily: 'That's not funny!'

Irwin then turned in the direction of newly engaged Karen Thompson (19), immediately opening fire; she was hit in the face and mortally wounded. Her fiancé, Steve Mullan* (20), was hit and killed, as he stood next to his future bride. John Burns (54), a former soldier, having reacted to the gunmen, was immediately hit in the stomach; he was mortally wounded, dying shortly afterwards in the operating theatre at Altnagelvin Hospital.

Next to be hit, as far as can be ascertained, was James Moore (81), who died at the scene. The indiscriminate spray of bullets then cut down Joseph McDermott (60). Next to die was Moira Dudley (59), downed with shots to her legs before being hit again; killed as she lay defenceless. One of the revellers, John Moyne (50), threw his wife to the floor but he was fatally hit, protecting her from Irwin's bullets. Samuel Montgomery (76) was fatally wounded, dying on 14 April the following year from his wounds. Knight, meanwhile, was standing at the front door, armed with a double-barrelled shotgun, which he was unable to use. Deeney fired one round from a Browning 9mm, but after that first round, it mercifully jammed. Almost as soon as the firing had started, it suddenly stopped. As the echoes of the gunshots died away, the three killers ran outside, laughing and joking before speeding off in the stolen Opel. In what seemed an eternity but in reality was only one hundred seconds, a total of forty-seven rounds had been fired, leaving nineteen people dead, dying or wounded.

Within minutes of the shooting, a fleet of ambulances was speeding to the scene of carnage; as fast as was possible, dead and dying as well as those who would survive were being 'blue-lighted' to Altnagelvin Hospital in Londonderry. One of the paramedics who attended that night was Adrian McAuley, who was on duty. He said:

---

* The young couple who had intended to be married, were instead buried side by side at the same church where their wedding was to have taken place. Karen Thompson's father died the following January; he had been ill but it was anticipated that a recovery was forthcoming. He is often considered the unofficial eighth victim of the attack.

*Murder scene at the Rising Sun pub, Greysteel. (*Belfast Telegraph*)*

We came back to our base when we got a call to go to the Rising Sun bar to a shooting. We turned off the main road and there were about 20 or 30 people outside the bar. They were absolutely frantic, waving their arms in shock. I saw people shot and wounded lying on the floor and slumped in their seats. The sound of crying and screaming was overwhelming. Shootings were nothing new to the ambulance service, but this was on a scale that I had never seen before.[*]

One survivor said: 'It was pandemonium, everybody was screaming. It was all over in two minutes, just two minutes, four bursts of machine-gun fire, all over, seven people dead, two minutes is all it took.'[**]

The killers were eventually caught, although those who ordered the attack were never convicted. UFF members Torrens Knight, Stephen Irwin, Jeffrey Deeney and Brian McNeill were jailed for their part in the murders. They were all released early under the terms of the Good Friday Agreement.

Among the injured were Lorraine Murray, who was shot in the arm, and her mother, Mary McKeever, who was hit in the stomach; both were in recovery for many years afterwards. Mrs Nellie Burns, wife of John, was also extremely badly injured in the attack. Jillian is the daughter of John Burns, who was murdered that night, and whose mother was terribly injured.

Jillian's Story

It was 30 October 1993; a very normal Halloween, or so we all thought. I was 14 years old; I had just lost my granny the April before, and with The Troubles going on, my childhood wasn't what you called a normal one.

My family were originally from Greysteel, but due to our family's home being under attack every marching season because of our

---

[*] Greysteel massacre, twenty-five years on: 'The smell of gun smoke has never left me' (irishtimes.com)

[**] Ibid.

John Burns, killed by the UFF in the Greysteel massacre. (Jillian Burns)

Jillian Burns, daughter of John Burns, killed in the Greysteel massacre. (Jillian Burns)

over and have the life we were having, without the fear of our house coming under attack. So, from the age of 8 to 14, the place where we lived felt like a safe environment, away from the conflict of division. Every Saturday night, my mum and dad went out to the Rising Sun bar at Greysteel for a drink with their friends. It was the only time Mum and Dad drank or socialised; it was their escape for a few hours a week.

So, during the day of the 30th, my dad took me into Derry shopping; I remember that we went to H. Samuels, where he bought me a wee chain that said: 'Daddy's little angel'. For some strange reason, and I really don't know why, but all day I thought something was going to happen; it was just out of character for Daddy to take me to Derry. But as the day and evening went on everything was a just a normal family day. We just had our dinner and Mum and Dad started to get ready. My big bro' Gregory (God rest him) was looking after me but as soon as Mum and Dad went out, I was straight over to my friend Mandy Carton's house, as you do. Mandy had been out that night with her friends for Halloween, so I was just in with her mum. They were a great family that I will never forget.

While I was with them, there was a knock at the front door, which I went to answer, but when I opened the door, two fellas from the village were standing there. One said: 'Jillian, get to the house. There has been a mass shooting in the Rising Sun.' My first reaction was: what the fuck? But I bolted out the back door to make my way over to the house.

I met Mandy, and she told me that both my parents had been shot; I dropped to my knees. When I finally got up, I ran to the house but all I could see was people everywhere; they were coming from everywhere; it was like a scene from a movie. Mandy and me rang a local taxi man, George Hamilton, to take us into Altnagelvin because I needed to see my daddy. When the taxi arrived, George immediately told us that Daddy was dead, which made me run back to the house, where I threw up for a solid hour.

Another taxi driver arrived. This time it was Martin Mcnerlin, and he took me to Altnagelvin Hospital, although looking back, I should have been there ages ago. As we approached there were ambulances, doctors, nurses everywhere. There was the smell of blood in the air and it has stuck with me ever since. There was the sound of screaming and gunshot wounds everywhere. My head just couldn't cope, so Martin took me home. But when we got there I had to deal with coming out of one door and out of the other because the media was there as well. My world had been torn to pieces at the age of just 14, and it didn't stop there as Mummy had also been shot at the scene; she was critical in intensive care. It was a strange time for me, having lost my daddy, murdered in cold blood, and knowing that Mummy was fighting for her life.

Words cannot express my feelings and emotions which I was going through and what myself and my brothers were facing; there were challenging days ahead. We were dealing with Daddy's wake as well as having to visit Mummy twice a day and not being able to tell her that Daddy was dead. She was too sick to be told and had she known, it would have killed her. She could only communicate with us by writing on a board as she had tubes going down her throat, preventing her from speaking. I remember her writing down a message asking how Daddy was, but all I could tell her was not to worry as someone was sitting with him. I think that she knew though, because she lifted her arms in the air and then dropped them on the bed; it broke my heart.

The family took turns with her whilst the wake was going on; I had never seen anything like it in my life, people coming in and out to pay their respects. This went on twenty-four hours a day for a full three days. I seriously thought that my head would go as it was a whirlwind with friends as well as the media. Then the day of the funerals arrived, but as they were largely all at the same time, we unfortunately were unable to attend their burials. By the time of Daddy's funeral, I still hadn't slept; I was just a child on auto mode. On the day, there were people everywhere as well as reporters; it was one of the biggest funerals in Limavady. The local high school did a guard of honour at the end of St Canices, which is where I totally broke down and couldn't walk anymore. I had to use the funeral car. The service was lovely and though Daddy got the send-off and the dignity he deserved, my mammy wasn't there.

Then sadly, the minister had to go to the hospital and inform her that her husband and the father of her three children hadn't made it and was being laid to rest. The staff in the ICU were so amazing and understanding, moving Mum to a little room of her own so that she could watch TV in privacy.

Following the funeral, I was facing the future and didn't know what it held in store for me. All of these questions were buzzing around my head whilst at the same time, I didn't even know if Mummy was going to make it. How was I going to make it without Daddy; why did this happen to us; why wasn't this stopped; have I even got a future? My mum was still critical, we had just buried my dad and my head was finding it impossible to soak up everything that was going on around me. I had to realise that I needed to forget my teenage years and grow up fast; I lost out on my late childhood because of the circumstances. I was a 14-year-old girl who had to try to turn into an adult overnight.

With Mum in hospital, I went to stay in Ballykelly with mum's sister and her family. I spent four years with them on and off over the next four years, but it was tricky because their niece – Karen Thompson – was also shot in the bar that night. The family pulled together as much as possible, with me eventually returning to school, where I found it quite hard to really interact with people.

I was dealing with grief, loss, confusion, anger, frustration, stress, worry as well as trying to cope with helping Mum as much as I could. She was confined to a chair for four years, having to have all her insides rebuilt back up again. So when it was time for Mum to come home, I moved back in and helped as much as I could. This only lasted for short periods of time as she was in and out of hospital over the years, having 174 operations to help her to recover as much as possible.

The experience has left me with so many issues and will always affect my day-to-day living. I have so many unanswered questions which I'll never get answers to and to live knowing that kills me inside. I have been left with PTSD, excessive OCD, depression, anxiety and psychogenic seizures. What the world doesn't realise is that it's not only the massacre and the death that families have to live with, but it's also the lifetime of the aftermath that is left behind to deal with too.

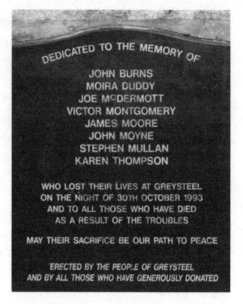

DEDICATED TO THE MEMORY OF

JOHN BURNS
MOIRA DUDDY
JOE McDERMOTT
VICTOR MONTGOMERY
JAMES MOORE
JOHN MOYNE
STEPHEN MULLAN
KAREN THOMPSON

WHO LOST THEIR LIVES AT GREYSTEEL
ON THE NIGHT OF 30TH OCTOBER 1993
AND TO ALL THOSE WHO HAVE DIED
AS A RESULT OF THE TROUBLES

MAY THEIR SACRIFICE BE OUR PATH TO PEACE

ERECTED BY THE PEOPLE OF GREYSTEEL
AND BY ALL THOSE WHO HAVE GENEROUSLY DONATED

Memorial to those murdered by the UVF at Greysteel. (Ken Wharton)

I battle every day with constant demons because of that night, and some images and the smell of blood will never leave me. It did teach me one thing and that is that everyone is equal and we all bleed the same.

✦

We have previously discussed the expression 'dial a Catholic', which is probably one of the English language's foulest obscenities. It is certainly one for which there can be neither condonation nor forgiveness. It was the darkest of the dark practices used by Loyalist paramilitaries; it was one honed into a malevolent art form by the Ulster Freedom Fighters (UFF). Although this author has previously described this practice, in light of the absolute anonymity demanded by the next contributor, it is correct that we should touch upon it again.

In cities such as Belfast and Londonderry, and in towns such as Strabane and Newry, areas were and still are, delineated according to 'tribal loyalty', demarcation enforced on sectarian lines. For the purpose of this specific sub-narrative, we are discussing only Roman Catholic areas. Where Belfast had the Ardoyne, New Lodge, Ballymurphy, Andersonstown, Poleglass and Twinbrook, Londonderry had the Bogside, Shantallow, Creggan and Gobnascale. Where Newry had the Derrybeg, Strabane had the 'Heads of the Town'. These were areas in which 100 per cent of the residents would be Catholics and, if not regular churchgoers, their sympathies would certainly be with the Roman Catholic Church, or with the Republican movement. One hastens to add that the two were not always synonymous. Some of these areas may at one time have been mixed areas, but the polarisation of the communities, exacerbated in the main by the onset and worsening of The Troubles, had ensured that sectarian boundaries had been drawn in the sand.

The names of some of the Loyalist assassins are written in the folklore of the UDA and UVF and these men, in spite of the murder campaigns in which they participated, will be as equally revered as they are reviled by the decent people of Northern Ireland. Johnny 'Red' Adair, Commander of the UFF's 'C' company based on the Shankill in Belfast, had two prolific killers among his subordinates in Stephen McKeag and Steven McFerran. These two are known to have participated in many sectarian murders and it is alleged that they took part in the 'dial a Catholic' murder campaign from 1990 onwards. The UDA/UFF gave an annual volunteer of the year award to the organisation's top gunman. It was generally a trophy in the shape of a handgun mounted on a plaque. McKeag is known to have won this so many times that he acquired the soubriquet 'Top Gun'. McFerran, also known by the nickname 'Inch', was never far behind him as the number of innocent Catholic victims began to fill the cemeteries of West Belfast.

On 7 September 1993, McKeag, accompanied by two other UFF gunmen, shot and killed Sean Hughes, a barber who ran his own hairdressers on the Upper Donegall Road. The next day, McKeag killed a shopkeeper, Michael Edwards, at his home in Finaghy. The following month, he murdered Paddy McMahon, a Catholic, in Newington Avenue in North Belfast. He was arrested by the RUC for this and other murders. Unfortunately for his many victims, poor courtroom appearances by eyewitnesses led to his acquittal. However, while he was being held in custody, another UFF gunman, Gary 'Smickers' Smyth, took on the mantle of top Catholic killer. This was the backdrop to the spate of sectarian killings that marked this period of The Troubles. To the uninformed eye, this almost inconceivable competition to kill innocents for the most spurious of reasons was the reality that faced the Catholic community in Northern Ireland. Tragically, this was but the tip of a degenerate iceberg, to borrow a cliché from the wonderful writer Simon Sebag Montefiore.

Due to the demographics of the hitherto mentioned 'tribal areas' the UFF leadership knew that if a taxi company was based in, say the Andersonstown area of Belfast, their employees would be highly, highly likely to be Catholics. They were also cognisant of the caution that would be exercised by these taxi companies, especially if the caller requested a pick-up in Protestant areas such as Woodvale, Shankill or Crumlin Road. A unit would be dispatched to – and here one must be careful not to unwittingly give clues as to the identity of the following contributor – for example, the Lower Kennedy Way, before calling a local taxi firm and requesting a pick-up in the local area.

Additionally, the killers always ensured that the name for the pick-up would be a 'Catholic' name, for example Murphy or O'Brien or Bryson, to further lull the dispatcher into a false sense of security. The gang would arrive in a stolen car, having carried out a reconnaissance of the area. Once in situ, they would lie in wait for their victim; as soon as he had arrived at the pick-up address, the gunmen would shoot him dead, before fleeing in both their own car as well as the dead man's vehicle. It would be later found burned out, almost unfailingly in a Loyalist area. After that, it would be back to Adair and 'Company HQ' in the Shankill to 'celebrate' the death of another Catholic. Somewhat cynically, the dead man would be elevated to the status of a 'senior Provisional IRA officer' in order to justify the murder. However, what followed would be a lifetime of grief and financial struggle for the unfortunate man's family.

One such murder victim was a father of several young children, living in the West Belfast area; he was a taxi driver who was killed in the post-1990 period. I am most grateful for the following story told by the dead man's son. I will not name him, nor will I give any clues as to his identity; we have changed elements of his testimony in order that he will be unrecognised and totally anonymous.

My Story

I have thought long and hard about talking to you and I was reluctant to give my story to one of the enemy. I am sorry but I don't have fond memories of you English soldiers. I have matured a bit in the last few years and a good friend told me that I can trust you. Anyway, I was only a young boy at the time and I was one of many children to my mammy and daddy, living in part of the west of the city. Daddy had worked at a big factory in Belfast but had been forced out by intimidation and threats and ended up buying an old banger to get a job with a local taxi firm.

As I say, we were a big family, very close to each other, but it meant that there were many mouths to feed, so Daddy worked every hour that God sent, and some more besides. He was a man who feared God and he treated us firmly but fairly. He was always tired, but never too tired to take us to school after a night shift or tell us a bedtime yarn or two before he went off driving.

On the night that he was murdered, he had gone to a nearby area to pick up a fare and wasn't afeared of the job. When he arrived, he was shot from behind and died almost instantly. They left him lying in a pool of blood and even stole his car, his pride and joy, burning it out near the Shankill. I don't want to say how old I was at the time, but I was old enough to understand that he wasn't coming back; I would never again smell the beer on his breath – he always permitted himself a couple a week – or the stale cigarette smell from him or his passengers of the previous night. I would never hear his stories of his favourite soccer team, Celtic, and how great they were and about the Lisbon invincibles. He was a lovely man with no hatred for any man; he didn't hate the Protestants and he didn't even hate the soldiers who were always outside our house. He loved us and he loved Celtic; the Prods killed a good man.

We had his wake at home – there were dozens and dozens of cousins, aunts, uncles and lots of neighbours – but the coffin was sealed because of the injuries to his head. The Peelers had explained and they were trying to be kind about it, but my older brother told them to 'fuck off', and called them 'Huns' and all the insults he could think off; Mammy was too distressed to tell him off. There was next to no money coming in except the 'brew'* and even the insurance didn't pay out, although I don't believe that he had any anyway. The neighbours helped and we always had clothes, always second-hand because 'Sean has grown out of his trousers', and old patched-up jumpers, even shoes given to us with good faith. We had so little money that even second-hand shoes – which gave me verrucas – then had to be handed down to the next sibling.

As I grew older, my hatred for the 'Hun' grew also; I hated fucking Proddies and the English soldiers. I was always out throwing stones and carrying ammo (ball bearings) for the boys with the catapults. I got many an Englishman with the odd rock as I developed a skill and a taste for it. I was out of control and the next step would be joining the RA, which seemed only a natural progression from rioting. I helped out occasionally, once carrying part of an automatic weapon stuffed into my underpants! The soldiers were shits and called us 'Irish c****' and '*Taig* bastards', all the usual sectarian insults, which they had probably learned from the Hun Peelers.

I saw death and destruction and by my teens, I had seen a dead Peeler and bits of a body after a bomb went off prematurely and I think that was what changed me and the direction my life was going in. I saw teeth still in the bloodied gums, fingers and a bit of a penis. I imagined Mammy seeing these little bits of me and trying to identify me by the scraps of the clothing I had been wearing. I turned my back on things and tried to ignore all the crap and destruction going on around me. I went away to family elsewhere in the North, but if I say much more, that will help some of the local boyos – and yes, they are still around – to realise who I am. I did come back in more peaceful times to try to get a job, but I am on and off the brew even now and trying to support my own wains.

I am hoping for peace and reconciliation, but I am very pessimistic as to whether it will ever come about. I never hated before Daddy was killed, but boy I have hated ever since. I wasn't alone in not having a man about the house. There were plenty of children whose fathers were either dead,

---

* Fortnightly unemployment benefit.

in the Kesh or over the border, sleeping rough in Dundalk on the run from the Peelers or the SAS. Sometimes when I was growing up, soldiers would walk up and down our street, occasionally taking cover in the gateways; we would hear them shouting to each other and we would mimic them, you know, take the piss out of their accents. Every now and then, I might forget that they were Huns and that they might even know who killed my daddy and see in their faces that they were scared, like us, and just wanted to go home to England. But most of the time, I hated them, and I hated the black bastards who accompanied them. I'm not being racist: I mean the Peelers who we called 'black bastards'.

I will never forgive because they destroyed my life and my mammy's life and my brothers and sisters' lives as well, but like John Lennon said, I'll give peace a chance. Do I believe that it will happen? Not in my lifetime it won't.

8

1998 – Good Friday and Beyond

The final mass atrocity of The Troubles produced the biggest loss of life from a single bomb. Dublin and Monaghan, it is true, saw more fatalities, but that was from four separate bombs, both inside the capital city as well as in the rural border area. On 15 August 1998, a bombing team from one of the dissident Republican factions, the Real Irish Republican Army (RIRA), left a stolen Vauxhall Cavalier outside Kell's shop in Lower Market Street, Omagh in Co. Tyrone. Inside the boot was a bomb containing both Semtex and other home-made explosives; it weighed 510lb (232kg). It is widely considered that their intended target was the town's courthouse; however, as parking had not been available, they were forced to change their plans, leaving the car outside Kell's, as it was the only free spot in the centre. It was a fateful decision that has impacted on so many lives over the last two decades and more. That impact will be felt for generations to come.

Security forces were cognisant of potential dissident Republican threats, particularly in light of an RIRA explosion in Banbridge, Co. Down, some two weeks earlier. The group's actions had ensured that they were very much considered a very real threat to the fledgling peace process. At 1432, some thirteen minutes after the car was parked, a call was made to a local television studio. The caller warned that a bomb had been left at the Omagh courthouse; they warned that it would explode in thirty minutes. Within minutes, a further call was received, contradicting the first call, stating that the bomb would explode in fifteen minutes, in 'Omagh Town'. Finally, in an identical manner to the way in which, historically, the Provisional IRA had cynically sought to confuse the authorities, a further call was received. This time, the call was to the Samaritans Office in Coleraine, some 56 miles away, warning that a bomb had been placed in Market Street. It was against this background of utter confusion, brought about by deliberately misleading warnings, that RUC officers inadvertently evacuated shoppers in the wrong direction. Moreover, they directed them away from the courthouse – and relative safety – towards the actual bomb.

At 1510 hours, a massive explosion tore Lower Market Street apart, obliterating people, vehicles and buildings. Twenty-one people were killed instantly, with a further eight being fatally wounded; between 200 and 300 other people were injured. Seven of the wounded died shortly afterwards, with the twenty-ninth victim dying three weeks later. One of the dead women was Avril Monaghan (30), who was pregnant with twins. One survivor spoke of hearing 'an unearthly bang followed by an eeriness, a darkness that had just come over the place'. Another eyewitness, who didn't wish her name included in this book, told the author: 'There was some panicked voices as people tried to get their kids and themselves away from where they thought that the bomb was. Then, and it was uncanny, there was a split second of silence and I felt my heart just sink and then there was a flash, no noise and the world just ended.' After this silence, other eyewitnesses spoke of hearing screams and seeing body parts everywhere among the rubble and wrecked vehicles. Marion Radford searched desperately for her son, Alan (16), with whom she had been shopping in the seconds before the blast; he was killed.

Those killed either in the blast or subsequently were: Samantha McFarland (17), Veda Short (56), Fred White (60), Bryan White (26), Avril Monaghan (30), Philomena Skelton (39), Deborah-Anne Cartwright (20), Esther Gibson (36), Mary Grimes (65), Brenda Logue (17), Brian McCrory (54), Jolene Marlow (17), Seán McLaughlin (12), Oran Doherty (8), James Barker (12), Fernando Blasco Baselga (12), Rocío Abad Ramos (23), Geraldine Breslin (43), Gareth Conway (18), Breda Devine (1), Aidan Gallagher (21), Maura Monaghan (1), Elizabeth Rush (57), Olive Hawkes (60), Julia Hughes (21), Lorraine Wilson (15), Ann McCombe (48), Seán McGrath (61) and Alan Radford (16).

Laura Hamilton was injured in the Omagh bomb; she was 14 at the time; her younger sister, Nicola (12), was with her at the moment of the blast.

Laura Hamilton's Story

On the day of the Omagh bomb blast, I was with friends and my younger sister, Nicola, doing some shopping. We both needed new school shoes and so it was that fate placed us right next to that device which wrecked our town and our lives. We met up with a school friend at the bus depot, which is where we saw the Spanish tourists[*] arrive on a bus. At that time we didn't know that they were Spanish, but we knew that they were foreigners. Shortly afterwards we were walking towards Campsie when I saw a friend from school, so crossed the road to speak to her. When I got to my friend, my sister and I spotted our auntie further up the main street and went to speak to her. She quickly told us that the area was being cordoned off and that we should get away. Little did she know that she was sending us back towards the actual bomb.

I recall that Nicola was about 6ft in front of me when the bomb exploded. I didn't know until later that she had been badly injured in her legs and her kneecap, which had to be surgically rebuilt. She also had a hole on the side of her head. I wrote a poem with Nicola later in hospital and I have given the author permission to use it in this book:

There were bodies all around me. Some crying out for help. It was the quiet ones who scared me. Just lying deathly still. The men of evil came to our town that day. They stole the lives of many.

---

[*] This refers to a party of thirty-four Spanish nationals visiting Omagh and Buncrana on a friendship trip from Madrid. Two of the party were killed, with a further twelve being injured. Amongst the Omagh dead were several Northern Irish children who had travelled with the party from Buncrana. The bodies of Fernando Blasco Baselga (12) and Rocío Abad Ramos (23) were flown back to Madrid in a military aircraft; their coffins draped with the Bandera de España. A second military aircraft fitted with hospital beds took eight more of the injured home; four others remained in Northern Ireland, too ill to travel at that stage.

At the time, I didn't realise the true extent of my injuries, which included multiple pieces of shrapnel in my buttocks and both legs. I still to this day have multiple bits of shrapnel in my hips and legs, mainly embedded in the muscle behind my left knee.

I couldn't find Nicola immediately after the bomb; I didn't even think about her until my mother came running from a nearby hairdressers and found me; she pleaded with me, asking where my younger sister was. She didn't realise the extent of my injuries as I was still walking and I had taken my jacket off, wrapping it around my waist so that no one could see just how much blood there was. Anyway, Mum sent me towards a shop, which my cousin worked in, and from there I was taken to the hospital in a stranger's car. Once at the hospital I remember being really cold, probably due to blood loss, so I was laid on the warm bonnet of a car with a cushion under my head. At that time, I was drifting in and out of consciousness, but remember being outside the hospital doors, where I was laid on the ground. A doctor finally came along as I was losing consciousness and he was shown my injuries; it was then that they realised the extent of how seriously hurt I was. I recall being took into a ward and having my clothes cut off. Both my sister and aunt ended up on that same ward. Both were then transported to other hospitals, via ambulance.

Not long afterwards, I was airlifted to Altnagelvin Hospital in Londonderry; I was put into an Army helicopter with other seriously injured people. A young soldier held my hand until I lost consciousness; I will never ever forget that young man and would love to thank him for his kindness. If he happens to be reading this and can remember me, please, please get in touch. I will never forget you.

I was in a coma for up to seven days, awaking to find myself in intensive care in the next bed to Nicola. Neither of us really knew what was happening, but she seemed OK. We both did. During my time in hospital, Clive, the son of Ann McCombe, came to visit, but as I was aware at that time that she had been killed in the blast, I just couldn't face seeing him. I was in pain and didn't want him to see me suffer, as he was suffering enough already after losing his mother. It was then I realised the extent of what had happened, knowing that people had died, and myself and Nicola could have been one of them; we were just children.

Three weeks later, Nicola was released just in time to see the US President Clinton visit Omagh. I was also released but only for the day. I was told that I needed skin grafts and plastic surgery and was transferred to Dundonald for extensive treatment. I had dead flesh and muscle removed as they repaired the lower half of my body. I was in hospitals for a total of seven and a half weeks before I was finally discharged. I had to use a wheelchair and we had our living room converted into a bedroom for me. I learned to walk again using crutches.

I lost eight months of schooling, never being able to finish my GCSEs, turning into a bit of a tearaway for a while. A year later I suffered the loss of my first boyfriend and his best friend to suicide. Exactly one year after that, I lost my grandmother; she was my rock and my best friend. I tried to put the bomb behind me, even returning to Market Street, the scene of my nightmares. The bomb had happened and I had to get over it. We don't dwell on things in my house, you move on.

What I will never be able to understand is how grown men could sit around a table, planning to murder women and children. You just know that they are evil; there is no other words to describe them. Incidentally, I was never once questioned by the RUC; we never once saw them and no one came to take our statements. Maybe they tried to but our parents probably didn't want it all being brought up again as we tried to get on with our lives and tried to overcome our injuries.

I should tell you that I am a product of a mixed marriage; in Northern Ireland that means that we had one parent who was a Protestant and the other was a Catholic. One week it was a Roman Catholic mass and the next was a Presbyterian service; we lived on both sides of the community. In a way, we were kept well away from the horrors of The Troubles, until that fateful day in Omagh that is.

How am I today you ask? I have seen many orthopaedic surgeons, all of whom have just shrugged their shoulders and told me to accept the pain. I also had bungled surgery in London, but that's another story. I am on morphine patches for the pain, but even the vibrations from brushing my teeth can cause spasms of pain. Because the shrapnel is so close to the femoral artery, they won't take the chance of removing it but why can't I make the choice myself? In the meantime, I have to live with the pain.

Forgiveness? It's funny that I have never really thought about forgiveness. What I don't forgive is how I am being left to struggle without proper treatment and care; that I can't forgive. I can't accept a life of pain when they haven't even tried to remove the shrapnel. I didn't do this to myself.

✦

Claire Monteith is the sister of 16-year-old Alan Radford, who was killed in the same blast in Omagh.

Claire's Story: Part of Me has Died with Him, I Still Feel Lost

That day is so vivid in my heart, soul and mind. The morning of 15 August 1998, I had awoke in my friend's house after staying there the night before. I was 15, and had attended a disco, whilst my brother went babysitting for a neighbour who lived in the same housing estate as us.

Unlike any other Saturday I had returned home mid-morning rather than late evening; my friend was also with me. I went into my home to find my mother, getting ready to go into town. This was her and my brother Alan's usual Saturday routine, unlike myself, a typical teenager who went out with friends at the weekend. Alan, who was 16, was dedicated to being there for my mum as well as helping out anyone else he could. We were rarely ever apart; being so close in age, we shared life. Alan was not only my brother but my best friend, my world, my protector, as I was his. I asked Mum where he was, as he would normally greet me as I came home, and would want to know the gossip from the night I had had out. Alan, being Alan, was concerned for the mother whose children he had cared for the night previous, so he had went back down to check on her and her kids. He had stayed longer than anticipated, but soon returned home to also get changed for town with Mum. That Saturday was the most beautiful sunny day that we had seen in quite some time.

That beautiful boy came in the door bright and full of life as always, calling out: 'Hello Sisa.' Mum had reminded him that they were going into town so Alan had got one of his new T-shirts out to iron. We were having our usual talk about how his and my own night had gone; he also had chased me round the house with a hot iron, jokingly telling me my tight trousers would stick to my ass with the heat of it. His laugh was infectious; the light that shone out of him when he was happy is indescribable. Mum had told us to stop messing around; typical us!

Alan was putting on his socks, sitting over by the far window in the living room; the sun was just shining down on his face, the normal antics and laughing going on with us. As Alan and Mum were leaving through the back door, I was telling him what way to get his hair cut, and to remember to buy gel; he replied: 'OK Sisa, I love you, see you later, nah, I'll see you sometime.' He left with Mum out the back door, went up the garden path to then run down, knock the window and shouted a personal phrase which was funny to both of us. He walked back up the path laughing, locked the gate. That was the last time I saw him alive.

My friend and I usually got the 1.20 bus into town, but for some odd reason we had decided not to bother going into town. My older brother, Paul, was asleep in his room upstairs and as it was a lovely day, we went to sit on the wall opposite my home. We were talking away when, all of a sudden the wall shook beneath us; a loud explosion had startled us and followed with the sky being filled with black smoke. In that moment my heart had hit my stomach and something didn't feel right. My brother Paul had been awakened by this, and came running out of the house; he had instantly thought the police or Army barracks had been blown up and proceeded to run round the road to see what had happened. The barracks were only about a mile away from us. Not long after, I could see friends of mine coming through the park, telling me that a bomb had been at the courthouse, which was at the top of Omagh's main street. This had worried me as Mum and Alan were in town, but they rarely visited that end of the town; yet I felt sick! Soon after, I had been given news that the bomb had exploded at the opposite end of the town, which was somewhere that I knew Mum and Alan would have been. I went into the house, repeating to my friend that I felt sick and was worried about Mum and Alan.

The phone rang: 'Claire, it's Mum; I'm at the hospital! Where is Paul? Tell him to come here; I was in the Salad Bowl. The bomb went off, outside; I can't find Alan; he went up the street; I can't find Alan!'

'I will look for him, Mum, I will find him, I will tell Paul to go to you.'

In the space of minutes, my brother Paul's best friend had come to our house, completely unaware of the events that had unfolded as he had driven from the airport. I was in shock, telling him of my phone call and to find Paul, but moments later Paul returned to instruct me to sit by the phone and do not use it; to keep the line free.

I went in search of Alan along with my friend and sister, searching the walkway, as we thought he may have tried to walk home, and passed out as he hated the sight of blood. We couldn't drive far, as there was cars parked everywhere in the direction of the local hospital. We walked to the bottom of the steep hospital hill; we held hands and ran to the top of it. Carnage, chaotic carnage was unfolding before me; a child's foot blown off inside its tiny shoe, helicopters landing overhead, friends with blood-stained clothes, people everywhere and I kept asking: 'Have you seen Alan?'

The hospital floors were awash with blood, the injured sitting outside on walls surrounding Casualty; stretchers with bodies, limbs abandoned. 'Alan, have you seen Alan?' I saw my brother-in-law, Dickie; he had been in with Mum, but he told me not to go and see her. Then my brother, Paul, was there; he had been lifting the dead and injured, along with his friend Davie. He told me to put Alan's name on the missing person list, as I knew what he was wearing. Back and forth I went, from the hospital to town, to the leisure centre, searching for him and adding his name to the lists in both places. I checked the new names being added to a board in the leisure centre of the people who had been found: 'Have you seen Alan?'

My brother Paul, now covered in other people's blood, had seen me close to home, on the park beside us. His face told me all I needed to know about what he was going through; he had been told that all the bodies of the dead were being taken to the bubble gym, in the Army barracks. As we knew some of the Army personnel, he told me to try to get into the Army camp. I left and went to the Army camp, only to be refused entry. 'I need to find my brother; I need to see if he is in there; I need to know!' I told the security officer.

Mum returned home later that day, badly injured, covered in blood and asking if I had found Alan. Each time I went into the house, Mum would call out: 'Alan! Is that you Alan?' My reply always being: 'No Mum, it's just me.' Mum rocked back and forth in front of the fireplace, waiting on her son's return. My friend and I went out yet again to check the lists at the leisure centre. I said to her: 'There's no way Alan would have Mum worrying of his whereabouts; he has his wallet with him, and he would call or make someone let her know if he was OK. I know he isn't coming home alive, Paula.' A long night was ahead; my mum was distraught as we awaited news: nothing!

The phone rang the following morning around 10 a.m. My brother-in-law, Dickie, answered the call. I watched him as he put down the phone receiver, opened the front door and cried, before coming in to tell us what we never wanted to hear. My brother Paul, sister Elaine and two close family friends went to identify Alan's body.

My whole world collapsed. I couldn't breathe, when my brother and sister returned to confirm it was Alan. He wasn't coming home, my boy, our boy wasn't coming home, as he lay covered in a tartan blanket in the Army barracks. Paul knew it was him just by his hair; he never got to get it cut. His life was cut short instead!

His body returned home on Monday evening. My brother and sister had said it would not be an open coffin, if Alan looked as he did in the morgue. His face was covered in shrapnel marks, plasters over his nose and his eye. I looked at my brother and what they had done to him; I touched his body, he was so, so cold; I pleaded for him to wake up, I wanted to see his eyes open, to hear his voice, to feel his touch, to hear his laughter. He never did; I still yearn for all of him, for my hugs when I cry, for the nightly chats, for the laugh, to feel at home. Home was where we were together. Since that day my life altered; a part of me died with him.

The Omagh Bomb: Author's Postscript

The dead included both Protestants and Catholics; two of the dead were Spanish tourists. Six children aged 12 and under were killed, as well as the unborn Monaghan twins. The then Prime Minister, Tony Blair, described the act as: 'an appalling act of savagery and evil', while the normally tight-lipped Sinn Fein pair of Martin McGuinness and Gerry Adams both condemned the attack, without their usual prevarication. On this occasion, they avoided using their standard perma-justification.

Irish Republican paramilitary groups have often relied on flags of convenience to disguise their participation in an attack that has spectacularly backfired on them in terms of public relations. There have been several salient examples of this: the Kingsmill massacre of ten Protestant workers in January 1976 was an embarrassment to the movement; they later used the term South Armagh Republican Action Force to claim the attack. The Tullyvallen massacre the previous year, which bore all the hallmarks of the Provisional IRA, was claimed by the Republican Action Force. Similarly, Loyalist paramilitaries have frequently used flag of convenience terms, such as Red Hand Commando as well as Loyalist Action Force, to disguise their involvement in particularly gruesome sectarian attacks. Indeed, all of the Northern Ireland terror groups have employed their own nom de plumes, at one time or another to cover up public relations disasters.

However, it would appear that there is perhaps something deeper than mere masking of involvement in the case of the RIRA's bomb attack in Omagh. The year before the outrage, five members of the Provisional IRA's Army Council resigned their positions in protest against Sinn Fein's involvement in the peace process, and their willingness to attack the British only via the ballot box. Many observers have also made the claim that the RIRA was made up of several former senior Provisionals, including their quartermaster general. The esteemed but flawed *Lost Lives* reported that several RIRA prisoners at Portlaoise Prison in the Irish Republic had approached PIRA representatives requesting a transfer to their wings. On 18 August, just three days after the Omagh bomb, the RIRA declared a full and immediate ceasefire.

The RIRA, however, did not admit to the blame – several of their members were later charged, but of those convicted, all have had their sentences quashed on appeal. However, in 2007 they finally made a public statement. Their spokesman said: 'The IRA [sic] had minimal involvement in Omagh. Our code word was used; nothing more. To have stated this at the time would have been lost in an understandable wave of emotion; Omagh was an absolute tragedy. Any loss of civilian life is regrettable.' This author believes that both the RUC as well as An Gardaí Siochana have the names of the bombing team; BBC's *Panorama* team named the suspected killers, and families of the dead have several times tried to bring about the prosecution of those named. It would seem that the killers of twenty-nine civilians, as well as two unborn children, will never be brought to justice.

✦

On Sunday, 29 July 2001, a full three years after the signing of the Good Friday Agreement, the Ulster Defence Association (UDA) killed a young man in an apparently random sectarian attack. Gavin Brett (18), a Protestant student, was standing with a friend outside St Enda's GAA (Gaelic Athletic Association) club in Hightown Road, Glengormley. Gavin was keeping his friend company while he awaited the arrival of a taxi. As they chatted, gunmen pulled alongside in a stolen car, opening fire with automatic weapons without any warning whatsoever. It was a random sectarian attack, with the masked men simply assuming that the boys were Catholics because of their location. A young man, innocent in every respect had lost his life to a sectarian murder gang.

Gavin was mortally wounded and his friend was wounded; the killers sped away, later abandoning the car in the centre of Glengormley, burning it to destroy forensic evidence. Gavin's father, a local paramedic, was alerted by the police and dashed to the spot, where he fought desperately to save his son's life. Tragically, for all his efforts, Gavin died at the scene. The other boy was hit in the foot as he leapt over a wall. An eyewitness quoted him as saying: 'Tell Gavin's mummy that I am sorry. Tell her that I'm sorry that he died and I didn't.'

The night ended with several sectarian attacks of vandalism as the paramilitaries attempted to intimidate Catholics in the area. The murder was claimed by the Red Hand Commando, considered a flag of convenience for the Loyalist Volunteer Force (LVF). According to BelfastDaily. co.uk, the murder was carried out by the UDA's south-east Antrim brigade under the command of John 'Grug' Gregg. Gregg met his own demise on 1 February 2003. He was killed in an internal Loyalist feud in Belfast. Twelve years after the murder of Gavin, a Loyalist activist was arrested in the West Midlands; he was released without charge.*

Phyllis Brett is the mother of the murdered student Gavin Brett.

Phyllis' Story

My son, Gavin, was a genuine person; he loved life and he loved his friends and his family. My husband, Michael, and I returned from a wedding anniversary trip away around teatime. Gavin and Tara were in the house tidying up after a birthday party for a friend; they were in for most of the evening, although Tara left for her little part-time job. Around 10.50, Gavin announced that he was going to walk his friend Michael Brown to pick up a taxi in Hightown Road. It was a beautifully warm summer's evening as the two walked out of the door; Gavin said: 'I love you, Mummy' and those were the last words he spoke to me.

Gavin Brett, murdered by the UFF.
(Phyllis Brett)

A short while later, the phone rang; I answered and remember the caller's words: 'Is that the Brett's house? Your son has been shot; come to the front of the estate.' I was so shocked that I just handed the phone to Michael. He listened, before grabbing the car keys and taking off

---

* Source: www.belfastdaily.co.uk/2013/03/13/loyalist-released-over-uda-double-murder

in the car. I couldn't leave because my youngest son, Phillip – then aged 9 – was sleeping upstairs. I was so worried; I just couldn't content myself. I called a neighbour, who then came round to watch over him as I dashed to Hightown Road.

When I arrived, there were lots of people milling around, and one woman asked me if I was Gavin's mum; at that moment I knew that it was bad. I could see where Michael was, but people held me back, stopped me from getting to my son. He saw me and came running over to me to tell me that Gavin was gone. It was all a blur, but before the RUC came to take us home, some of the local politicians came over, supposedly to comfort me, but when I told them what had happened, they quickly lost interest and walked away.

The officer who took us home was a man whom I had been to school with. Later we were taken to see Gavin's body. We then had to go find Tara at her part-time job to give her the awful news about her brother. When we got back home, it was like a jungle, with masses of friends and neighbours coming to comfort us, but it still hadn't sunk in. We went to bed, but as you can imagine, sleep was next to impossible; there were far more questions than answers which tormented us.

The following morning, we received more information which allowed us to piece together what had happened the night before. There had been an attempted child abduction in the area, resulting in the Army stepping up their patrols. They had attended the scene of Gavin's murder within half a minute, but the killers had already sped away. A few days later, the Ulster Defence Association (UDA) admitted that they had carried out the murder; their pathetic excuse was that they had thought that Gavin and Michael were Catholic boys. Incidentally, there were two more sectarian murders in the area over the next twelve months.[**]

No one was ever charged, although there was a man arrested a few years later, but he was released. People get charged and released or they serve piddly little sentences and are out in eighteen months or so; this

---

[**] A young Catholic, Daniel McColgan (20), was murdered by the UFF at Barna Square, Rathcoole, on 12 January 2002, some 3 miles from the scene of Gavin's murder. Six months later, on 21 July, Gerard Lawlor (19), also a Catholic, was murdered by the UFF at Floral Road, which is just 1.4 miles from where the UFF took Gavin's life.

adds insult to injury because it should be a life sentence. I try not to let it eat me up, because it can if you let it. At the time of the murder, I had children of 9 and 13 and I had to go on living for them. I remember the outcry at the time; the friends and neighbours who came to help us; letters and postcards from all over the world, even as far away as the USA. Archbishop Tutu came to the house to comfort us.

The day of the funeral was very difficult for all of us; there were hundreds there and friends and neighbours carried Gavin's coffin for the 2 miles from home to the cemetery. It was only afterwards that I began to feel the sense of loss and the grief kicked in. I also have to tell you that there was some nastiness towards Tara at her school when she was taunted by some bullies who told her that she would end up the same as her brother. She was very angry; she had enough to contend with without all that. We sorted it out in the end, but how can people be so cruel?

Incidentally, there was a young boy from the estate who was a bit of a hoodlum. He went to the local Catholic estate, where he began throwing stones at cars. One woman driver deliberately drove her car at the boy, killing him. Our minister visited the driver's home to chat to them. He later came to see us; he told us that there was no love at all in her house, whereas he felt the love in ours.

My Michael died in 2007, aged 51, as a result of cancer which took him very quickly. It was the fact that he couldn't do anything and I think he carried a lot of guilt about that. He felt he was there and he had saved other people, but when it came to his own son he couldn't do anything, but it wasn't his fault at all. I have always blamed the grief over my son's death for the cancer which took Michael.

Paramilitaries don't realise that they're not only murdering one person, they're tearing a whole family apart. It has been a very difficult thing for us to live with, but talking about Gavin helps me. It is difficult even now to realise that he has been dead longer than he was alive.

✦

In 2008, a very worrying trend began to emerge, showing that several splinter groups from the Irish Republican movement were planning a new campaign of terrorism. Groups such as the Real IRA, Continuity

IRA and Óglaigh na hÉireann had all threatened a return to violence, and had pledged to continue the paramilitary campaign aimed at removing Northern Ireland from the United Kingdom. The RIRA, like their dissident sister groups, were never far from the radar, but since the Omagh bombing, some nine and a half years earlier, they had done little to alert the world's media.

During 2008, there were three separate gun and bomb attacks on PSNI officers in the Republican hotspots of Londonderry, Dungannon and Spamount near Castlederg. All three officers involved were seriously injured. The following January, a bombing team planted a viable device under the car of a police officer in Castlewellan, Co. Down; bomb disposal experts were called in to make the vehicle safe. This disturbing trend was clearly on the increase. Indeed, just days before there had been an attack in Antrim. The then PSNI Chief Constable, Sir Hugh Orde, warned that there was a growing threat of violence from dissident Republicans.

Officially, the last soldier to die in Operation Banner at the hands of terrorists was Lance Bombardier Stephen Restorick (23), shot dead by a PIRA sniper at a VCP at Bessbrook Mill, Co. Armagh, on 12 February 1997. However, it is true that several other soldiers also died from a variety of causes between the so-called IRA ceasefire and the cessation of Operation Banner in 2007.

On the evening of Saturday, 7 March 2009, some 145 months since the murder of Restorick, two British soldiers were killed by Irish Republicans in Northern Ireland. At 2140 hours, four off-duty soldiers from the Royal Engineers – on the eve of deployment to Afghanistan – were waiting outside the front gate of Massereene Barracks in Antrim. What the four soldiers did not know was that in a nearby parked car were several men waiting for the optimum moment to attack them. The four men had ordered pizzas from two local companies. As the drivers from both delivery firms arrived, the four soldiers eagerly gathered around to collect their orders. The customers crowded around the drivers, but as they did so, several men, armed with Romanian-manufactured automatic weapons, jumped out of their parked car, opening fire, hitting all six men.

Around sixty shots were fired over a brief sixty-second period, in which time all six men were hit, slumping to the ground. The attackers walked over to the wounded, firing further shots into their helpless bodies. The gunmen then fled in their car, abandoning it in nearby Randalstown, a dozen miles or so from the barracks. Medics quickly dashed out to treat the wounded men, but sadly, two of the soldiers died: Sapper Mark Quinsey (23), from Birmingham, and Londoner Patrick Azimkar (21) were beyond saving. Ambulances rushed the dead and wounded to hospital; the other soldiers and the delivery men – Anthony Watson, 19, from Antrim, and an unnamed Polish man in his 30s – eventually recovered.

The attack was claimed by one of the main dissident Republican groups, the Real Irish Republican Army (RIRA), whose spokesman said that the shootings were 'executions' and that the pizza delivery-men were legitimate targets as they were: 'collaborating with the British by servicing them'. Two Republicans, Colin Duffy and Brian Shivers, were arrested and tried for the murders. Duffy was found not guilty and Shivers, although convicted, was later released after a successful appeal. To date no other person has stood trial for the Massereene killings.

Geraldine Ferguson is the mother of Patrick Azimkar.

Geraldine's Story

My husband, Mehmet, and I had been out with friends and got to bed in the early hours. At 5 a.m. someone knocked on the door. When I opened it there were two men dressed in black suits. They asked to come in. In those seconds between our front door and our kitchen I wondered if Patrick had got into some sort of trouble (I didn't dare think of any other possibility). They told me to sit down and they just said: 'I'm sorry to tell you that Patrick is dead.' Mehmet came down and I remember him asking them if this was some kind of joke. They said: 'No sir, it's not a joke.'

I couldn't speak and I felt I was going to pass out. Mehmet took me to lie down on the sofa. All I could hear was loud swirling noises in my ears, I seemed to be unable to speak at all, it felt like I was inside a nightmare. Mehmet asked what happened to Patrick and all they would say is that he died of gunshot wounds. They couldn't give any more details. As far as we knew Patrick had arrived in Afghanistan a few hours earlier, how could he already have died from gunshot wounds. He'd only just arrived? We didn't know then that the plane taking the boys to Afghanistan had been delayed. We never thought of Northern Ireland terrorism. We were shocked and confused and we didn't really believe what they said. It seemed impossible to believe that Pat was dead.

After a couple of hours the men left. Mehmet and I stared at the wall in silence, there were no words. Eventually, when I could, I phoned my two sisters and they and their families arrived

Patrick Azimkar, killed at Massereene Barracks by dissidents. (Geraldine Ferguson)

quickly. When James (then aged 25) came downstairs I had to do the hardest thing I ever had to do, to tell James that his one and only sibling, his little brother, was dead.

My memory of the early days and weeks after Patrick's murder are hazy. I remember, sitting in the sitting room staring at the door willing Patrick to appear. For days I waited, hoped and expected Patrick to walk through the door with his cheerful smile and that massive black bag, called a Bergen, that he always had with him on his weekends home. I honestly thought he would, because I was convinced there had been a mistake. It was another young soldier who had died, not Patrick! We were all stunned and in a state of disbelief. Then I was hit with a great river of unstoppable grief. I cried for weeks, day and night, the tears just didn't stop.

It's hard to find words that can describe the horror and desolation we suddenly found ourselves in. Patrick's death was also a kind of death for us three too. We were in this other place between life and death, a living hell, and there seemed to be no way out. We were surrounded by our close family and friends, love and great care lavished on us from all sides, but nothing mattered because Patrick was gone. We were broken people, I wasn't sure how to go on.

A man was sent to help us from the Army. His name was Lee, he was a casualty visiting officer. He arrived on the morning of that first day. His job was to assist and support us in any way he could. Lee turned out to be little less than an angel sent from God and without his support, at that time, I think we would have sunk. He was our crutch so we could stand, he helped us to be able to think straight (about the funeral), so plans could be made. When we could hardly breathe from grief he was there, in the background. Everything was under control because Lee had it in hand. He was quiet, calm and kind and we could not have wished for someone better than him.

The PSNI did a thorough and professional investigation. They visited us at home regularly to keep us up to date with the developments. We were appointed two PSNI family support officers who looked after us with enormous kindness and dedication and were there with us every step of the way. Those men (and their families) are now firm friends of ours.

Eventually, after a two-year investigation, the date for the trial arrived. It was eagerly awaited in NI because one of the defendants was well known there. There was no jury allowed because of fears of intimidation of jury members, so it all came down to one elderly judge, on his last ever case. The verdict was a shock to everyone in NI, and even more so for us. Despite DNA evidence on both suspects, plus over 1,000 exhibits, one defendant was acquitted there and then, and the other defendant was acquitted one year later, on appeal. For whatever reason, astonishingly, no one was ever found guilty of the brutal murders of Pat and Mark and the attempted murder of six other innocent young men. The effect of that injustice had huge consequences for both families.

Injustice is a heavy burden to carry; for us it affected every aspect of our lives and our family relationships. It can drive you mad with anger and rage but there is absolutely nothing you can do about it. Rage is a difficult thing to live with, in yourself and in others. You can't think about anything else and it can eat away at you. We lost our trust in the criminal justice system and a lot more too! For Pam, mother of Mark Quinsey, the injustice was literally too much for her to bear. A few weeks after the second defendant got off on appeal she died of a broken heart.

It's been an immensely difficult twelve years for us three but at least we have survived, it could easily have been a different story. I think we may be different people now because of the suffering we have had to endure but we learned a lot about the best of humanity and the worst. For me, my strength comes from my faith and that same faith gives me hope that we will see Patrick again, one day. Finding faith has

Patrick Azimkar. (Geraldine Ferguson)

been unexpected for me, I was an atheist for forty-six years but in desperation I called out to God and God answered me in ways I could not ignore. That faith has been transforming and I thank God for it.

Twelve years on James has married his sweetheart and our first grandchild is on the way. Mehmet and I have moved away from London. We live our lives fully, we enjoy life. Patrick will always be right in the middle of us all, we love him as we always have. To live well, without bitterness, that's now our life's work.

✦

Approximately forty-eight hours after the murders of the two soldiers at Massereene, at around 2145 hours, a PSNI patrol car arrived outside a house in Lismore Manor in Craigavon. Minutes earlier, the police had received a 999 call from a terrified woman whose windows had been broken in an apparently random attack. It was unknown at the time that members of another dissident Republican group, the Continuity IRA (CIRA), had deliberately smashed the window to lure a police patrol into an ambush.

As the officers arrived in their unmarked Skoda Octavia, waiting gunmen opened fire from the rear, some 50m away. Using a 'decommissioned'

AK–47, two rounds shattered the rear windscreen; one of the rounds struck Constable Stephen Carroll (48), killing him instantly.*

The CIRA claimed responsibility for the murder, with a spokesman stating: 'As long as there is British involvement in Ireland, these attacks will continue.' Two members of the CIRA, John Paul Wootton and Brendan McConville, were convicted in 2012 of Steve Carroll's murder. Wootton's tariff was raised from fourteen to eighteen years in 2014, due to the aggravating factors of his still undefined role in the terrorist killing; McConville was told that he would serve a minimum twenty-five-year sentence. They were also convicted of possession of an AK–47 assault rifle and ammunition with intent to endanger life. Wootton was further found guilty of attempting to collect information likely to be of use to terrorists.

Kate Carroll is the widow of the murdered policeman.

Kate's Story

Steve was a very, very happy type of man; he had a wonderful smile and red cheeks and he was always singing, even though he couldn't sing a note. When he went out that morning, he was standing at the door and he was humming away to himself. I remember saying: 'Hey, Mr Carroll, why are you always so happy?' He said: 'Well, Kate, I'm happy with my lot and I love you very much, so I suppose that's why I am so happy.' I replied: 'Oh, good, at least I'm good for something.'

Two soldiers had been shot a couple of days prior to that, and I felt that Steve might be in danger. That particular day, I can remember feeling really, really anxious, so I told him to be careful. He said to me: 'Don't worry, I'll be fine.' I just thought OK, and got ready for work. He asked

---

* Prior to the murder of Constable Carroll, the last police officers murdered by terrorists during The Troubles were RUC Constables Roland John Graham and David Andrew Johnston; the two officers were shot dead by PIRA gunmen outside the RUC station in Church Walk, Lurgan, Co. Armagh, on 16 June 1997. Constable Frank O'Reilly was fatally wounded by a UFF/Red Hand Commando blast bomb on 5 September 1998, during disturbances linked to the Drumcree dispute in Co. Armagh; he died of his injuries on 6 October that same year.

PSNI Officer Stephen Carroll,
murdered by dissidents, Craigavon.
(Kate Carroll)

Kate and Stephen Carroll, PSNI officer
murdered by dissidents. (Kate Carroll)

me for a kiss before I went off and then he asked me for another, because it would keep him right all day. I remember him saying: 'If I die now, I will die a happy man,' and I told him not to talk like that. When I went off to work, he would stand at the door and wave to me until I was round the corner. That was the last time that I saw Steve alive. His final words to me were: 'I can't wait to see you at home tonight; drive carefully.'

Later that evening, two police officers came to the house and told me that Steve had been shot. I begged them: 'Please, please, don't tell me he's dead.' That was just like the end of my world had come about. He had such a great heart and he was so well-known in our community. On the day of his funeral, the whole town stopped; Bainbridge Town just stopped.

The first year would have been the absolutely worst year I can remember. One night, I was lying in bed; all I wanted was my husband; I just wanted Steve. When we went to bed, we would have laid down together and I would have put my hand across his chest; we would have just cuddled up and slept like that. That particular night, I was just inconsolable; I didn't want to ring anyone, I just wanted Steve. That night, the weather was very cold, with snow on the ground. I knew that I wanted to open the grave; I wanted to feel his chest. I went down to my shed and got my shovel, and was almost at the gate when I realised that I couldn't do it; I knew that it was terrible, awful; what would people think? The grief was so bad, that I said to God – I fell out with God – 'Why did you take him? Why didn't you take me? The suffering is terrible.'

I remember my granddaughter coming into the conservatory with a photo of Steve; she was just 3. She said: 'Nanny, where's my Pappy?' I told her: 'Pappy is up in Heaven,' and she asked me why. I said he was in Heaven because he was taken away, and she asked: 'Who took him away, Nanny? I told her: 'Bad men.' She again asked why, and the purity of her question was everything; so innocent. I had no answer. There aren't any good answers. I took her to the graveyard and she put a wee rose on Pappy's grave. She never got to meet her grandfather and she never will. It's so sad to think she was denied all his love.

So I try to document everything and put it into a scrap book, for when my grandchildren are older. They'll understand the difference between good and evil. They'll not destroy lives; they'll never be the reason for anyone's question: why?

I'm alone in my head reliving the past, saying this time twenty years ago Steve and I were doing this, planning that; it just never seems to end. I'll never make sense of what happened, but I still have to put my feet on the floor, and get out of bed every morning. So I have to be determined to live in hope. But it's hard, so very hard. People ask me how I forgive what happened to my husband, but I tell them it's not up to me to forgive. I don't want hatred in my soul. I don't need anything tap-tapping on my head, telling me to hate people.

As Steve was being put into the ground, I silently promised him: 'I want your name to be remembered and I'll never forget what you've done for all of us, and the family and I'll never become bitter.' He was a good man, so bitterness will never take an effect on me. It never has. It never will. It's up to a higher being than me to forgive, and the people who took Steve away are not going to take up space in my head.

But sometimes I get into this rut because what's hurting me is that he's not here. People want me to heal and I can't expect people to be where I am, only I'm in my own head and heart and I just have to deal with it. No matter how many people I have in my life, or how good, loving and caring they are, no one can or will ever take the place of Steve Carroll in my heart ever. I have this pain because I had him and I lost him.

His murder completely took my future away, obliterated it; there are times I wonder if there's any future for me? Today I'm living one day at a time, just to put the time in. I don't sleep well because I have bad dreams, then I get up and this feeling of doom and gloom hits me. It's like a big, heavy cloud coming down around me. I can't see where I'm going and then it's like a physical weight descending. I get up with plans but end up back in the rut with my pain and sorrow, everything going around in my head, day after day after day. What if? ... But ... Why? And twenty years on it hasn't changed. It's just something I'll never get over in my lifetime. The only time it won't be in my head is when I'm in my grave.

What do I think about the people who did it? People say to me: 'How can you forgive them?' I don't forgive them, but I have forgiven myself, because I don't want to carry this cancerous feeling inside my head, just eating away. Those years were dreadful and might be a lifetime ago to the people who killed Steve, but to me, I am still suffering at their hands; I have got a bigger jail sentence than they have.

✦

The main Loyalist paramilitary groups and the Provisional IRA both targeted off-duty prison officers for assassinations. Between 1975 and 1988, twenty-six prison officers were killed – the vast majority by Republicans – between their place of work and home. David Black (52) worked as a PO at Maghaberry Prison; he lived in Cookstown, driving the 34.4 miles (55km) to work each day. On the morning of 1 November 2012, he set off in his black Audi, but at approximately 07.30, as he neared the junction for Craigavon/Lurgan, A76, on the M1 motorway, a Toyota Camry bearing Dublin number plates pulled alongside him. A gunman in the car opened fire, hitting the PO several times. His injuries forced him to lose control of the car, which crashed at the side of the motorway; he was fatally injured and died at the scene. The car used in the attack was later found burned out in a Nationalist area of Lurgan.

David Black. (Yvonne Black)

A dissident Republican group that referred to itself as 'the New IRA' admitted the murder, claiming that it had been carried out to 'protect and defend Republican prisoners'. The previously unheard of paramilitary group had been formed from an amalgamation of other disparate dissident paramilitary organisations, including the perpetrators of the 1998 Omagh bomb, the Real IRA. There was an on-going dispute at the prison, where forty-one dissident Republican prisoners were detained at the time, with many of them refusing to wash in protest at strip searches. The terrorists and suspected terrorist prisoners were seeking to secure political status. Why PO Black was singled out has never been ascertained. He became the first PO to be killed by paramilitaries since the Belfast/Good Friday Agreement, some fourteen years earlier, and the thirtieth PO killed in Northern Ireland since 1974. He left a widow and two teenage children.

Then UK Prime Minister, David Cameron, said: 'First and foremost, this is a dreadful tragedy for the family and friends of David Black, who has been so brutally murdered as he went about his work keeping the people of Northern Ireland safe. My heart goes out to them.' Unionist

MP Jeffrey Donaldson commented: 'This is a terrible tragedy. Once again, a small minority are trying to drag us back to the dark days.'

One man, Vincent Banks of Dublin, was arrested, although he was only convicted of IRA membership. There have been other charges of involvement in the murder, but to date no one has been convicted of David Black's murder. It is suspected that the terrorist group's intel came from an accumulation of information gathered by dickers – possibly neighbours who lived close to the Blacks – and from carrying out recce runs along the M1 motorway, surveying routes and driving habits before deciding when to strike. As the reader will see from the following testimony, PO Black had not worked that week, with Thursday being his first journey to the prison. To have carried out this operation, there must have been an element of leaked information.

Yvonne Black is the widow of the murdered man.

Yvonne's Story

The first of November was a Thursday; it was a freezing, cold day and David had gone out to defrost our three cars. He had been off work on the Monday, Tuesday and Wednesday, rostered to work half a day on the Thursday. He set off at about 7 a.m., followed by our son, Kyle, who was travelling to Belfast on the same route as his dad, to his work placement from university, and then myself; our daughter, Kyra, was at home as she was off school that day. I worked as a palliative care nurse at Altnagelvin Hospital in Londonderry. My drive was about an hour, but I loved my job and didn't mind the journey.

Not long after I left, David called on his way to work, advising me that he had forgotten to leave some money for Kyra. Little did I know that this would be my last conversation with him. It was approaching the anniversary of my father's death. He had died in a farm accident the previous year. I was not in the best frame of mind. In work, while I was with a patient, my bleep went, but I ignored it as the patient was my priority. A short while later as I was at the nurses' station, it went again and it was Kyle. He asked if I had spoken to his dad, as there had been

David and Yvonne Black. (Yvonne Black)

an accident on the motorway and a prison officer had been killed. I was very calm and told him that it wasn't his daddy; I promised that I would ring David straight away and telephone him back, but didn't think that anything was wrong.

I walked at first, however, I soon found myself running back to the office to get my mobile with the direct number for the prison. In the office was Sylvia, my colleague, so I quickly told her what had happened so she offered to call the prison. My heart was thumping, praying that David would come to the phone. But she was given another number to dial; at that moment I knew something was wrong. Just at that minute Michele, another colleague, opened the door and stood back to allow a smartly dressed man and woman to enter the room. My stomach plunged, as I knew that they were police and that something awful was about to unfold.

They began asking me about my husband; what job he did, what car he drove, things like that, before informing me that he had been killed on the motorway on his way to work. My mind went into a spin; my world fell apart. I remember saying: 'This can't be happening; we are at peace!' I know that the police wanted me and the children to be informed of the news, before the media or Facebook did.

My priority were our two children. I asked my colleague to ring my brother, Ivor, to ask him to go to our home to be with Kyra, who was there all alone. I also asked him to speak to my friend Dorothy, to organise her son – Kyle's best friend Ryan – to go to Belfast and bring him home. I remember leaving the hospital that day flanked by Michele and Sylvia, who travelled home in the police car with me. One of the officers drove us to my home, whilst his colleague followed behind in my car. That journey home just seemed to take hours, and though part of me wanted to get home, the other part of me wanted to just run away. The reality truly hit me when we turned into the roadway to our home. It was filled with police cars and other vehicles. Michele and Sylvia got out of the car but my legs were like jelly. I couldn't move as I became overwhelmed with emotion. This was real. I remember sitting in the back seat of the police car, looking at my house with so many people all around and thinking: 'Why are you all here?' even though I knew exactly why. Then my brother Ivor came out and with his help I entered my home.

I can't remember any of the faces, as I walked through to the conservatory where Kyra was waiting; we hugged and cried but didn't say much. Kyle arrived home and came straight to us in the conservatory. We all hugged and held each other. I remember going out into the living room and hugging David's dad, mum and sister Lorraine. We were all broken. The rest of the day was mostly a blur, with the police liaison and the prison officers' benevolent people being around, helping with everything and giving us support. It was just so surreal. We wanted David home, but had to wait for the post mortem and eventually were able to bring him home on the Saturday evening. Over the next four days hundreds of family, friends, colleagues, neighbours and people we didn't even know, came to our home to pay respects and in total disbelief at what had happened. I would like to say thank you to Kyle and his friends who rallied around each of them, not only over the wake but ever since. Also to my precious, precious friends and family, who not only supported me then but who have faithfully remained by my side. They have continued this journey with me, through many, many dark, difficult days (and nights).

The morning of the funeral I was sitting in the room with David. I could not stand as I was so emotional. How could I say goodbye to my soulmate, my best friend, the father of my children, my world? About an hour before the service was about to start, something came over me and I can only describe it as if oil was being poured over my head and it ran down all over my body. A serenity and calm settled over and in me and I stood up. I didn't realise that people all around the world were praying and this was the peace from God that surpasses all understanding. I asked all those people standing around to please put on a poppy. I gathered Kyle and Kyra together and I remember saying that, due to David's security, we always had to hide the fact that their dad was a prison officer and that we didn't need to do this anymore. We would walk behind their dad, so, so proud of the husband and dad he was.

I remember the overwhelming emotion I felt as the procession drove into Cookstown. The whole town was still and quiet. Cars had just stopped in the streets, the shopkeepers closed their shops and hundreds of people lined the route through the town to where we were having the service. I was just overwhelmed by their respect and support. As we arrived, just before the church, the prison officers' guard of honour had formed and was waiting for us. But I could see a gap in their ranks; it was where David would have normally stood as he had taken a proud part of the guard of honour for quite a few years. My heart broke. As David's colleagues carried his coffin, we walked behind in silence, other than the sound of the marching boots of the guard, and then the click, click, click of the press cameras. At the door of the church we had requested that family take over and at that point to see David's elderly dad, our son Kyle and other family carrying David's coffin was so, so raw and surreal.

After the service, we drove to the cemetery, where David's coffin, draped in the Union flag, with his hat and gloves placed on top, was taken for burial. The honour guard folded the flag and passed it to me with his hat and gloves, which I will treasure forever. As they handed them to me at the graveside, I remember thinking, this is something

David Black's funeral in Cookstown. (Yvonne Black)

that happens on TV, but not to me. At that minute it felt that this was all I had left of David and this was so cruel.

I never thought that this would ever happen to our wee family now. After the Peace Agreement in 1997, we had remained cautious, but as time wore on we did relax our security somewhat in light of being told that threats were low and subsequently lost security and protection measures we had at our home just one year previously in 2011.

How do I feel today? I feel really sad and lonely. I have lost my life partner, my best friend, my confidante and the person who truly cared about me. Kyle and Kyra have lost their dad who loved them so, so much. We lost our future. All that we had planned; to have quality time together as our children flew the nest. David and I had so many plans and places to travel to after his early retirement. We had our kids' futures to look forward to; our lives were good, but that all changed in a split second; I can't believe that it has been nearly nine years, as it still feels as raw as yesterday.

I am just so, so sad that David isn't here, but proud of the man he was. When people speak highly of his life and his work, I am so proud that he was the same person outside the home that he was inside it. He deeply appreciated and loved his family and friends. He worked hard for anything he had and took nothing for granted. He had high morals, principals and standards. He was always fair and said that if you treat others with respect and dignity, you will get the same in return. How ironic that this was not the case for those who planned and carried out his murder. We received thousands of letters and cards, including some from ex-prisoners. One thing that stands out was that the prisoners at Maghaberry asked for a book of condolence for David, so well liked and respected he was amongst them. The paramilitary prisoners didn't sign, of course.

I am so proud how our children have dealt with their dad's murder. Kyle and Kyra have worked so hard to achieve the life that David would have wished for them. They could have been pulled into a life of bitterness that would have destroyed them but they chose not to. They succeeded through university into their chosen professions. They did this because they knew how happy it would make David and to make him proud. I know that I am so proud of them and that their dad is too.

I feel so let down by the justice system in Northern Ireland. It hasn't ensured that we have seen justice. But I pray that someday this will happen as someone will gain a conscience and give information that leads to convictions. However, I rest in the knowledge that when we leave this world, we all will have to face the judgement of God, our creator. Those who murdered David will face God's ultimate judgement. There will be no more lies, no more hiding.

My future and that of our family was lost on 1 November 2012. Those who murdered David made choices that day, but we have been left to face every day with the consequences.

Is it Peace?

The author returned to Belfast in November 2008, his first return to that troubled province since 1973. At Leeds-Bradford Airport, he was greeted by family, where the questions centred inevitably around the state of Northern Ireland in these early days of peace. I recall telling my daughter that it 'isn't over yet', and one day you will understand what I mean.

Kenny Donaldson, Head of SEFF, has expressed his frustration at the naïvety of people outside of the country who have claimed that Northern Ireland is at peace. Indeed, their insistence that the country has been at peace in the two decades since the Belfast/Good Friday Agreement greatly irks him. There is a naïve assertion from those who would rather not face reality that the land is enjoying the fruits of that 'peace'. The words of this chapter, and the oral testimony contained therein, should adequately underline the frustration that both Mr Donaldson and this author feel.

The ceasefires of 1997, the stated Republican and Loyalist paramilitaries' commitment to peace, and the alleged decommissioning of their weapons are now twenty-four years in the past (at the time of publications). It is true that soldiers and police officers are no longer being gunned down on a daily basis, in the streets and fields of Northern Ireland; there are no longer the regular sounds of yet another car bomb exploding in the commercial hearts of Belfast and Londonderry, and innocents living in the sectarian interfaces no longer need to cower behind their curtained windows of a night time. However, the continued internal score-settling by both the Republicans and the Loyalists, the carnage at Omagh, combined with the murders of Sappers Azimkar and Quinsey, Police Constable Carroll and Prison Officer Black, resonate beyond the small country of Northern Ireland. They point to an underlying and festering malevolence that pours cold water over claims of 'peace at last'.

The Irish Republican movement has spent those twenty-plus years settling some of their internal scores, the most notable being Denis

Donaldson, killed by the IRA in March or April 2006.* He had been a leading Provisional in the heady days of 1972, and had also been elevated into PIRA folklore by his part in the murders of Protestants in the Newtownards Road area of Belfast in 1970. In late 2005, it was revealed that he had been 'turned' by British Army Intelligence, having been an informant for many years, operating in the Nationalist heartland of West Belfast. It was revealed via the press that Donaldson was hiding at Glenties in the Republic. Once they were in possession of the information, the RIRA moved to have this particular score settled.

Donaldson's death was just one of an estimated twenty-five other score-settling acts carried out by the IRA.** Indeed, the *Irish Independent* claimed that the IRA had carried out thirty-nine murders since the 1994 ceasefire, with twenty-six committed since the Belfast/Good Friday Agreement.

Some of the other 'internal murders' carried out by the IRA between 1998 and 2007 were:

Gerard Moran, Dublin, in 1998; Eamon Collins, Newry; Brendan 'Speedy' Fagan, Newry; Paul 'Bull' Downey, South Armagh, in 1999; Edmund McCoy, Dunmurry; Nicholas 'Mad Nicky' O'Hare, Dundalk; Patrick Quinn, Magherafelt; Joseph O'Connor, Belfast; Trevor Kells, Belfast; Thomas 'Tomo' Byrne, Dublin, in 2000; Seamus 'Shavo' Hogan, Dublin; Bobby McGuigan, Lurgan; Kieran Smyth, Co. Meath; Michael Magee, Downpatrick; Paul Daly, Belfast; Christopher O'Kane, Londonderry; Mark Robinson, Londonderry, in 2001; Mathew Burns, Castlewellan; Brian McDonald, Dungannon, in 2002; Gareth O'Connor, Co. Armagh; Jimmy McGinley, Londonderry, in 2003; Robert McCartney, Belfast, in 2005; Paul Quinn, Castleblaney, in 2007; Kevin McGuigan, Belfast; and Jock Davison, Belfast, in 2015. Each one of these deaths were either score-settling from the days of The Troubles, local paramilitary rivalries over drug distribution and other criminal activities, or in the case of Robert McCartney, a pub dispute that ended fatally. In the case of

---

* His body was discovered at a remote farmhouse in Co. Donegal on 4 April 2006; he had been blasted with a shotgun at his hiding place.

** 'Paul Quinn murder: IRA kills 26 people since Good Friday Agreement, but looking backwards could be "dangerous" says Rev Harold Good', *Belfast News Letter*.

the last two murders, McGuigan, a former PIRA member who had morphed into a violent criminal gang leader, shot and killed the top Short Strand and Markets areas commander, Jock Davison (46). Just four months later, on 12 August, the Provisional IRA ambushed McGuigan near his home in the Short Strand, shooting him dead, claiming that the killing was in revenge for the death of Davison. The families of those men might well argue that, whatever the post-GFA situation was, it certainly wasn't 'peace in our time'.

It is estimated that the aforementioned deaths are but the tip of an enormous iceberg, indicating that claims of widespread peace are highly exaggerated. Studies reported on by the *Belfast Telegraph* indicate that the number of paramilitary killings, when taking into account 'ordinary' gangster killings and drugs-related dealer deaths, is extraordinary. The study showed that a total of 158 murders, including the Omagh bombing, have been carried out by former combatants in the conflict, on both the Loyalist and Republican sides.[***]

Professor Paul Nolan, Queen's University, Belfast, conducted this study of post-Troubles Ulster, reporting in April 2018 that these murders had been carried out in the twenty years of what some call 'the whitewash' of the GFA. The study showed that Republicans were responsible for seventy-four of these, Loyalists for seventy-one, with the remaining thirteen being committed by indeterminable organisations.

Additionally, the murder of Robert McCartney following a dispute outside Magennis's Pub in Belfast with Republican paramilitaries in early 2005 is a case in point, epitomising the uneasy peace. The Republican movement's post-murder actions led to worrying accusations about the continued lawless attitudes still held by them. The IRA said it gave the murdered man's family the names of the man who stabbed Mr McCartney, as well as a second man who supplied, and later destroyed, the murder weapon. It requested that the family did not prosecute the case through the PSNI, but promised instead to shoot those responsible. The McCartney family rejected the IRA's 'offer'. The late Ian Paisley said at the time: 'The offer to shoot those responsible for the

---

[***] Figures show 158 paramilitary killings since the Good Friday Agreement, *BelfastTelegraph.co.uk*

murder of Robert McCartney confirms again that terrorism is the only stock and trade of Sinn Fein/IRA.'

This author wrote the following for his 2019 book, *Torn Apart: 50 Years of The Troubles*:

> Disconcertingly, a 2016 PSNI investigation showed that the Provisional IRA still had an intact Army Council; this leadership group still had the final say in any activities or announcements for Sinn Fein. Moreover, it stated that PIRA still existed, with the other dissidents (DRs) being responsible for the murder of 5 members of the security forces and a prison officer in the post-Troubles era. In short, they – the Republicans – were practising and profiting from the very same criminal activities in which their Loyalist counterparts were engaged. There are areas in West Belfast, Londonderry and Lurgan which are almost totally under the control of the respective paramilitaries; in those parts of Northern Ireland, they represent 'law and order', not the PSNI.

At around 2230 hours on the evening of Friday, 28 September 2001, Owen O'Hagan (51), a Northern Irish journalist, was returning home to Westfield Gardens in Lurgan following an evening out with his wife. As the couple neared their destination, gunmen from the LVF shot him three times in the back. A second or so earlier, he had bravely pushed his wife to safety as he saw his attackers. He was mortally wounded, dying shortly afterwards, even as medical help was being summoned. He was the first journalist to be killed in Northern Ireland during The Troubles and the aftermath of the Belfast/Good Friday Agreement.

O'Hagan was an investigative reporter, specialising in looking into paramilitary activity. He had once been a member of the OIRA, serving time in the Maze for firearms offences, before his release in 1978. He had angered the Loyalists, as well as incurring the wrath of the Provisional IRA, during the twenty-three years of his post-paramilitary career. He was a thorn in the side of the paramilitaries, unafraid of reporting their rapid descent into gangsterism. No one has ever been convicted of his murder.

Almost eighteen years later, with the Belfast/Good Friday Agreement some two decades old, Lyra McKee (29), an author and journalist from Belfast, was killed as she covered rioting in Londonderry. On the evening of Thursday, 18 April 2019, the PSNI had entered the Creggan Estate, with the objective of raiding the homes of dissident Republicans to seize arms and explosives. Their presence prompted mass rioting, as swarms of youths from the fiercely Nationalist estate attacked police officers and vehicles with rocks and petrol bombs.

As the confrontation was raging, McKee was standing next to a PSNI Land Rover in Fanad Drive when a masked gunman – believed to be from the New IRA (NIRA) – opened fire with a handgun. It is thought that he fired around a dozen shots at the officers, but one round struck the journalist in the head, fatally wounding her. Police officers

Lyra McKee, shot dead by dissidents in Londonderry. (Sent to me by one of the contributors to an earlier book, taken by International Journalism Festival from Perugia, Italia CC BY-SA 2.0, via Wikimedia Commons)

carried her into one of their armoured vehicles, rushing her the 4.2miles (7km) to Altnagelvin Hospital; she died shortly afterwards.

The then UK Prime Minister, Theresa May, denounced the killing, stating that the journalist 'died doing her job with great courage' and that her death was: 'shocking and senseless'. A leading journalist, Séamus Dooley, wrote that she was 'a journalist of courage, style and integrity'.

Two men were arrested, but released the following day without charge, as was a 57-year-old female from the same area. Shortly afterwards, demonstrating that hollow apologies haven't gone away, a spokesman for the NIRA told the *Irish News* that the journalist was not the intended target, offering apologies to her partner and their family. The weapon – a Hämmerli X-esse pistol – was recovered over a year after the murder following a PSNI raid on the Ballymagroarty Estate, close to the Creggan in Londonderry.

In February 2020, four men were arrested under the Terrorism Act and charged with murder; there have been no convictions at the time of publication. However, in a statement in the Belfast High Court, shortly before this book was finished, it was revealed that the weapon had been used in dissident Republican activity on at least four occasions in four paramilitary attacks between September 2018 and March 2019.

There is a growing unease amongst the Protestant Unionist Loyalist population (PUL) at the increasing strength of the Republican narrative, which has at its heart the rewriting of history; in this instance, the complete reinvention of their role in The Troubles. Sinn Fein have seemingly armed themselves with the biggest airbrush in history, similar to the Loyalist paramilitary tactic of sweeping outrages such as the Reavey murders, Greysteel and Dublin and Monaghan under an increasingly lumpy carpet. The PUL still represent the majority – albeit a shrinking one – in Northern Ireland, but their discomfort increases at the seemingly irrevocable growth and influence of the aforementioned Sinn Fein.

There are many examples of post-Troubles 'truth and reconciliation' that both the partisan and non-partisan find unpalatable; for example, the naming of a children's playground after a man suspected of killing Protestant workmen in the Kingsmills massacre. There were further examples, such as the now disgraced Sinn Fein politician who poked fun at the Kingsmills dead by balancing a Kingsmill-branded loaf on his head on the anniversary of the murders.

Loyalist paramilitary groups didn't disband en masse after the 1998 Agreement; in the same vein as their Republican counterparts, they merely paid lip service to the decommissioning of their vast weapons caches. Their organisations tend to concentrate on the control of the illegal drug trade, protection rackets and the supply of prostitution as well as – it is rumoured – controlling the vile business of human trafficking. There is a growing consensus that they are preparing for the next constitutional crisis, maintaining themselves in a state of readiness for another 'Doomsday situation'. It is neither encouraged – and certainly not recommended – for Catholic families to move on to predominantly Protestant estates; it is also very much the same for Protestants who might consider relocating to a Catholic-dominated area.

In 2021, the *Belfast Sunday World* warned against a resurgence of Loyalist groups prepared to begin a terror campaign against the 'Irish Sea Border'. They quoted a member of Orange Vanguard who said:

> groups are starting to organise … there's deep anger and frustration at the leaders of loyalism who appear to be doing nothing while Northern Ireland is separated from the UK. Pressure is going to be put on the commanders of the UDA and the UVF to get involved in some form of action – otherwise what's the point of calling themselves loyalists? There is a small minority who are ready to go back to war over this, that's the truth.[*]

The author has revisited Northern Ireland a further eight times since 2008, and admits to never truly feeling completely safe, even in the company of trusted and loyal friends such as MC and BR. There are areas in which he would never walk unaccompanied, and there are even 'safe' Loyalist areas where he knows to keep his private thoughts to himself. The situation in Northern Ireland can occasionally be described as a knife edge, although the peace that came at a tremendous price is at times fragile. There is mutual suspicion on both sides, with accusations and counter-accusations that the respective narratives seek to rewrite the terrible history of those three bloody decades. One can only hope that the writer of a future history of The Troubles can present a more optimistic picture.

A former UDR soldier told the author:

> If it is peace now, why do I have to be careful in front of who I speak about my military career? Why do I still check under my car; why would I not feel safe walking through most of the Catholic estates? If this is peace, why do I feel like a stranger in my own country?

A female RUC officer who served in North Antrim also told me: 'Where I work, there are people from some of the Nationalist areas and I would

---

[*] Source: www.sundayworld.com/news/northern-ireland-news/lorry-driver-blinded-in-brick-attack-may-be-first-victim-of-violent-loyalist-anti-protocol-group-40041721.html

never dream of telling them that I was a policewoman.' One PUL confided in the author: 'I do get frustrated when I hear Republicans use the phrase "north of Ireland" because that just shows no respect for the Unionist side.'

This book will close with one final and salient fact for the reader to ponder: Before the Belfast/Good Friday Agreement, there were eighteen peace walls in Belfast; now there are forty-eight.

Selected Bibliography

Adams, J., Morgan, R. & Bainbridge, A., *Ambush: The War Between the SAS and the IRA* (Pan Books, 1988).

Barzilay, David, *The British Army in Ulster Vol. I* (Century Books, 1973).

Barzilay, David, *The British Army in Ulster Vol. II* (Century Books, 1975).

Beresford, David, *Ten Men Dead* (Harper Collins, 1994).

Breen, Colin, *A Force Like No Other* (Blackstaff Press, 2017).

Breen, Colin, *A Force Like No Other: The Next Shift* (Blackstaff Press, 2019).

Brown, Johnston, *Into the Dark: 30 Years in the RUC* (Gill & MacMillan, 2005).

Burgess, Jonathan, *The Exodus* (Causeway Press, 2011).

Burleigh, Michael, *Blood and Rage: A Cultural History of Terrorism* (Harper Collins, 2009).

Campbell, John, *The Iron Lady* (Vintage, 2012).

Clarke, A.F.N., *Contact* (Secker & Warburg, 1983).

Clarke, George, *Border Crossing* (Gill & MacMillan, 2009).

Clarke, L.; Johnston, K., *Martin McGuinness: From Guns to Government* (Mainstream, 2001).

Collins, Eamon, *Killing Rage* (Granta Books, 1997).

Conway, Kieran, *Southside Provisional* (Orpen Press, 2014).

Cusack, Jim; McDonald, Henry, *UVF: The Endgame* (Poolberg Press, 2008).

Davies, Nicholas, *Dead Men Talking: Collusion, Cover-Up and Murder in Northern Ireland's Dirty War* (Random House, 2011).

Dillon, Martin, *25 Years of Terror* (Bantam, 1994).

Dillon, Martin, *God and the Gun* (Routledge, 1999).

Dillon, Martin, *Killer in Clowntown* (Arrow Books, 1992).

Dillon, Martin, *Political Murder in Northern Ireland* (Penguin, 1973).

Dillon, Martin, *Stone Cold* (Hutchinson, 1992).

Dillon, Martin, *The Dirty War* (Arrow Books, 1990).

Dillon, Martin, *The Shankill Butchers* (Arrow Books, 1991).

Dillon, Martin, *The Trigger Men* (Mainstream, 2003).

Doherty, Richard, *The Thin Green Line: History of the RUC* (Pen & Sword, 2004).

East Belfast H&CS, *Murder in Ballymacarrett* (Self-Published, 2003).

Edwards, Aaron, *Agents of Influence* (Merrion Press, 2021).

Edwards, Aaron, *UVF: Behind the Mask* (Merrion Press, 2017).

Feeney, Brian; Bradley, Gerry, *Insider: Gerry Bradley's Life in the IRA* (O'Brien, 2009).

Geraghty, Tony, *The Irish War* (Harper Collins, 1998).

Gilmour, Raymond, *Dead Ground; Infiltrating the IRA* (Little, Brown & Co., 1998).

Hamill, Desmond, *Pig in the Middle* (Methuen Books, 1985).

Harnden, Toby, *Bandit Country* (Hodder & Stoughton, 1999).

Holland & Phoenix, *Phoenix: Policing the Shadows* (Hodder & Stoughton, 1996).

Jordan, Hugh, *Milestones in Murder* (Mainstream, 2002).

Larmour, George, *They Killed the Ice Cream Man* (Colourpoint, 2016).

Latham, Richard, *Deadly Beat* (Mainstream, 2001).

Leslie, David, *Lighting Candles* (Black & White Publishing, 2014).

McDaniel, Denzil, *Enniskillen: The Remembrance Day Bombing* (Wolfhound Press, 1997).

McDonald, H.; Holland, J., *INLA: Deadly Divisions* (Poolberg, 2010).

McGartland, Marty, *Fifty Dead Men Walking* (Blake Publishing, 1997).

McKittrick, D. et al, *Lost Lives* (Mainstream, 2007).

Moloney, Ed, *Voices from the Grave* (Faber & Faber, 2010).

Myers, Kevin, *Watching the Door: Cheating Death in 70s Belfast* (Atlantic Books, 2008).

O'Callaghan, Sean, *The Informer* (Corgi Books, 1999).

O'Doherty, Malachi, *The Telling Year: Belfast 1972* (Gill & Co., 2007).

Parker, John, *Secret Hero* (Metro Books, 2004).

Phoenix Project, *Stories of Sacrifice* (2015).

Potter, John, *A Testimony to Courage* (Pen & Sword, 2001).

Sanders, A.; Wood, I., *Times of Troubles* (Edinburgh UP, 2012).

SEFF, *For God and Ulster* (SEFF, 2015).

Simpson, Alan, *Murder Madness* (GM Books, 1997).

South East Fermanagh Foundation, *I'll Never Forget* (2011).

Stone, Michael, *None Shall Divide Us* (John Blake, 2003).

Taylor, Peter, *Loyalists* (Bloomsbury, 1999).

Urban, Mark, *Big Boys' Rules* (Faber & Faber, 1993).

Van der Bilj, Nick, *Operation Banner* (Pen & Sword, 2009).

Walsh, Andrew, *From Hope to Hatred* (The History Press, 2013).

Ware, Darren, *A Rendezvous with the Enemy* (Helion Books, 2010).

Wharton, Ken, *A Long Long War: Voices from the British Army* (Helion Books, 2008).

Wharton, Ken, *An Agony Continued: Northern Ireland 1980–83* (Helion Books, 2015).

Wharton, Ken, *Bloody Belfast: An Oral History of the British Army's War Against the IRA* (The History Press, 2010).

Wharton, Ken, *Bullets, Bombs and Cups of Tea: Further Voices of the British Army in Northern Ireland* (Helion Books, 2009).

Wharton, Ken, Sir, *They're Taking the Kids Indoors* (Helion Books, 2011).

Wharton, Ken, *The Bloodiest Year: Northern Ireland 1972* (The History Press, 2011).

Wharton, Ken, *Wasted Years, Wasted Lives (Vol. I)* (Helion Books, 2013).

Wharton, Ken, *Wasted Years, Wasted Lives (Vol. II)* (Helion Books, 2014).

Wilson, Barbara N., *A Quiet Courage: UDR Greenfinch* (Shanway Press, 2011).

If you enjoyed this title from
The History Press

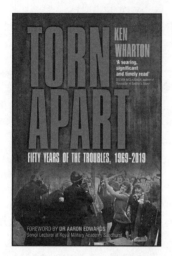

978 0 7509 9728 7

978 0 7509 8547 5

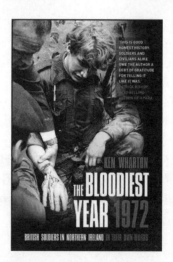

978 0 7509 8546 8